United States
Department of
Agriculture

Forest Service
Pacific Northwest
Research Station

Research Paper
PNW-RP-567

August 2006

Learning to Manage a Complex Ecosystem: Adaptive Management and the Northwest Forest Plan

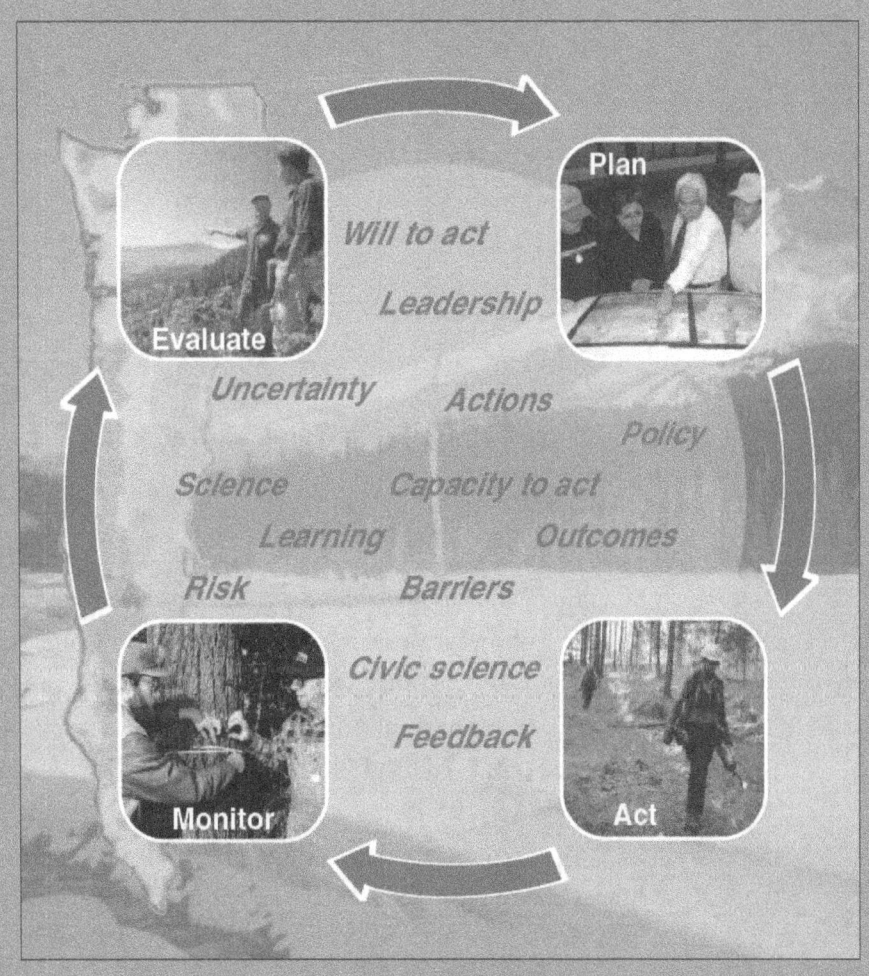

Editors

George H. Stankey is a research social scientist (retired), and **Bernard T. Bormann** is a principal plant physiologist, U.S. Department of Agriculture, Forest Service, Pacific Northwest Research Station, Forestry Sciences Laboratory, 3200 SW Jefferson Way, Corvallis, OR 97331; **Roger N. Clark** is a research social scientist (retired), Department of Agriculture, Forest Service, Pacific Northwest Research Station, Pacific Wildland Fire Sciences Laboratory, 400 N 34th Ave., Suite 201, Seattle, WA 98103.

Cover credits

Mount Hood photo taken by Ron Nicols, Natural Resources Conservation Service; top left photo taken by Dave Powell, USDA Forest Service, www.forestry images.org; top right photo taken by Jeff Vanuga, USDA Natural Resources Conservation Service; lower left photo taken by USDA Natural Resources Conservation Service; lower right photo taken by Roger Ottmar, PNW Research Station. Cover design by Kelly Lawrence.

Learning to Manage a Complex Ecosystem: Adaptive Management and the Northwest Forest Plan

Editors
George H. Stankey
Roger N. Clark
Bernard T. Bormann

U.S. Department of Agriculture
Forest Service
Pacific Northwest Research Station
Portland, Oregon
Research Paper
PNW-RP-567
August 2006

Abstract

Stankey, George H.; Clark, Roger N.; Bormann, Bernard T., eds. Learning to manage a complex ecosystem: adaptive management and the Northwest Forest Plan. Res. Pap. PNW-RP-567. Portland, OR: U.S. Department of Agriculture, Forest Service, Pacific Northwest Research Station. 194 p.

The Northwest Forest Plan (the Plan) identifies adaptive management as a central strategy for effective implementation. Despite this, there has been a lack of any systematic evaluation of its performance. This study is based on an extensive literature review, 50 interviews with resource managers and scientists involved with the Plan's implementation, and a survey of over 400 citizens in Oregon and Washington who participated in public involvement programs related to the adaptive management elements of the Plan. The study documents experiences with adaptive approaches, identifies key facilitators of, and barriers to, implementation of such approaches, and suggests needed changes to enhance implementation. Major problems confront efforts to undertake adaptive approaches, and these derive from a complex set of factors including a risk-averse organizational culture; a restrictive legal-political environment; and inadequate training, staffing, and financial resources.

Keywords: Adaptive management, decisionmaking, complexity, risk and uncertainty, social learning, precautionary principle.

Research Paper PNW-RP-567

Preface

This project originated from discussions between Clark, Stankey, and Bormann regarding the need for a critical assessment of the extent to which the concept of adaptive management had been successfully integrated into the Northwest Forest Plan. It was apparent that a team approach would be necessary to provide a diversity of perspectives for the evaluation. This led to an invitation to the other authors of this report to participate. A number of meetings involving the team took place, discussing methods, strategies, and results. Completion of the final report was overseen by the three coordinating authors; authorship of the individual chapters is recognized at the outset of each chapter.

Summary

This Research Paper assesses the performance of the adaptive management concept and the 10 allocated adaptive management areas (AMAs) across California, Oregon, and Washington that provided a diverse range of biophysical and socio-economic conditions and were to be used as test-beds for the application of adaptive management principles to meet certain technical and social objectives in the Northwest Forest Plan (the Plan). Particular attention focuses on evidence of implementation of adaptive practices that treat policies as experiments, the factors that facilitate or constrain implementation of adaptive management, and suggestions for changes to enhance its performance.

The incorporation of adaptive management in the Plan is the product of a long-evolving series of efforts to improve management of the region's forests and to secure adequate protection of a range of public values and uses, including endangered species, old-growth, commodity production, and community resiliency. Despite several efforts in recent years to ensure appropriate forest management regimes for the maintenance and restoration of species such as the northern spotted owl (*strix occidentalis caurina*), evidence mounted that the species status continued to decline. Despite major reductions in harvesting levels, with associated impacts on rural communities and people, the decline in habitat and species continued. It reached sufficient proportions to attract attention in the 1992 presidential campaign, leading to the 1993 Forest Summit hosted by President Clinton in Portland, Oregon. He called for creation of a team of experts to identify options to help break the gridlock that paralyzed forest management in the region. In response, the Forest Ecosystem Management Assessment Team (FEMAT) prepared a series of options; the selected alternative—the foundation of the Plan—imbedded the idea of adaptive management as a key element in its overall approach.

Although the concept of adaptive management has an appealing simplicity to it, it remains primarily an ideal rather than a demonstrated reality. A wide variety of definitions of adaptive management exist, ranging from traditional, incremental approaches and trial and error to more rigorous, hypothesis-based tests. The core of contemporary visions of adaptive management involve the explicit design of a protocol that involves an inclusive process of problem-framing, documentation and monitoring procedures, and assessment and evaluation processes. All these are designed to enhance learning from the implementation of policies. Although adaptive management in a natural resource context, including the Plan, has focused on resolving problems related to the management of biophysical systems, it nonetheless has an equally important sociopolitical dimension that manifests itself in both the problem-framing stage as well as in the evaluation and interpretation of the outcomes of policy implementation. Adaptive management is particularly suited for dealing with problems involving high levels of uncertainty, limited knowledge, and unpredictability. The goal of adaptive approaches is to enhance learning about these complex systems that enables more informed policy formulation and design and implementation of policies in a manner that enhances the learning that will derive from them. However, despite the great potential of an adaptive approach, significant barriers confront efforts to implement it: institutional constraints, including legal and political (e.g., legal requirements to protect endangered species), socio-psychological barriers (e.g., risk-aversion), and technical-scientific constraints (e.g., lack of adequate knowledge bases). Effective implementation of adaptive management requires strong organizational leadership and political support coupled with skilled advocates and champions at the field level. It also requires transition strategies that enable the transformation from traditional command-control systems to one built on learning, collaboration, and integration.

Incorporating adaptive management in the Plan was a strategy for fostering the knowledge needed to manage a complex ecosystem at a regional level. Although the Plan is weighted to terrestrial and aquatic reserves—a strategy grounded in the precautionary principle—a key allocation involved creation of the 10 AMAs across the three-state region. These areas, ranging from less than 100,000 acres to nearly half a million acres, were intended to provide a diverse range of biophysical and socioeconomic conditions. The overall objective of the AMAs was to "learn how to manage on an ecosystem basis in terms of both technical and social challenges… consistent with applicable laws." Technical objectives involved development, demonstration, implementation, and evaluation of monitoring programs and innovative management practices. The AMAs were sites where the Plan's standards and guidelines (S&Gs), applicable to management throughout the region, could be tested, validated, and revised as appropriate. The social objectives of the AMAs focused on provision of flexible experimentation with policies and management and the development of innovative links and relations with local communities in managing the region's forests. Although each AMA was assigned a principal area of emphasis (e.g., the relative efficacy of alternative silvicultural systems in restoring old-growth habitat), these were not to limit the work conducted in any area. Moreover, the AMAs were to be treated as an interrelated system, wherein lessons learned in any area were communicated to other areas.

To enhance the ability of the AMAs to meet the objectives assigned to them, each area was assigned one or two coordinators from the land management agencies (Forest Service and Bureau of Land Management). In Oregon and Washington, the Pacific Northwest Research Station assigned a lead scientist to each AMA, except the Finney, to facilitate interactions between land managers and researchers. Although the two California AMAs did not have lead scientists, local scientists were involved with them.

In addition to interviews with resource managers and scientists regarding efforts to incorporate an adaptive management strategy into the Plan, a region-wide survey of citizen interest and involvement in management of the AMAs was conducted. Over 400 so-called "attentive publics"—people who had been directly engaged in a problem, project, or issue related to the adaptive management program—provided information about their experiences. The survey also was administered to over 100 managers who had responsibilities in the AMAs. This provided an opportunity to compare responses between managers and citizens regarding their respective assessments of adaptive management.

There were significant differences between managers and citizens with regard to the extent they felt that the agencies had identified what the AMAs were intended to be or the role citizens should play in their management. For example, less than half of the citizen respondents believed they could participate in AMA planning, and even fewer thought that agencies had used suggestions they had provided in making decisions. There were also sharp differences between the two groups with regard to their assessment of the extent to which the AMAs had fostered productive interactions between citizens and managers; in no case did a majority of citizens agree that public involvement goals were being met. A particularly distressing statistic was that slightly less than one-third of citizens thought that the AMA program was effective in building trust and cooperation, whereas about half of the managers believed it had.

Four major conclusions emerged from the survey. First, although citizens have made gains in the extent to which their views, concerns, and knowledge are included in planning and decision processes, much remains to be done; many citizens remain convinced their input is neither sought nor used. Second, improved procedural performance is required; accurate data are provided, timelines are defined and followed, roles are identified and respected. A specific element here regards the visible participation in planning efforts by agency leadership; such engagement is an important symbol of organizational commitment and an indication to citizens that their participation is worth the time it takes and that their input is likely to be acknowledged and used.

Third, creation of the AMAs and the definition of their purposes have created high expectations among many citizens. The notion that the AMAs would offer more flexible, creative opportunities has been well-received, but failure to follow through on this has been disappointing to many, suggesting that despite organizational rhetoric, AMA management is "business as usual." Finally, there is a need for management agencies to reach internal agreement and understanding as to the purposes of the AMAs. There has been a low level of organizational support for personnel in adaptive management functions, and that appears directly related to the lack of results the public can observe. Clearly, there is a need for agencies to deliver on what it is they have said they will do.

To assess the impact of the adaptive management program on the Plan's implementation, 50 interviews were undertaken with managers and scientists directly involved with the effort. An open-ended interview schedule was developed and administered to these people in sessions that ranged from half an hour to 3 hours. Interviews were recorded and evaluated for content and key themes. Five major findings emerged from them. First, multiple definitions existed as to the meaning of adaptive management. For many, there was a strong belief that management agencies had always been adaptive and that the current attention given to the idea simply affirmed this long-term tradition. For others, adaptive management was principally a means of enhancing relations with public groups. There was also a strong undercurrent of confusion as to what the term meant for land managers. In general, there was a sense that adaptive management called for a new way of doing business, but the specific nature of that "new" way was not entirely clear.

A second finding relates to the question as to what institutional structures and processes would be required to support an adaptive approach. Consistent with the belief that agencies always had been adaptive, some argued little change was required. Others acknowledged that current management approaches were not well-suited to an adaptive approach. Although many agreed that learning was a key element of an adaptive approach, they acknowledged that little had been accomplished in developing processes and protocols to document and integrate learning with subsequent action. Many concurred that documentation was rare; moreover, the lack of specific examples of on-the-ground projects meant there was little to document. The interviews revealed that despite the objective of using the AMAs as venues for the testing and validation of the S&Gs, virtually no such work had occurred; moreover, there was a strong belief that in the absence of a more substantive involvement by either the regulatory agencies or environmental interests, the likelihood of using information, were it to be available, for modifying the S&Gs was remote.

Third, important achievements did occur. The AMAs and the AMA coordinators helped foster improved and extended efforts to work with the public, particularly in local communities. Field trips, small group meetings, and other forms of one-on-one or small group interactions improved understanding of the respective groups' concerns and interests. In summary, the AMA program provided an important mechanism that facilitated public involvement efforts.

Fourth, both internal and external barriers constrain effective implementation of adaptive management. Despite the comments above regarding improved public involvement, there were concerns regarding the limited ability of management agencies to implement plans and to convert rhetoric to reality. Agency personnel expressed frustration with opposition from external interest groups and the associated lack of trust or inclination to collaborate, either with the agencies or with one another. Many individuals expressed a sense of uncertainty and a lack of clarity with regard to the mission and direction of the AMAs; some expressed the belief AMAs were an ephemeral phenomenon, existing only because of current political whims. There was widespread concern that despite the rhetoric given to the importance of innovation and creativity in an adaptive approach in general, and in AMA management in particular, little in the way of these qualities had materialized. Some of this was attributed to the impact of external factors, such as the requirements for management of endangered species; the fear of litigation and lawsuits was commonly expressed.

There was candid acknowledgment that a risk-averse institutional culture stymied creative and innovative approaches. Some saw a shifting burden of proof argument as a critical change, in that managers were now required to demonstrate no adverse effects would result from an action prior to implementation. The theme of risk-aversion also extended beyond the agency culture; there was a widespread conviction that regulatory agencies, environmental interest groups, and the public in general were opposed to actions whose outcomes were uncertain. The perceived need for an ability to be certain in an uncertain environment was seen as a critical challenge to acting adaptively. Finally, agency personnel frequently cited the lack of institutional support—funding, training, staff—as a challenge to the adaptive management program. A lack of organizational commitment to adaptive management and an associated failure for organizational leadership to take a strong, proactive stance with regard to its importance in Plan implementation was cited.

A fifth finding was that a number of steps would be required to make adaptive management an effective, successful program. This included a clarification of the definition, goals, and objectives for the program; clear evidence of organizational commitment, capacity, and leadership; enhanced organizational resources in terms of funding, training, and most importantly, time to do the job; improved public participation processes; and an increased emphasis on the delivery of on-the-ground, visible projects.

There remain major challenges and barriers to implementing adaptive management, both in general and in terms of the Plan. In the case of the Plan, many of these problems took form in the process of converting the FEMAT recommendations into specific and legal actions identified in the record of decision (ROD). Concerns remain about the organizational leadership, willingness, and capacity to implement an adaptive approach, particularly as a strategy involving experimentation and risk-taking. The challenges of building an adaptive organization are substantial and will require changes beyond simply tinkering with current organizational structures, processes, and skill sets. Particularly challenging is developing a mind set that is accepting of risk and uncertainty, especially given the risk-averse nature of the larger political context. Adaptive management is also challenged by the asymmetry between the costs of such an approach, which typically are revealed in the short term, and the benefits, which might not be revealed for a long time.

At the outset of this report, we identified four key evaluative criteria. First, is adaptive management conceptually sound and is the idea, at its core, sensible? We conclude that it is a conceptually sound, sensible idea, at least in the abstract. It represents a viable, productive complement (not a replacement) to traditional management approaches. Having said that, it remains problematic as to whether it is an academic, intellectually-robust notion, but one whose utility is diminished by political and legal realities.

Second, does adaptive management translate into practice well? A variety of problems and barriers—structural, organizational, social-psychological, political, and legal—stymie implementation. The inability or unwillingness to acknowledge the limits of knowledge and capacity, the inevitability of mistakes coupled with a lack of forbearance and tolerance, the difficulty of letting go of conventional ways of organizing and behaving all combine to foster resistance to experimentation and implementing innovation.

The third criterion involves the ethical aspects of adaptive management and the associated costs and benefits and their distribution associated with its application. New knowledge and the management implications associated with it are not always seen as a benefit. Not all interests will consider new understanding of ecological processes and functions, for example, as necessarily a good thing. And when costs are revealed, resistance is often not far behind. An adaptive approach also implies that multiple forms of knowledge about the world exist. In traditional management, expertise was considered as largely held by scientists and specialists. Knowledge long has been a currency of power, but in an adaptive world, this currency becomes universal and shared, meaning that power is distributed across a wide range of players, rather than concentrated in the hands of a few.

The final criterion concerns the pragmatic aspects of adaptive management; Does it work? In general, the answer is "we do not yet know." Given the time scales involved in both ecological and social processes, it might be some time before we do. However, the nature of the larger political and social environment is one in which ambiguity is not easily accepted or tolerated. An innovative policy such as adaptive management will take time, perhaps measured in many years, before we have a good understanding of its practicality. The expectation that the adaptive management directives in the Plan will produce demonstrable evidence of success in only a few years is unrealistic. However, given the larger social, political, and legal environment within which the Plan is imbedded, such an inability to unequivocally document success might prove a major liability.

What will be needed to improve the performance of adaptive management in the Plan? A number of requisite attributes can be identified. These include a closer alignment of adaptive management with organizational goals; a demonstrated organizational commitment and will to act adaptively; increased capacity (skills, resources); a clear, shared language; an agreement on expectations, both within and outside the management organizations; a reasonable likelihood of continuity to allow the process a fair chance to succeed; clear performance benchmarks; and formal and explicit documentation protocols.

These requisite attributes also need to be pursued within a strategic policy environment. At its core, we must find ways to revitalize the vision of adaptive management spelled out in FEMAT and the ROD. Organizational leadership must publicly declare adaptive management as a new way in which business will be conducted. An increased focus must be placed on building effective processes, relationships (with citizens, regulators, politicians), and outcomes. Within the organizations, there is a need to provide the skills, tools, and protocols necessary to be adaptive. The focus on learning needs to better link with actions and how those actions are justified or how they might need to be altered in light of new knowledge. Adaptive management, like all types of resource management, is ultimately a political undertaking and there is a need to build increased political understanding and support among the host of actors, internal and external, involved in resource management. Finally, greater emphases need to be placed on the phases and steps in which we engage to practice adaptive management. This includes improved processes to frame problems; to document intentions, processes, and outcomes; to interpret what was learned in a policy-relevant manner; and to continually appraise what was learned and its implications for examining new questions and uncertainties and thereby renew the adaptive management cycle.

Contents

Chapter 1: Toward the Future

George H. Stankey, Roger N. Clark, Bernard T. Bormann, Clare Ryan, Bruce Shindler, Victoria Sturtevant, and Charles Philpot[1]

Key Findings

- Adaptive management and adaptive management areas were central elements of the Plan. Over time, adaptive management would generate new knowledge and understanding that could lead to changes in the Plan.

- Concerns about the effectiveness of implementing an adaptive approach led to calls for an evaluation of its performance, including an understanding of barriers and solutions to them.

- An evaluation team, representing agency and nonagency participants, undertook this project to document experiences in implementing an adaptive approach and the factors that facilitated or constrained these efforts.

- The evaluation addressed four dimensions of policy design: (1) conceptual soundness (i.e., Is the adaptive management idea sensible?); (2) technical (i.e., Does the idea translate into practice well?); (3) ethical (i.e., Who loses and who wins when adaptive management is implemented?); and (4) pragmatic (i.e., Does adaptive management work?).

Introduction

In April 1993, President Clinton convened a Forest Summit in Portland, Oregon, to discuss the "gridlock" gripping federal forest management in the Pacific Northwest. Following the summit, the President established the Forest Ecosystem Management Assessment Team (FEMAT) to frame a set of alternatives designed to resolve that gridlock. Their efforts were guided by a mission statement (FEMAT 1993: i-iv) directing the team to consider a range of issues and uses, including

---

[1] George H. Stankey is a research social scientist (retired), and Bernard T. Bormann is a principal plant physiologist, U.S. Department of Agriculture, Forest Service, Pacific Northwest Research Station, Forestry Sciences Laboratory, 3200 SW Jefferson Way, Corvallis, OR 97331; Roger N. Clark is a research social scientist (retired), U.S. Department of Agriculture, Forest Service, Pacific Northwest Research Station, Pacific Wildland Fire Sciences Laboratory, 400 N 34th Ave, Suite 201, Seattle, WA 98103. Clare Ryan is an associate professor, College of Forest Resources, University of Washington, Seattle, WA 98105, Tel. 206 616 3987, e mail: cmryan@u.washington.edu; Bruce Shindler is a professor, College of Forestry, Oregon State University, Corvallis, OR 97331, Tel. 541 737 3299, e mail: Bruce.Shindler@oregonstate.edu; Victoria Sturtevant is a pro fessor, Department of Sociology and Anthropology, Southern Oregon University, Ashland, OR 97520 Tel. 541 552 6762, e mail: Sturtevant@sou.edu; Charles Philpot is a retired director, U.S. Department of Agriculture, Forest Service, Pacific Northwest Research Station, Sherwood, OR 97140.

The AMAs were to be used "to develop and test new management approaches to achieve the desired ecological, economic, and other social objectives... and to offer the opportunity for creative, voluntary participation in forest management activities by willing participants."

environmental and ecological values as well as the economic and social effects of proposed policies.

That statement also provided the following direction: "...your assessment should include suggestions for adaptive management that would identify high priority inventory, research, and monitoring needed to assess success over time, and essential or allowable modifications in approach as new information becomes available" (FEMAT 1993: iii). The FEMAT report responded in two ways. First, it discussed the adaptive management concept, arguing it was a "crucial element of any ecosystem-based strategy" (FEMAT 1993: VIII-17). Second, it incorporated a specific land allocation—adaptive management areas (AMAs)—in its discussion of option 9, the alternative eventually selected. The AMAs were to be used "to develop and test new management approaches to achieve the desired ecological, economic, and other social objectives... and to offer the opportunity for creative, voluntary participation in forest management activities by willing participants" (USDA and USDI 1994: 28).

Ten AMAs were established, accounting for 6 percent of the land area of the 24-million acre (9.7-million hectare) owl habitat region across western Washington and Oregon and northern California (fig. 1). They range in size from 90,000 acres (36 400 hectares) to nearly half a million acres (202 000 hectares), providing a diverse range of biophysical and socioeconomic conditions. Each area was assigned a particular emphasis (table 1). Although it was not the intention of FEMAT that the emphasis assigned to any one area would preclude or restrict flexibility and innovation within that AMA, those emphases typically have been interpreted as prescriptive and binding.

Adaptive Management and the Northwest Forest Plan

At present, the Northwest Forest Plan (the Plan) is grounded in a set of allocations and specific land management prescriptions (standards and guidelines [S&Gs]) that direct management across the region. As envisioned in FEMAT, in the longer term, the Plan was to be the means through which the elusive notion of ecosystem management would be achieved (Pipkin 1998). However problematic the definition of ecosystem management might be, its principal attributes stand in contrast to conventional management models and traditions; e.g., it favors a holistic approach, recognizes the stochastic, nonlinear, and dynamic nature of biophysical and socioeconomic systems, treats theory and practice as intertwined, and favors decentralized, flexible, and bottom-up management (Cortner and Moote 1999). Although the explicit concept of ecosystem management has faded from the contemporary agency lexicon, these core elements remain important.

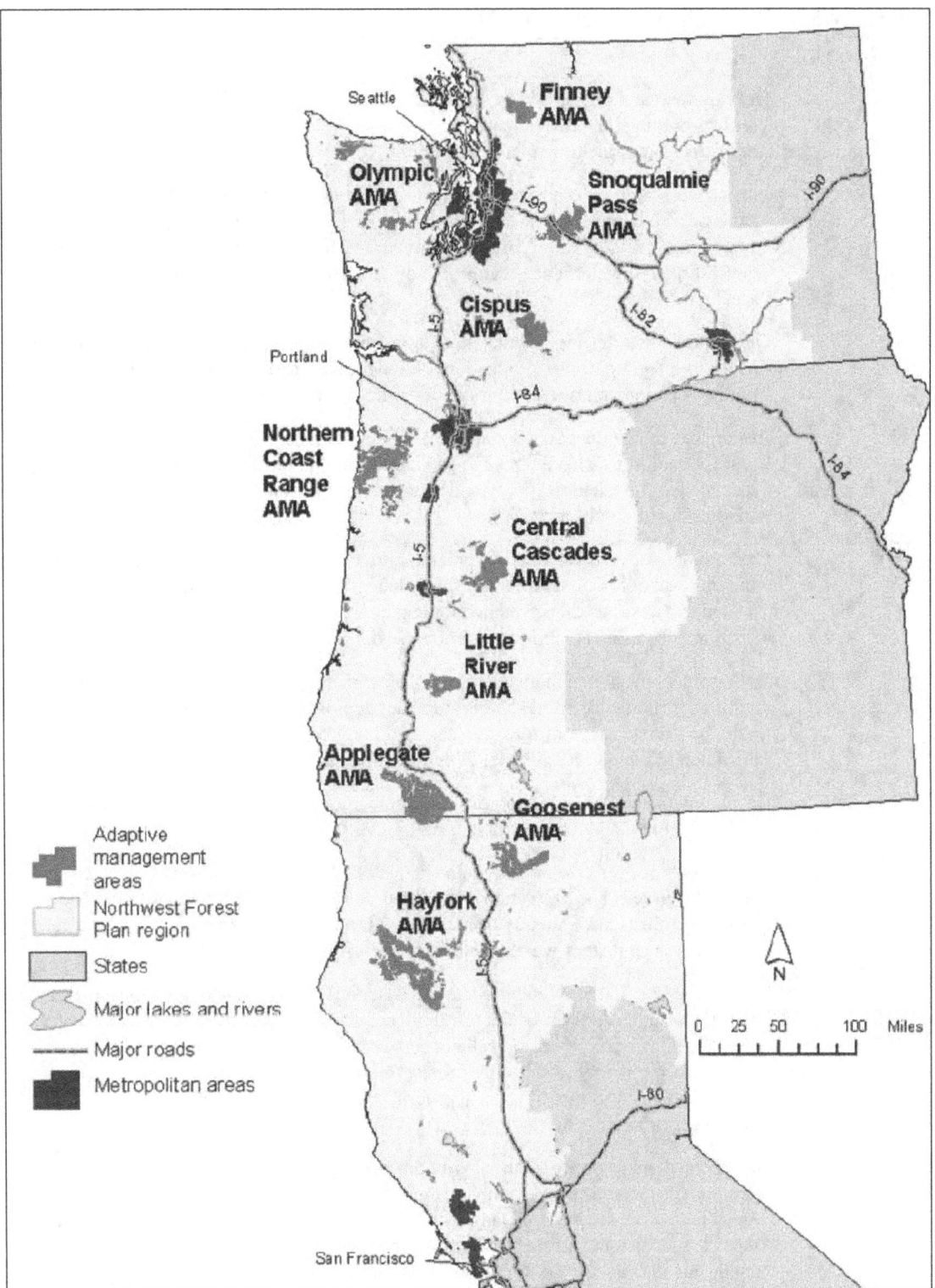

Figure 1   The 10 adaptive management areas in the Northwest Forest Plan provide a diverse range of biophysical, political, and socioeconomic conditions.

Table 1—Emphases assigned to adaptive management areas

Adaptive management area	Emphasis
Applegate	Development and testing of forest management practices, including partial cutting, prescribed burning, and low-impact approaches to forest harvest to provide a broad range of forest values, including late-successional forest and high-quality riparian habitat.
Central Cascades	Intensive research on ecosystem and landscape processes and its application to forest management in experiments and demonstrations at the stand and watershed level; approaches for integrating forest and stream management objectives and on implications of natural disturbance regimes; and management of young and mature stands to accelerate development of late-successional conditions.
Cispus	Development and testing of innovative approaches at stand, landscape, and watershed levels to integrate timber production with maintenance of late-successional forests, healthy riparian zones, and high-quality recreational values.
Finney	Restoration of late-successional and riparian habitat components. (Given that most late-successional forests have already been harvested, the record of decision directed that special steps be taken to survey and protect marbled murrelets and the retention of areas critical to owl survival).
Goosenest	Development of ecosystem management approaches, including use of prescribed burning and other silvicultural techniques, for management of pine forests, including objectives related to forest health, production and maintenance of late-successional forest and riparian habitat, and commercial timber production.
Hayfork	Development, testing, and application of forest management practices, including partial cutting, prescribed burning, and low-impact approaches to forest harvest, which provide for a broad range of forest values, including commercial timber production and provision of late-successional and high-quality riparian habitat.
Little River	Development and testing of approaches to integration of intensive timber production with restoration and maintenance of high-quality riparian habitat.
North Coast	Management for restoration and maintenance of late-successional forest habitat, consistent with surveys and protection of marbled murrelet. (Like the Finney, most late-successional forests have already been harvested in the North Coast adaptive management area; thus special steps were called for to protect murrelets and owls).
Olympic	In partnership with the Olympic State Experimental Forest, Washington Department of Natural Resources, develop and test innovative approaches at the stand and landscape level for integration of ecological and economic objectives, including restoration of structural complexity to simplified forests and streams and development of more diverse managed forests through appropriate silvicultural approaches such as long rotations and partial retention.
Snoqualmie Pass	Development and implementation, with the participation of the U.S. Fish and Wildlife Service, of a scientifically credible, comprehensive plan for providing late-successional forest on the "checkerboard" lands (i.e., mixed public and private tenure). This plan should recognize the area as a critical connective link in north-south movement of organisms in the Cascade Range.

Adopted from USDA and USDI 1994: D 12 16.

In the short term, however, the Plan acknowledged limitations in the ability to implement an ecosystem management approach. Both the current levels of scientific knowledge as well as institutional structures and processes are inadequate to move from the stand-level, commodity-oriented model of past management to something approximating the characteristics of ecosystem management described above. Thus, the Plan's short-term strategy is grounded in a precautionary approach, designed to prevent irreversible errors and ensure the maintenance of options. This is reflected in the allocation of over three-fourths of the region into reserves (congressional or administrative) and a set of standards and guidelines (S&Gs) that are restrictive, conservative, and largely mandatory.

Such actions are not unusual in the face of high levels of uncertainty and where the possibility of irreversible consequences exists. However, the Plan also envisioned a **phased** approach to implementation; as time passed and knowledge grew, allocations and prescriptions could be revised. "The Northwest Forest Plan was not intended to be a static creation. It was intended to **evolve**...." (Pipkin 1998: 71). The knowledge driving this evolution will derive from both traditional scientific inquiry and through implementation of **adaptive management processes**. Adaptive management is a "cornerstone of any long-term plan, like the Northwest Forest Plan... where the intention is to modify and improve the plan as experience is gained" (Pipkin 1998: 9).

The Plan acknowledged that improving understanding of the complex biophysical, socioeconomic, and political systems in the region would require an increased emphasis on new knowledge. As a result, it called for adoption of an adaptive management strategy to gain new understanding. It proposed a four-phase adaptive management cycle (fig. 2). In the first phase, plans are framed, based on existing knowledge, organizational goals, current technology, and existing inventories. In phase two, on-the-ground actions are initiated. Phase three involves monitoring results of those actions and, in phase four, results are evaluated. The cycle could then reinitiate, driven by emerging knowledge and experience. Results could validate existing practices and policies or reveal the need for alterations in the allocations, S&Gs, or both.

Adaptive management is embodied within the Plan as both a strategy and an allocation. Supporting the role of adaptive management as a strategy for achieving the objectives of the Plan, the AMAs provide places where learning "how to manage on an ecosystem basis in terms of both technical and social challenges, and in a manner consistent with applicable laws" can occur. The record of decision (ROD) (USDA and USDI 1994: D-1) noted:

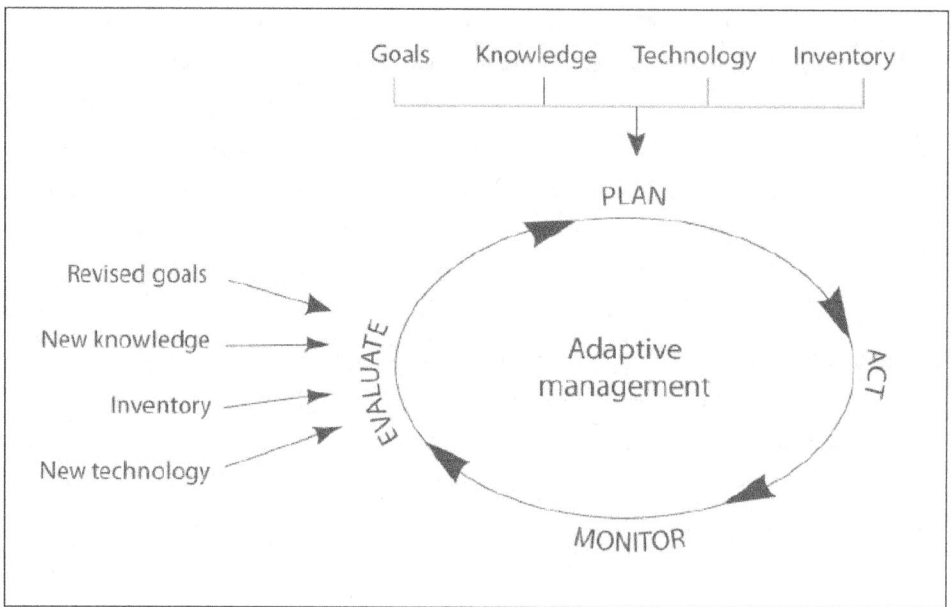

Figure 2   The adaptive management cycle (USDA and USDI 1994: E 14).

It is hoped that localized, idiosyncratic approaches that may achieve the conservation objectives of these standards and guidelines can be pursued. These approaches rely on the experience and ingenuity of resource managers and communities rather than traditionally derived and tightly prescriptive approaches that are generally applied in management of forests.

Thus, AMAs serve as an end in themselves **and** as a means to an end; they provide an innovative institutional structure in the short term for developing knowledge among citizens, managers, and scientists; applying the knowledge; and learning and adapting based on those applications. The cycle results in improved knowledge about the region's biophysical and socioeconomic systems as well as about the adaptive management process.

The Problem

Although adaptive management and the AMAs hold considerable potential and promise (Stankey and Shindler 1997), to what extent, and under what conditions, have these qualities been realized? At present, any answer can only be tentative and qualified. Some preliminary efforts to provide a more systematic evaluation have been undertaken (Shannon et al. 1995, 1997; Shindler 2003; Shindler and Aldred-Cheek 1999). A 1996 report, *Adaptive Management Areas: 1996 Success Stories*

(USDA Forest Service 1996), presents a series of brief, self-defined successes across the AMA system. Clearly, the AMAs provided opportunities that have been seized upon by local managers, citizens, and scientists to explore new ideas, including research, collaboration, and management. Yet it is unclear the extent to which such efforts are simply innovative and creative project-level activities or if they constitute measures that enhance, facilitate, and communicate learning and its systematic integration into subsequent action, key elements of an adaptive approach.

There are three levels at which adaptive management is appraised in this report. First, there is the generic concept of adaptive management. As noted earlier, the concept has gained attention in recent years, and efforts to apply it in varying resource sectors have been undertaken. This body of experience and evaluations relative to implementation efforts is primarily examined in the companion literature review (Stankey et al. 2005). Second, and more directly a component of this evaluation, there are questions concerning the extent to which adaptive management has become the critical component of the Plan, as envisioned in both FEMAT and the ROD. Finally, the extent to which the AMAs have served to provide an allocation in which adaptive management practices and processes could be implemented on the ground is examined.

Any assessment of the effectiveness and utility of adaptive management must be framed within the particular level of analysis. In this evaluation, we are primarily concerned with the latter two levels; adaptive management as a general strategy within the Plan and the performance of the AMAs. However, we have attempted to draw lessons and experiences from the wider body of literature and experience where appropriate to assess experiences in the Northwest and as a basis for identifying needed actions and strategies.

The difficulty of documenting success, improvement, or even examples of an adaptive approach within the context of the Plan or the AMAs is not unexpected or unique to the situation in the Pacific Northwest. A review of the adaptive management literature (Stankey et al. 2005) revealed similar challenges to measuring progress. An array of problems have been documented: e.g., difficulties in developing acceptable predictive models, inadequate designs to facilitate and communicate learning, conflicts regarding ecological/social values and management goals, inadequate attention to nonscientific knowledge, and risk-averse organizations (Johnson 1999, Miller 1999). Such challenges have stymied efforts to practice an adaptive approach in a host of geographic, sociopolitical, and resource sector situations.

Although it is important to recognize the widespread, generic nature of the challenges confronting adaptive management, we need to capitalize on, and build from, the insight these experiences provide as a basis for assessing, evaluating, and enhancing the practice of adaptive management in the Plan. However, a core problem is that we lack a rigorous, systematic assessment and evaluation of adaptive management and the AMAs and their impact on resource management practices, organizations, and users. Pipkin (1998) noted that the extent to which the purpose of AMAs envisioned in the Plan (i.e., to test, validate, refine, and implement S&Gs) has occurred is problematic and that the full potential of the AMAs has yet to be realized. He suggests that progress has been constrained by a persistent "top-down," and often statutory or procedurally grounded management approach. He concluded "there appears to be a need to institute some form of **evaluation process** that would allow agency personnel to terminate practices that are not working and establish new practices that might be more effective" (Pipkin 1998: 71).

The arguable success or failure of adaptive management and the AMAs, however, is only symptomatic of more fundamental questions: In what ways has the concept of adaptive management been undertaken and tested? More to the point, what body of knowledge has emerged as to how to effectively translate the best state of knowledge into management decisions and how have we been able to use this implementation process as a source of feedback, problem reformulation, and learning? Conversely, what factors and forces constrain such a process?

The inability to answer such questions is aggravated by a continuing failure to find instructive models where the core concept of adaptive management has been implemented. Despite its intuitive appeal, examples of effective adaptive management remain elusive. Walters (1997: 2) observed:

> Unfortunately, adaptive-management planning has seldom proceeded beyond the initial stage of model development, to actual field experimentation. I have participated in 25 planning exercises for adaptive management of riparian and coastal ecosystems over the last 20 years; only seven of these have resulted in relatively large-scale management experiments, and only two of these…would be considered well planned in terms of statistical design…. The rest have either vanished with no visible product, or are trapped in an apparently endless process of model development and refinement. Various reasons have been offered for low success rates in implementing adaptive management, mainly having to do with cost and institutional barriers.

In light of these factors—the importance of an adaptive approach to the long-term success of the Plan and the apparent inability to implement adaptive approaches, despite its potential and promise—we undertook the following evaluation.

Study Objectives

This evaluation addresses several objectives.

- Develop a critical discussion and analysis of the historical and socio-political context within which the Plan was framed.
- Identify and clarify the premises and assumptions within the Plan upon which the concept of adaptive management was based and that underlay creation of the adaptive management areas.
- Develop a critical evaluation of the experience in application of adaptive management and in the implementation of the AMAs.
- Identify factors that facilitate or constrain implementation and application.

Our purpose was to undertake a rigorous, systematic evaluation of the core adaptive management concept, identifying its potential, limitations, and the institutional requirements for effective implementation. By evaluation, we mean a "purposeful activity, undertaken to affect policy development, to shape the design and implementation of social interventions, and to improve the management of social programs" (Rossi and Freeman 1993: 403).

There is particular interest in understanding how the current best knowledge—based on science, management experience, or local knowledge—has been applied in the adaptive management cycle, how such knowledge has shaped the definition of management questions, the context under which the findings have been applied, the role of science and scientists in the adaptation of findings in applied contexts (Graham and Kruger 2002), and the dynamics of feedback, evaluation, and reformulation (as appropriate) of practices in light of outcomes. In short, our concern is with documenting the learning and feedback process and the nature of facilitating, as well as constraining, structures and processes.

Within this broader undertaking, we also assess the institutional structure of the AMAs. As Pipkin (1998) noted, the AMAs now possess a sufficient history and body of experience to warrant systematic evaluation regarding what they have accomplished and what directions should be undertaken in the future.

It is important to acknowledge the role of timing on this evaluation. Although the concept of adaptive management has been discussed in the literature for nearly

30 years, its specific application to the Plan is less than a decade old. If we think of adaptive management as an innovation, the diffusion-adoption literature (Rogers 1995) would suggest insufficient time has passed to appraise fully the extent to which this policy experiment has proved fruitful or not; typically, innovations require 12 to 15 years before it is possible to assess their relative impact.

We are hopeful that this review comes at an opportune time; much of the budget support for adaptive management and the AMAs has been discontinued, and current efforts to practice adaptive management are being undertaken primarily through the efforts of committed field-level managers and scientists. On a more positive note, there appears renewed interest in adaptive management and the AMAs on the part of the Regional Ecosystem Office (REO), the Regional Interagency Executive Committee, and the Intergovernmental Advisory Committee (these groups provide oversight and policy advice for implementation of the Plan). Thus, this evaluation has the potential of demonstrating the key values of an adaptive approach as well as providing an improved understanding of the factors that facilitate, as well as constrain, implementation, and this could prove critical to efforts to revitalize the adaptive management effort. Abandoning the adaptive management experiment at this time could constitute a premature closure that would waste the resources, financial as well as intellectual, invested to this point and forego a legitimate opportunity to implement adaptive management as a rigorous, appropriate, and effective management strategy.

Approach

Our review of adaptive management as a policy innovation is grounded in a framework discussed by Lee (1999). Citing earlier work by Brewer (1973), Lee argues that successful policies are responsive to four key dimensions.

First, is the policy **conceptually sound**? That is, are the underlying concepts and precepts of the policy sensible? Do they satisfy generally accepted standards of logic and clarity? Does the policy allow for hypotheses, controls, and replication, the standard tools of scientific inquiry and verification? As Lee (1999) reminds us, learning is valuable, but it is a precarious value compared to action.

Second, how well does the idea **translate into practice**? Here, we are concerned with the extent to which there are models and mechanisms for translating ideas—however compelling and appealing—into effective action. The absence of such models and mechanisms, or the difficulty, costs, and time required to employ them can stymie the most attractive idea.

Third, with any policy, under any circumstance, there will be winners and losers associated with its implementation. Thus, there is a need to be concerned about the **ethical and equity aspects of the policy**. When the costs of policy implementation are ignored or discounted, any benefits associated with it become tenuous and provisional, especially in systems of democratic governance.

Fourth, **will the idea actually work on the ground**? This is a measure of pragmatism and argues that irrespective of the conceptual soundness, the availability of models and mechanisms, and a full cost accounting of any policy, it is the ability to turn the idea into demonstrable, on-the-ground results that ultimately establishes its utility.

Lee (1993: 163) adds a fifth dimension to those above, identifying the idea of **vulnerability**, which embraces "the limitations and cautions necessary because learning in large ecosystems is not an established policy but an idea whose feasibility is being assessed." This dimension acknowledges there can be high levels of skepticism, denial, or outright opposition to changes in the way business is undertaken. It also highlights the importance of evaluation as a process to provide unbiased feedback on performance, but this also indicates how such evaluations can be resisted, discounted, or ignored, given their potential to challenge convention and accepted practices.

These basic criteria provide the basic framework within which our evaluation of adaptive management has been undertaken. The criteria are broad; for example, in chapter 5, Shindler reports on the extent to which citizens evaluated the efficacy of agency efforts to implement programs in the AMAs. Efficacy deals with the extent to which ideas translate into practice well and with the notion of pragmatism.

Policy evaluations typically involve multiple stakeholders, representing multiple interests, concerns, and perspectives (Rossi and Freeman 1993). In such an environment, one must acknowledge that the conclusions and recommendations that emerge from the evaluation represent only one input in a complex set of factors affecting a final decision. One also must recognize, and anticipate, the inevitable strains that result from any set of conclusions and recommendations because of conflicts with the multiple stakeholders. "To evaluate is to make judgments…" (Rossi and Freeman (1993: 407). Because judgments are inevitably involved, evaluations can be seen as a threat (Michael 1973). Ironically, such an interpretation, particularly in the case of this evaluation of adaptive processes, fails to acknowledge the value of treating the untried programs of adaptive management and the AMAs as an experiment that could inform future actions.

Because judgments are inevitably involved, evaluations can be seen as a threat (Michael 1973). Ironically, such an interpretation, particularly in the case of this evaluation of adaptive processes, fails to acknowledge the value of treating the untried programs of adaptive management and the AMAs as an experiment that could inform future actions.

In response to such concerns, the evaluation used various information sources. First, we undertook an extensive literature review, including a review of the growing body of literature dealing specifically with adaptive management (including other resource sectors, such as agriculture), as well as cognate fields, such as evaluation research, diffusion-adoption, and public policy. This helped identify key issues and questions our evaluation needed to consider in examining efforts to implement an adaptive approach in the Plan. That review is summarized in chapter 3 of this report, with the full review available as a General Technical Report (Stankey et al. 2005).

Second, we conducted interviews with 50 agency personnel involved in implementation of the adaptive management program. This included the AMA coordinators (representing the Bureau of Land Management and Forest Service), lead scientists (Pacific Northwest and Pacific Southwest Research Stations), key policymakers and line officers, REO members, regulatory staff and technical specialists, and selected citizens. The perspective of citizens on efforts to implement adaptive management was further assessed by an analysis of both quantitative and qualitative information obtained from a series of public surveys undertaken by Shindler (2003).

Third, we reviewed a variety of documents developed during implementation of the AMAs. This included research proposals, AMA plans and guides, the AMA business plan, and policy papers issued by the REO. We have also reviewed existing evaluations of the AMAs undertaken earlier by independent investigators.

Fourth, the evaluation team involved agency staff as well as university cooperators. This team approach enabled us to combine a diversity of disciplinary backgrounds, experiences, and independent observation with the high level of familiarity with the AMAs and adaptive management our internal review group possesses.

Chapter Outline

How adaptive management came to be a central component of the Plan, and the specific creation of the AMAs, is a product of debate and conflict over management of Pacific Northwest forests. Chapter 2 provides a historical analysis of this situation.

Given the importance of adaptive management to the Plan, an extensive review was undertaken of the adaptive management literature and its application across a wide range of resource sectors (e.g., water and riparian management, agriculture) and as well as a wide range of sociopolitical and cultural settings. The purpose of this review was to provide the evaluation team with a better understanding of the variety of problems to which adaptive management methods have been applied and to better understand the factors that affect (i.e., either facilitate or constrain) effective implementation. As noted above, that review is reported in a General Technical Report (Stankey et al. 2005); in this report, chapter 3 summarizes key findings.

Chapter 4 focuses on the AMAs and provides descriptive background on the system, including the assigned emphases as identified in the ROD as well as the organizational structure imposed on them by the management and research organizations. This chapter also reviews management and research activities undertaken within the AMAs, budget background, and an assessment of progress.

Chapter 5 reports on the results of a survey of citizens and managers involved with each of the AMAs. This includes information regarding expectations and experiences in working with the AMAs as well as evaluations of both positive and negative aspects and ideas for change in their administration.

In chapter 6 we analyze results of the interviews regarding efforts to implement adaptive management under terms of the Plan. This provides a detailed accounting of the experiences—for managers, researchers, line officers, the regulatory agencies—reported in efforts to implement the AMA program.

Chapter 7 is organized around two major components. First, based on the literature review, surveys with citizens, and interviews with agency officials, it presents a summary of conclusions regarding the effectiveness with which adaptive management and the AMAs have contributed to the implementation of the Plan. It also assesses the Plan's performance in light of the evaluative criteria introduced in chapter 1. In the second component, it presents a critical assessment of the challenges facing efforts to implement an adaptive management approach in the Plan. It discusses the key attributes that must be present for such an approach to succeed. Then, given that these conditions have been satisfied, the discussion identifies the steps of an adaptive approach: what they would entail and what roles and responsibilities individuals and groups within management and research organizations need to undertake. The challenge is that the barriers to adaptive management often are systemic in character, and any hope for long-term success must address these challenges at the systemic level. Without leadership and courage, such changes are unlikely to be successful.

This project is grounded in the tradition of evaluation research: "a purposeful activity, undertaken to affect policy development, to shape the design and implementation of social interventions, and to improve the management of social programs" (Rossi and Freeman 1993: 403). Policy evaluations are undertaken to identify what works and what does not as well as the factors contributing to these outcomes. They provide information on what kinds of changes might be most appropriate and efficacious (e.g., statutes, regulations, organizational structures, and processes) (Wallace et al. 1995). Ultimately, evaluation is a political activity involving judgments; policy evaluation research has come to acknowledge that policies and programs are creatures of political decisions and, therefore, subject to political pressure (Birman and Kennedy 1989). To ignore or remove this political aspect in policy evaluation is to handicap and debilitate the potential value of the evaluation in fashioning policy reform and change.

Chapter 2: Federal Forestry in the Pacific Northwest: Changing Uses, Changing Values, Changing Institutions

Charles Philpot, George H. Stankey, and Roger N. Clark[2]

Key Findings

- Conflicts over forest management in the Pacific Northwest derive from a long-term national debate regarding the values, goods, and services for which forest are managed and the means through which those desired ends are achieved.

- Despite a decade of intensive scientific involvement in the region, disputes over forest management remain, reflecting limits to the ability of science to resolve the technically-complex scientific questions or the sociopolitical value conflicts.

- The precautionary principle was the basis for specification of the initial standards and guidelines (S&Gs). The intent was to use adaptive management approaches, particularly in the adaptive management areas (AMAs), to validate whether the initial S&Gs were appropriate across the area covered by the Northwest Forest Plan (the Plan). The initial conditions imposed by the S&Gs limited, sometimes severely, the range of acceptable management activities.

- In the Plan, adaptive management and the AMAs were envisioned as strategies to develop improved knowledge and guidelines for forest resources management and to improve links with forest-dependent communities and interested citizens. They also provided venues to test and validate the Plan's S&Gs.

- The learning-based approach of adaptive management, based on systematic monitoring of feedback from applications and adapting subsequent applications in response to those outcomes, stands in contrast to the technical-rational planning model upon which contemporary forest planning relies.

---

[2] Charles Philpot is a retired director, U.S. Department of Agriculture, Forest Service, Pacific Northwest Research Station, Sherwood, OR 97140. George H. Stankey is a research social scientist (retired), U.S. Department of Agriculture, Forest Service, Pacific Northwest Research Station, Forestry Sciences Laboratory, 3200 SW Jefferson Way, Corvallis, OR 97331; and Roger N. Clark is a research social scientist (retired), U.S. Department of Agriculture, Forest Service, Pacific Northwest Research Station, Pacific Wildland Fire Sciences Laboratory, 400 N 34th Ave, Suite 201, Seattle, WA 98103.

Introduction

The Forest Ecosystem Management Assessment Team (FEMAT) and the resulting Northwest Forest Plan (the Plan) are only the most recent chapter in a long history of forest management in the Pacific Northwest. In this chapter, we describe the key events that led to President Clinton coming to Portland, Oregon, in 1993 with the purpose of breaking the gridlock gripping federal forest management. Understanding this historical context is crucial to understanding not only why FEMAT was developed, but also in understanding the evolving nature of the demands, uses, and values associated with the region's forests and of the relation of science to forest management in this changing milieu. It also is key to understanding the biophysical as well as sociopolitical environment that an adaptive management approach must accommodate.

The chapter draws on work presented in chapter 7 of FEMAT, "Social Assessment of the Options," especially pages VII-11-22; Wondolleck's *Public Lands Conflict and Management: Managing National Forest Disputes* (1988, esp. chapter 2); and Yaffee's *The Wisdom of the Spotted Owl* (1994). It also benefited from interviews with Charles Philpot, Director of the Pacific Northwest Research Station during FEMAT, and Jack Ward Thomas, FEMAT Team Leader, and Chief, USDA Forest Service, during the first years of the Plan's implementation.

The Early Years

With the rapid westward expansion of the 19th century, the Nation's natural resources faced a host of demands. Wood and water, in particular, fueled much of the Nation's growth and development. During this period, forestry, in the modern sense of the term, did not exist; forests were mined, with a "cut-and-get-out" mentality, always with the knowledge that more forests lay across the mountains.

However, at the end of the century, concerns about these rapacious practices, coupled with a growing sense that forests were limited, not limitless, prompted a push for policies and institutions to impose a more orderly pattern of forest development. Key to the development of such policies and institutions was the incorporation of science. Gifford Pinchot, fresh from forestry school in France, helped frame the central elements of scientific forestry in this country; by 1905, he was the head of the Bureau of Forestry, forerunner of the modern Forest Service. With Teddy Roosevelt, Pinchot drew the boundaries of the present-day National Forest System and Roosevelt signed them into law.

This history is well known, but its implications are less obvious. Our present system of national forests and the primary institution through which these lands are managed is, at least in American terms, old; they were created in a time and context that differs sharply from what prevails today. This historical legacy holds important values—an honored, stable organization, a legacy of proud public service, a source of strong identity and esprit de corps. But current events now challenge this legacy. Fairfax (2005: 266) recently argued that the Progressive Era ideology upon which the Forest Service is founded is no longer applicable; "sadly," she writes, "the agency's quest for a new management gospel has produced an uninspiring series of short-lived slogans…designed to protect the agency's eroding authority rather than to define its mission for a new age." Wilkinson (1992: 17) described many current policies as the "lords of yesterday," noting that they "arose under wholly different social and economic conditions but…remain in effect due to inertia, powerful lobbying forces, and lack of public awareness." Conceived and implemented a century ago, these lords of yesterday prevail today, and their inadequacies, limitations, and perspectives challenge our ability to respond to change. An inability or unwillingness to candidly and honestly confront these challenges carries great peril.

> **Conceived and implemented a century ago, these lords of yesterday prevail today, and their inadequacies, limitations, and perspectives challenge our ability to respond to change.**

Forestry in an Era of Post-War Expansion

The world changed dramatically after World War II. The Allied victory can be attributed in large part to America's extraordinary capacity in material production. However, one consequence of this concentrated output was that as timber supplies on private industrial lands were liquidated, growing demands for timber, generated by postwar expansion and prosperity increasingly were met by harvests from federal forests. The commodity production orientation of the Forest Service helped ensure the ability to respond to these demands.

This accelerated level of harvest was especially evident in the Pacific Northwest as the region possesses outstanding biological and physical attributes that support some of the most productive forest lands in the world. The result was an accelerated harvest of old-growth stands on the west side of the Cascades in Oregon and Washington. Much of the timber was harvested by using the same methods found on private lands; large clearcuts, extensive road systems, and minimal attention given to scenic, wildlife, watershed, recreation, or wilderness values.

Ironically, the postwar prosperity that fueled increased timber harvests also stimulated demands for nontimber goods and services from the same forests. The key drivers of increased demand for recreation and amenity values—a growing population, increased discretionary income and leisure time, increased education—coupled with structural changes such as improved transportation—led to unprecedented levels of use of forests and parks. Thus, traditional commodity values of forests, such as timber for housing construction, and emerging demands related to amenity values and uses combined to create new pressures on forests and the agencies that administered them.

Multiple Values and Multiple-Use Forestry

In 1960, Congress passed the Multiple Use-Sustained Yield Act (MU-SY). The act was intended to provide a framework within which the multiple values and uses found in forests could be managed and produced in a compatible fashion. Yet, in reality, these other uses and values entered into organizational decisionmaking processes largely in the form of either constraints on the primary output (i.e., timber) or only as secondary considerations. There was a prevalent notion that with rare exceptions, the practice of good timber management represented good management practices for a host of other values, such as wildlife and recreation. Thus, despite its name, the MU-SY Act, in large part, perpetuated a dominant-use philosophy.

As a result, the high levels of timber harvest in the Pacific Northwest continued. During the 1960s, harvest levels in the Pacific Northwest Region of the Forest Service, Region 6 (Oregon and Washington), approached 5 billion board feet per annum.

However, federal forest management in the Pacific Northwest faced new challenges. Some of these were rooted in events taking place outside the region, but their effects would reverberate throughout the forestry profession. In Montana's Bitterroot National Forest, timber harvesting had come under intense and critical public scrutiny. Initially, much of the public attention focused on the aesthetic impacts associated with the silvicultural practice of "terracing" steep slopes as a means of encouraging regeneration. However, these concerns quickly encompassed other issues as well; long-term site productivity, stand regeneration, and economics. At the request of Montana's U.S. Senator Lee Metcalf, an independent study of practices on the forest was commissioned under the leadership of Arnold Bolle, Dean of the School of Forestry at the University of Montana. The report (U.S. Senate 1963, often referred to as the "Bolle Report") was critical not only of the specific activity of terracing, but of the overall decisionmaking processes of the agency. The report concluded that timber harvest on the Bitterroot was more properly described as timber mining (i.e., it essentially involved a one-time, nonrenewable removal of trees, rather than sustained yield). Moreover, the authors concluded that "multiple use management, in fact, does not exist as the governing principle on the Bitterroot National Forest" (U.S. Senate 1963: 13). The resulting timber bias was seen as fundamentally at odds with the agency's capacity to operate under a multiple-use policy.

Three thousand miles away in West Virginia, another local controversy, but with similar national implications, was boiling. There, mixed hardwood stands were being clearcut, and local opposition, driven in part because of concerns by hunters of the effects of such a prescription on wild turkey populations, called for an end to the practice.

Congressional and Statutory Intervention in Forestry

Such events triggered increasing Congressional consideration of how to make federal forest management responsive to local as well as national constituencies. Congress responded by developing new legislation that gave even greater emphasis than before to the need for a rational system for both problem-framing and problemsolving. "Thus, the response to the obvious politicization of public forest management was more scientific management—rationality would be achieved when all of the values were placed in the same decision framework" (FEMAT 1993: VII-18).

The era of the 1970s saw two major Congressional initiatives to further this objective. The 1974 Resources Planning Act (RPA) emphasized the need for national thinking and planning on the federal lands, particularly as a strategy for improving the agency's ability to obtain long-term appropriations (Wilkinson and Anderson 1987). Among other requirements, it directed the Forest Service to develop an assessment of the Nation's renewable resources every 10 years; this would assess the status of resources on all lands (not just federal) as well as the current and expected demands for resources and forest products of all kinds. Based on the assessment, the Forest Service would prepare a program (updated each 5 years), describing activities in which the agency would be involved, consistent with legal constraints (e.g., private property) and the ecological, social, and economic context, as described in the assessment.

Although, RPA was intended, in part, to keep the agency out of court, ironically, less than a year after its passage, the Fourth Circuit United States Court of Appeals, ruling on a dispute over clearcutting on the Monongahela National Forest in West Virginia, found the activity illegal. This "crisis of authority" provided the impetus for yet another Congressional intervention to "…get the practice of forestry out of the courts and back to the forests" (Senator Hubert Humphrey in support of amendments to the RPA, quoted in Wondolleck 1988: 10).

In 1976, Congress enacted the National Forest Management Act (NFMA), technically an amendment to the RPA. The NFMA, like the RPA, was grounded in a belief in scientific management and rationality and relied on comprehensive assessments and planning processes to achieve these. The NFMA was more pre-scriptive than RPA, identifying acceptable management practices, restricting the use of clearcutting, and calling for suitability analyses for timber harvesting (e.g., harvested areas had to be capable of regeneration within 5 years). To facilitate implementation, the act called for creation of a committee of scientists (COS) to develop specific planning regulations.

The NFMA also shifted enduring emphases within the organization. For exam-ple, each national forest would be required to prepare a plan that focused on "values" as opposed to "uses." Formal public involvement was mandated as were the use of interdisciplinary teams (IDTs); both of these were consistent with direction con-tained in the National Environmental Policy Act (NEPA). Finally, a key element of NFMA was the requirement that plans prepared by individual forests had to ensure the long-term viability of all vertebrate species. Forests also were required to iden-tify the presence of any sensitive species, such as those classified as threatened and endangered, including those listed by the states.

It is important to note that the regulations developed by the COS were found by the courts to be part of the law (i.e., NFMA), rather than simply administrative regulations; thus, they were to be treated as such by the agency.

In summary, then, NFMA held these implications for the Pacific Northwest:

- It reduced clearcut size and defined biological, physical, and economic suitability for timber harvesting.
- It led to major shifts in organizational staff composition, moving from the traditional forester and civil engineer to nontraditional disciplines (wildlife, recreation, archaeology, etc.).
- It required formal identification of species that were "in trouble."
- It set the stage for the species viability clause in the regulations to take on a controlling role in defining acceptable forest management activities on the national forests.

- Although the agency retained final authority to make land management decisions, it reinforced public expectations (especially among nongovernmental organizations) for adequate and routine consideration of forest values and direct participation in, and influence upon, the decisionmaking process.

As the decade of the 1970s came to a close, a large planning effort was underway across the National Forest System. Not surprisingly, many problems were encountered. One of the most significant of these derived from the continuing pressure, oversight, and review by the Forest Service's Washington office that continually pressed for higher timber harvest levels associated with the preferred alternatives identified in forest plans than those calculated by local planning teams (Hirt 1994). Although the harvest levels identified in the plans were reduced from historical levels, agency planners as well as many interested stakeholders, were disturbed by pressures to increase the harvest. Thus, support to end clearcutting, and the conversion of old-growth stands, became even more intense, and calls for changes in decisionmaking processes grew.

Owls, Old-Growth, and Forestry

The changes began inauspiciously (Thomas and Verner 1992). Research by Eric Forsman, an M.S. student at Oregon State University in 1972, provided early evidence of the tenuous status of the northern spotted owl (*strix occidentalis caurina*) (fig. 3). Later, in 1975, the Oregon Department of Fish and Wildlife listed the spotted owl as threatened. In 1981, the U.S. Fish and Wildlife Service (FWS) described the subspecies as vulnerable, but argued that threatened status was not justified. In 1983, forest plans began to identify the owl as an indicator species for the health of old-growth forest ecosystems in the Pacific Northwest. Because much of the region's old-growth private forests had been liquidated, old-growth remnants found on Forest Service and Bureau of Land Management lands became critical to the owl's survival. However, even on these lands, approximately 70,000 acres (28 300 hectares) per year were being harvested, making the likelihood of an endangered listing for the owl virtually inevitable (Thomas et al. 1990).

Efforts to head off such listing continued, however. Both the Forest Service and the Bureau of Land Managrment were committed to the idea of instituting management regimes that would maintain "minimum viable populations" of owls. In 1984,

Figure 3 The northern spotted owl became an icon for growing public concerns about protection of old growth forests in the Pacific Northwest. *Photo by Burt Gildart.*

the Pacific Northwest Region of the Forest Service issued a regional guide designed to provide guidelines and prescriptions that would make listing unnecessary. It was appealed by environmental groups, who argued that the standard and guidelines were inadequate, and that an environmental impact statement (EIS) was required. A lengthy administrative appeals battle ensued, but in the final analysis, the Assistant Secretary of Agriculture ruled that an EIS was to be prepared. However, it too was challenged; e.g., all alternatives in this EIS were constrained by a limit of 15 percent maximum reduction in existing harvest. It also created spotted owl habitat areas, or SOHAs, although little scientific support for the concept existed (e.g., it attempted to apply the smallest documented SOHA size of 900 acres (365 hectares) across the entire owl range, disregarding research showing that the SOHAs varied from a minimum of 900 to over 4,000 acres [365 to 1600 hectares]). A court challenge eventually killed this EIS effort.

Conflicts continued over owl habitat and the effect of management activities on that habitat. In 1985, the National Audubon Society pressed for listing. Agencies continued to attempt to avoid both species listings and dramatic shifts in current practices. In 1986, the Bureau of Land Management considered preparation of a supplemental EIS to plans for managing owl habitat in western Oregon, but concluded that a supplement was not warranted, a decision later ruled inappropriate in Federal Court. In 1987, the FWS again was petitioned to list the owl as threatened, but for the second time, determined that listing was not warranted. That decision, in turn, was appealed and, once again, the Federal District Court concurred with the plaintiffs, ruling that the decision not to list the owl was arbitrary and capricious and directed FWS to once again review the issue. During this same period, the state of Washington officially declared the subspecies as endangered, while Oregon determined the owl to be threatened.

In 1988, the Forest Service issued a final supplemental EIS on owl protection. The selected alternative rated the long-term chance of successfully protecting the owl as poor; the rationale for selection of this alternative was that owl numbers would not be "seriously eroded" in the 5-year period covered by the management plan. Further, and a key assertion related to the issue of adaptive management, the recommended alternative was based on the assumption that information from research and monitoring efforts would lead to a more informed decision at the end of the 5-year period. In the meantime, logging of suitable owl habitat would continue at about the same level as before.

The Forest Service decision was appealed by environmental groups, as well as by the Washington Department of Wildlife, on the grounds that it provided inadequate protection for maintenance of viable numbers, as well as adequate distribution over its range on the national forests, as required by NFMA. The appeal was rejected by the Assistant Secretary of Agriculture.

Thus, at the close of the 1980s, forestry in the Pacific Northwest was embroiled in contentious debate. The questionable legality of many forest practices had resulted in major reductions in timber harvesting. Between 1987 and 1991, federal harvests declined from 5.6 to 3.1 billion board feet. Even more dramatic, whereas 5 billion board feet was offered for sale in 1990, only 1 billion board feet was offered in 1991, a decline largely attributable to a court injunction requiring the agency to justify harvest of remaining old-growth forests that provided habitat for associated species, as well as a range of other values and uses (FEMAT 1993: VII-21). Although the precise status of the spotted owl continued to be debated, it was clear the population was in decline. Moreover, concern was growing over the impacts of declining old-growth habitat on a host of other species and values. There was growing evidence that the policies and practices in place were inadequate to deal either with the levels of scientific uncertainty surrounding complex forest interactions or with the increasingly diverse range of societal demands and values (Wondolleck 1988). What remained unclear was what management strategies were most appropriate to respond to this situation.

The 1990s—An Era of Scientific Assessments

In 1989, as part of a rider to the appropriations bill for the Department of the Interior and related agencies (Section 318 of Public Law 101-121), a 1-year compromise was fashioned between environmentalists and timber industry interests. Commonly referred to as the "Northwest Compromise of 1989," it was intended to enhance existing owl habitat protection and establish a timber sale level for 1990. It also declared that Forest Service and Bureau Land Management plans for owl management were adequate (a decision challenged for its constitutionality, but eventually found to be so by the Supreme Court). For the purposes of this review, the most significant impact was that it acknowledged and incorporated provisions of the Interagency Scientific Committee (ISC) report and required federal agencies to respond to the results of that report (Thomas et al. 1990).

The ISC derived from an interagency agreement among the Forest Service, Bureau of Land Management, Fish and Wildlife Service, and National Park Service (NPS) calling for development of a scientifically credible conservation strategy for the northern spotted owl. Their report concluded the owl was "imperiled over significant portions of its range because of continuing losses of habitat from logging and natural disturbances" (Thomas et al. 1990: 1). It reported few options were available for managing owl habitat, and available alternatives were declining rapidly throughout the bird's range. "For these reasons, delay in implementing a conservation strategy cannot be justified on the basis of inadequate knowledge" (Thomas et al. 1990: 1).

The ISC recommended replacing the SOHA concept with habitat conservation areas (HCAs). These were large blocks of habitat capable of supporting, wherever possible, a minimum of 20 owl pairs, with no more than 12 miles (19 kilometers) separating one HCA from another to ensure connectivity. It also established the "50-40-11" rule (i.e., at least 50 percent of the forest land base outside of HCAs is maintained in timber stands with an average diameter at breast height of 11 inches

(28 centimeters) or greater and at least 40 percent canopy closure) in adjacent for-est lands, rather than dedicated corridors between HCAs. Finally, they noted that if healthy populations of owls could be sustained in the managed forest, HCAs even-tually would not be necessary.

The ISC report focused on the question of suitable owl habitat. However, other questions remained concerning the extent and condition of old-growth forests in the region and wildlife and fish species associated with them. Thus, in May 1991, two House of Representative committees (Agriculture and Merchant Marine and Fisheries) authorized formation of the Scientific Panel on Late-Successional Forest Ecosystems (known as "The Gang of Four," after the four principal authors, Norman Johnson, Jerry Franklin, Jack Ward Thomas, and John Gordon). The panel was given a variety of charges, but fundamentally, was to identify, map, and clas-sify the ecologically significant late-successional and old-growth (LS/OG) forests on federal lands within the range of the northern spotted owl and to propose and evaluate different alternatives for their protection (Johnson et al. 1991).

The panel proposed and evaluated 14 major alternatives, rating them on their ability to maintain and support viable populations of LS/OG-associated species, including the northern spotted owl and marbled murrelet (*Brachyramphus mar-moratus*). They also assessed the effects of these alternatives on timber harvest levels and regional employment and income. In the comparison between the alter-natives in terms of economic and environmental outcomes, the panel reported there was no free lunch; i.e., as the probability of retaining functional LS/OG networks and viable populations of owls and other threatened species and stocks went up, adverse impacts on employment and income would increase.

Two important conclusions from the panel presage the emerging importance of thinking adaptively. First, they noted that a major resource management need was to expand monitoring efforts in ways that ensured that forest plan objectives under NFMA were being achieved and that innovative management techniques, such as the 50-40-11 rule and green-tree retention, were working as hypothesized (the panel noted that effective monitoring programs "are almost nonexistent at this time," Johnson et al. 1991: 13). Second, they strongly encouraged research within the LS/OG reserve system, including stand manipulation and tree cutting. However, they cautioned, "research should represent bona fide scientific investigation based on appropriate statistical designs and led by qualified scientists. Uncontrolled and/ or large-scale management demonstrations should not be permitted" (Johnson et al.

1991: 13). The panel recommended the Forest Service and Bureau Land Management consider establishing additional experimental forests, across a range of locations and forest types, to facilitate needed research on LS/OG forests.

Following release of the ISC report, the FWS recommended listing of the northern spotted owl as threatened throughout its range. With the ISC report representing the only existing management strategy with at least some scientific credibility, the Forest Service announced it would rely on it as a strategy while the Bureau of Land Management opted for a modified version, called the Jamison Plan. Both agencies, however, were troubled by anticipated job losses associated with the ISC strategy, and both undertook a strategy to modify the ISC plan. This decision was challenged in Federal district court, on the grounds that it violated terms of the NFMA, Endangered Species Act (ESA), and NEPA. In May 1991, federal Judge William Dwyer ruled in favor of the plaintiffs, issuing an injunction against further timber harvesting in owl habitat on the national forests, pending adoption of a spotted owl management plan consistent with NEPA, NFMA, and ESA guidelines.

After Judge Dwyer's injunction, 1991-92 saw continuing efforts by management agencies to fashion a legally acceptable strategy for resuming timber harvesting while ensuring adequate owl habitat protection. In 1991, the FWS was ordered by Judge Thomas Zilly to map critical owl habitat. Initially, over 11 million acres (4.5 million hectares) were identified, later reduced to 8.2 million acres (3.3 million hectares), then again to 6.9 million acres (2.8 million hectares) (reductions were attributed to concerns about socioeconomic impacts, identified through public comment).

Listing of a species under the ESA requires a recovery plan, and an effort to prepare one began in early 1991, directed by Secretary of the Interior, Manual Lujan, Jr. Because of a variety of political concerns, that plan, although submitted to the Secretary's office at the end of 1991, and similar to the ISC report, was not signed. In 1992, an owl preservation plan was tabled by the administration; it resembled the unpublished recovery plan, but reduced the range of the northern spotted owl by about 50 percent. No action on this plan occurred.

Despite widespread recognition that owl habitat was in severe decline and the population under significant threat of extinction, at the end of 1992, no recovery plan was in place or even approved. As a consequence, court injunctions affecting both the Bureau of Land Management and the Forest Service remained in effect, halting all timber harvesting in spotted owl habitat.

In July 1992, then Chief of the Forest Service, Dale Robertson established yet another scientific team to address the questions raised by Judge Dwyer's ruling regarding the inadequacy of the Forest Service EIS on owl habitat protection. The Scientific Analysis Team (SAT) was asked to evaluate all the species associated with late-successional forests and to suggest mitigation measures to ensure high viability for those species. At-risk fish were included. The analysis in the report focused on the questions contained in Judge Dwyer's ruling:

- Does exemption of 13 Bureau of Land Management timber sales from the requirements of the ESA necessitate changes in viability assessments in the Forest Service's Final Environmental Impact Statement (FEIS)?
- Does new information necessitate changes in management proposed in the Forest Service's FEIS?
- What are the risks to other species associated with old-growth forests?
- What are appropriate mitigation measures?

Although it is not the purpose of this evaluation to describe in detail the find ings of the SAT in terms of these questions (detailed answers are found in the SAT report, 1993, chapters 2–5), it is important to note recognition by the team of the high levels of uncertainty surrounding the S&Gs contained in the various land and resource management plans guiding agency actions. A general tone in the answers to Judge Dwyer's questions was that exemptions would lead to increased risks for species survival, that understanding of the nature of those risks, as well as the species that would incur increased risk was minimal, and that the ability to specify appropriate mitigation strategies was limited.

Because of these risks and uncertainties, SAT called for monitoring and adaptive management as critical elements in its recommended management and mitigation measures (SAT 1993: 23). It noted "if, for whatever reason, no monitoring is instituted, the standards and guidelines we have suggested should be substantially enhanced to compensate for the risk of failure inherent in untested management strategies based to such a large extent on expert judgment" (SAT 1993: 24).

The response of the Forest Service to the SAT recommendations was equivocal. For example, in a letter dated March 1993 to recipients of the report, Deputy Chief James C. Overbay noted:

> This report does not represent any official position of the Forest
> Service....The report...presents one set of management proposals,
> based upon various scientific, legal, political, and administrative
> assumptions...that the scientific panel believes would raise the viability

Figure 4   In 1993, President Clinton convened a forest conference in Portland, Oregon, to discuss options for protecting the region's natural heritage and ensuring continued support for rural communities. The Forest Ecosystem Management Assessment Team report, which led to the Northwest Forest Plan, resulted from this conference.

rating to "high" for the northern spotted owl and all other native vertebrate species associated with late-successional forests...The report will be considered by the Forest Service...and will comprise an appendix to the DEIS, but...itself is not an alternative....

FEMAT and the Northwest Forest Plan

Despite three major scientific assessments in 3 years addressing the challenge of formulating a scientifically sound management program to protect the northern spotted owl and other old-growth-associated species and values, forest management in the region remained "in gridlock." During the 1992 presidential campaign, candidate Bill Clinton pledged that, if elected, he would host a forest conference as a first step in breaking that gridlock. On April 2, 1993, he fulfilled his promise, convening a forest conference in Portland, Oregon (fig. 4). At the close of the day, the President instructed that an assessment team be assembled to fashion a "balanced and comprehensive policy that recognizes the importance of the forests and timber to the economy and jobs in this region, and...preserve(s) our precious old-growth forest." The FEMAT was created in response to the President's challenge.

The team was given a broad mission statement. They were to undertake their work consistent with an ecosystem approach. There was a need to search for legally compliant solutions. Particular attention was to be given to maintenance and restoration of biodiversity and long-term site productivity. The NFMA's viability standard was to be applied to Bureau of Land Management lands as well. The mission statement called for maintenance of sustainable levels of renewable natural resource outputs, including commodities and other values and also emphasized maintenance of rural economies and communities.

A key element of the mission statement, particularly germane to this evaluation, followed: "Your assessment should include suggestions for **adaptive management** that would identify high priority inventory, research, and monitoring needed to assess success over time, and essential or allowable modifications in approach as new information becomes available" (FEMAT 1993: iii; emphasis added).

As envisioned in FEMAT, adaptive management was the mechanism through **which the validity and integrity of the assumptions underlying the policy and management recommendations could be assessed**. Adaptive management views policies as hypotheses; "policies are really questions masquerading as answers" (Light, quoted in Gunderson 1999: 35). It emphasizes that adaptive management is more than an ancillary management strategy to the reserve-based model emphasized in the Plan and the AMAs as more than a minor allocation of land, subject to the whims of changing priorities. Rather, these companion ideas were envisioned as the principal mechanisms through which the Plan's long-term, ecosystem-based goals would be achieved.

Scientific Assumptions Underlying the Northwest Forest Plan

In understanding any plan, an explicit exposition of underlying assumptions is critical. This includes the presumed relationship among variables (e.g., cause-and-effect relationships), the political context within which the plan is embedded (e.g., pressures for citizen-based decisionmaking vs. expert-driven), and the capacity of organizations to act in support of the plan's directives (e.g., sufficient financial and personnel resources, the availability of expertise). When such explicit discussion is absent, it is easy for assumptions to become accepted as fact or to act as constraints upon thinking. As Socolow (1976) observed, assumptions that might once have been formulated simply to enable applying a model can evolve into immutable constraints. Moreover, lacking explicit discussion of underlying assumptions leaves observers to make their own definitions, increasing the likelihood that conflicts and misunderstandings will occur.

A first step is simply identifying these assumptions. In the case of the Plan, this has escaped attention, with one exception (Busing 1994). Subsequently, Clark et al. (n.d.) cataloged what they considered to be the Plan's "higher order" assumptions—i.e., fundamental assumptions underlying the key components of the Plan, such as the reserves, allocations such as the AMAs, and the management processes used to implement the Plan. These assumptions are described below.

As envisioned in FEMAT, adaptive management was the mechanism through which the validity and integrity of the assumptions underlying the policy and management recommendations could be assessed.

Assumptions underlying reserve allocations of the Plan:

- The allocation of land within the region across reserves, matrix, and AMAs, and the associated management actions within each allocation, is sufficient to ensure legal compliance, species viability, economic stability, and protection of old growth.

- Needed management actions, and their consequences, to achieve the objectives of the respective allocations are understood, and there is an institutional capacity and willingness to undertake them.

- The terrestrial and aquatic reserve systems are not strict nature preserves, but can accommodate a variety of other uses and values.

- The size and distribution of reserves and connectivity corridors provided by riparian zone protection will provide sufficient dispersal habitat; therefore:
    * This will eliminate need for application of the 50-11-40 rules in the matrix.
    * Increased habitat and species protection afforded by the extensive reserve system will increase management discretion and flexibility in the matrix.

- After 150 years, stand conditions in reserves will exhibit old-growth characteristics, given active application of thinning, restoration, and management of disturbance regimes.

- The riparian reserves will provide adequate connectivity among reserves.

- In riparian reserves, potential site tree height would initially be used to define buffers, but onsite analysis will be undertaken to modify boundaries to accommodate local conditions.

- The principal conservation benefits for old-growth protection, endangered species, and noncommodity values will derive from reserves.

- There will be a capacity—scientifically, technically, and socially—to utilize disturbance regimes in the management of the reserves and that management of disturbance regimes is essential to the viability of both old growth and endangered species.

- Implementation of the riparian reserve system will not have a significant effect on the projected probable sale quantity (PSQ) of the Plan.

Assumptions underlying the AMA allocation:

- The AMAs are a fundamental allocation necessary to achieving objectives of the Plan; they serve as test beds for exploring options and approaches to applying ecosystem management across the region.

- The geographic distribution of the AMA system provides adequate bio-physical, social, and economic representation across the region.
- Managers, citizens, and regulatory agencies will understand and support the role of the AMAs and engage actively in their implementation.
- A key role of the AMAs is to provide a setting for validation, experimentation, and reformulation of management strategies, such as the S&Gs, that would be impossible to undertake in the reserves or matrix.
- The AMA system provides sufficient scale, biophysical and social diversity, and range of management conditions necessary to facilitate adequate experimentation.
- Budgetary support will be adequate to undertake appropriate levels of experimentation across the AMA system.

Assumptions underlying the matrix allocation:
- Harvest levels in the matrix will achieve the predicted PSQ level, and active management of these lands will be possible to ensure a sustained level of timber output.

In addition to the land allocations created by the Plan, it also set in motion several important **processes**. Forest planning and inventory and monitoring constitute a continuation of previous activities, while adaptive management, survey and manage (S&M) species assessment, and implementation processes are unique byproducts of the Plan.

Assumptions underlying the forest planning processes:
- Planning processes that encompass multivalue, -scale, and -tenure issues will be identified, implemented, and supported.
- New processes that integrate science into decisionmaking will be undertaken.
- New collaborative approaches to linking citizens, managers, and scientists will be formulated, adopted, and supported.

Assumptions underlying adaptive management:
- Adaptive management represents a core strategy to the eventual implementation of an ecosystem approach to management across the region.
- Effective adaptive management requires explicit documentation of problem/issue, rationale, treatment, and results in order to facilitate learning.

- Current representation of the adaptive management process, as outlined in FEMAT and the record of decision (ROD), is an accurate depiction of steps, linkages, and responsibilities.
- Adaptive management will foster effective new relationships among citizens, managers, and scientists.
- Current organizational structure and processes are adequate for implementing adaptive management; this includes operating under conditions of risk and uncertainty, integrating different forms of knowledge, and facilitating learning behaviors.

Assumptions underlying S&M species:
- The land allocations in the Plan and their intended management will provide adequate protection for all rare, old-growth-dependent species.
- The S&M guidelines and the adaptive management process will maintain viability for the listed species.
- The ecosystem functions of the various S&M species need better understanding, especially in terms of their contribution to ecosystem health and resiliency.
- The impacts on S&M species of disturbance and silvicultural treatments will not lead to adverse effects on PSQ.
- Population viability must be assessed at multiple scales.
- The levels of uncertainty and risk relative to S&M species will be quickly resolved.
- As onsite surveys are conducted, the number of S&M species will decline, as new information regarding their population status becomes known.

Assumptions underlying inventory and monitoring processes:
- Effective and legal implementation of the Plan will require an expanded, rigorous monitoring process.
- The role of research in monitoring is essential, both in developing credible, appropriate, rigorous, and operational monitoring protocols and in the analysis and evaluation of results.
- Effective monitoring requires processes to formulate appropriate and relevant questions and to serve as the basis for judgments of appropriate conditions.

Assumptions underlying implementation processes:

- Implementation of the Plan will be a priority task for all agencies across the region.
- There was an agreed-upon meaning and understanding of the Plan—its purposes, requirements, costs, and implications—among managers, scientists, and citizens.
- The conditions and factors that drove creation of the Plan are interpreted by agencies and programs as indicative of changing expectations and demands of forest management, thus establishing a precedent for a new way of doing business and defining priority needs.
- Management and regulatory agencies will work in concert to facilitate effective implementation of the Plan.
- Agencies have the technical capacity, legal authority, and political commitment to implement the Plan.
- Current organizational processes and structures, including interagency connections, are adequate to implement the Plan.
- Adequate indicators and standards to define satisfactory implementation of the Plan are in place.
- Successful implementation of the Plan requires a new conception of the role of research in the land management decisionmaking process; it also challenges research to think of the Plan as a "grand experiment" that poses both great responsibilities as well as opportunities.

The idea of adaptive management in FEMAT, and its incorporation into the Plan and the AMA allocation, is underlain by two fundamental premises:

- The store of knowledge required to implement a comprehensive, scientifically-grounded "ecosystem approach" to management is limited; the pace at which new problems develop will outstrip the capacity of existing research organizations and approaches.
- The strategies and approaches through which knowledge is acquired, developed, transmitted, and applied will require innovative institutional structures and processes.

These premises are distinct, but nonetheless linked. The first represents a technical-scientific problem; there is simply insufficient information about the region's complex ecological and socioeconomic systems to frame informed decisions that

Does the concept of adaptive management or the allocation of the AMAs represent the kind of innovative strategies upon which we might design structures and processes that more effectively cope with uncertainty and ambiguity?

anticipate the consequences and implications of any action. These information deficiencies become more debilitating when we act at large, multitenure spatial scales and over long temporal scales.

The second premise is sociopolitical in nature. Contrary to the assumption that current organizational processes and structures are adequate to implement the Plan, there is concern as to whether the institutional capacity and mechanisms exist to operate effectively in the face of high levels of scientific uncertainty and a pluralistic, ambiguous system of public uses and values. Taken together, the combination of scientific uncertainty and political ambiguity challenge traditional scientific-rational bureaucratic structures that typify natural resource management organizations today (Shannon and Antypas 1997). But if not these institutions, that have served us well for the past century, then what? Does the concept of adaptive management or the allocation of the AMAs represent the kind of innovative strategies upon which we might design structures and processes that more effectively cope with uncertainty and ambiguity? The challenges such a question raises are both theoretical and practical in nature and any answers are equally uncertain and ambiguous. In the literature review undertaken in support of this evaluation (Stankey et al. 2005), we examined the underlying concept of adaptive management, and reviewed the results of its application in a wide range of resource settings, biophysical regions, and sociopolitical entities; chapter 3 summarizes the key findings of that review. We close this chapter by reviewing the key dimensions and conclusions that emerge from the history of conflict, debate, and experience in the Pacific Northwest.

The last three decades witnessed an unprecedented level of investment, both monetary and intellectual, in developing a scientifically rigorous basis for natural resources management. From ISC to FEMAT, the scope of inquiry and the range of issues became more complex and interrelated. For example, although various sociopolitical issues permeated the conclusions and recommendations of ISC, Gang of Four, and SAT, it was only with the formation of FEMAT that the noneconomic social sciences both literally and figuratively were invited to "sit at the table."

Yet, despite this investment, controversy and conflict continues to characterize forest management. Despite significant efforts to develop better science to inform and guide land management, the challenges and complexities encountered both within the environmental and socioeconomic systems, as well as between them, have grown. Our capacity to work at larger spatial scales and longer temporal scales, generally taken as key attributes of ecosystem-based management (Grumbine 1994, Slocumbe 1993) is limited. Moreover, efforts to work in this substantively complex decision environment are further complicated by a pervasive atmosphere of distrust. The high levels of uncertainty that characterize many decisions and the consequences (real or perceived) of making a mistake have created and sustained risk-averse organizations and behaviors that constrain the ability to experiment and learn.

Forestry in the Pacific Northwest—The Perfect Storm?

In a scenario metaphorically similar to that described in The Perfect Storm (Junker 1999), the past years have seen a convergence of events that collectively have redefined the turbulent context within which the natural resource management professions and institutions operate. These include the following:

- There is a broadening array of demands and concerns for a diverse range of environmental goods and services. Traditional commodity emphases have not disappeared, but have been joined by demands for amenity, environmental, spiritual, subsistence, and other values and uses that alter the dynamic of forest management.

- There is widespread public perception that forest habitat has continued to decline, resulting in the loss of species and other forest values, despite wide-spread efforts to halt such losses and empirical evidence that habitat is not in decline.

- Despite large investments in science, there is an increasing recognition of both the absolute limits of knowledge (i.e., we simply do not understand enough about the systems with which we are working) and of the limits of science as a means of solving the problems with which we are confronted (i.e., even if we knew a lot more about these systems, it would not be sufficient to solve the problems).

- Because high levels of uncertainty characterize actions, the law of unintended consequences continues to plague us. For example, concerns about the impact of the ESA led many private landowners to accelerate rates of harvest, thus further diminishing critical habitat for many species.

- There is a growing sense that the current suite of institutions (agencies, laws, policies) is limited in its capacity to cope with the problems with which we are faced (Dryzek 1987, Wilkinson 1992). In many cases, these institutions constrain, rather than facilitate, effective problem resolution.

- Distrust between the governed and those who govern grows. Distrust is also a pervasive feature within and between interests, fostering strategic,

In a scenario metaphorically similar to that described in *The Perfect Storm...*, the past years have seen a convergence of events that collectively have redefined the turbulent context within which the natural resource management professions and institutions operate.

often self-serving objectives, rather than a search for some common good. It feeds the growing preference for legislative remedies for localized, idiosyncratic problems.

- The growth in real-time communications (TV, World Wide Web) means events and issues occurring at any place can be transmitted instantaneously around the region, Nation, and world. Thus, a controversial forest management action (e.g., the use of prescribed fire by the NPS in Los Alamos) is instantly communicated as a means of mobilizing political action and protest.

- There are growing demands for science-based decisionmaking, but there are unrealistic expectations as to what such an approach can do. Science involves description, explanation, and prediction, not prescription. Moreover, because science is concerned with describing what is and what might be, rather than what is right or true, it is only a necessary, not sufficient, agent in informing natural resource policy.

- There is an inability to portray the concept of risk in a socially acceptable manner. There are no risk-free solutions; all actions, including no action, involve risk. Yet, increasingly, resource managers are called on to avoid actions and policies that would lead to risk for species, conditions, and values. Because of this, innovation can be easily stifled; the irony is that attempting to maintain the status quo can itself be highly risky.

- Within natural resource organizations, a series of events are unfolding that collectively create high levels of stress at the institutional and individual level. These include the impacts of continued workforce downsizing, the increasingly political nature of the wider environment within which organizations exist, the fundamentally new philosophical and procedural directions imposed by the Plan, and a sharp discontinuity between the historical traditions, knowledge, and belief systems that characterized organizations for much of the past century and the demands for change to better operate in the future. This latter issue is exacerbated by criticisms and a lack of appreciation of these former qualities; often, they are denigrated and identified as responsible for the problems agencies face today.

Within this complex web of forces, implementation of the Plan was further confounded by two structural features regarding how the FEMAT assessment was undertaken. These issues are significant, given FEMAT's role in shaping the ROD and efforts to implement the Plan. First, agency planners were not included on the

FEMAT. This denied FEMAT authors the on-the-ground expertise and experience in many of the realities of the legal and administrative environment within which the Plan would need to perform. There was also no relief provided (or the need for such even anticipated) in such fundamental laws as NEPA, ESA, the Administrative Procedures Act, or Federal Advisory Committee Act.

Second, problems stemming from the speed with which FEMAT was put together became apparent as implementation began to unfold. Again, the lack of experience among FEMAT authors in implementing land management programs spawned a number of implementation challenges, including unrealistic assumptions (e.g., about agency resources and capacity), conflicting statements (e.g., the conflicts imbedded in overlapping allocations between reserves and AMAs), and unclear definitions (e.g., what the concept of adaptive management meant). There was also concern as to how the emphasis on species and habitat protection affected other traditional management concerns, such as recreation and lands and minerals management.

Forest Management in a Turbulent World

The collective effect of these factors severely challenges current institutional structures and processes. Over a decade ago, Wondolleck (1988) critiqued Forest Service planning and its continued reliance and dependence on the technical-rational planning model. This planning model, grounded in the notions of objectivity, rationality, centralization, and efficiency, was seen as a necessary remedy to the laissez faire environment that characterized the country up till the end of World War I. But the most critical attributes of the new technical (or social reform) model of planning were embodied in the twin ideas of **calculation** and **control**. Calculation involved the capacity to undertake comprehensive analysis; control referred to the ability of actors to carry out their intentions. Moreover, unless control emanated from a central directorate, "there would be only chaos" (Friedmann 1987: 94).

The social reform school of planning espoused scientific planning as a departure from the chaos and self-centeredness of a laissez faire mentality and the anarchy of the corporate-run market. "Only scientific planning," J.H. Robinson, an advocate of the approach, proclaimed in 1921, "can save the world from itself" (cited in Friedmann 1987: 92). Three assumptions underlay the concept: (1) the world is predictable and knowable; (2) management goals are clear; and (3) not only is there a "right answer," but it can be revealed through objective, technical analysis (Smith 1997). With expansion of science in the 20th century, combined with the growth of the progressive government movement, social reform-based planning did achieve major accomplishments. As noted earlier, the capacity of the United States to mobilize development of the Nation's natural resources to meet the demands generated by the war effort in the 1940s was a direct result of an efficient, centralized, and elite-directed planning effort.

But the social reform model rested on another critical, if implied, assumption: planning was a technical, avowedly nonpolitical, enterprise. Rexford Tugwell, an early advocate of social reform planning, described politics as having "a connotation of slight unscrupulousness" (Tugwell 1940: 98). Scientific planning, on the other hand, simply was an extension of contemporary business practices; politics would only confuse things. The questions addressed by planners had to be defined strictly in technical terms, or some means had to be found to give the appearance of being democratic or of "demobilizing public opinion" in order to create an apparent state of social consensus. This "engineering of consent" (Friedmann 1987: 114) would prevent scientific planning from being soiled by politics, while ensuring popular support.

It is not the purpose of this evaluation to provide a detailed critique of the technical-rational planning model (see Friedmann 1987: 87-137). However, it is important to understand both the roots of the planning ideology and culture that dominate current natural resource planning methodologies as well as the specific ways in which this traditional orientation is challenged by the contextual changes discussed here. Although planning itself is not a paradigm, it is a technology through which sense is made of the world, and this, in turn, impacts the choices that are considered, including how problems are framed, the organization's role, and the types of information needed to resolve problems (Westley 1995). For example, a simple yet profound shift in the underlying assumptions is that rather than defining politics as being "slightly unscrupulous," there is a growing recognition that planning is inextricably, a political activity. The technical-rational model treated scientific knowledge as objective and value-free. Today, there is a growing openness to acknowledge the value-laden nature of knowledge; what is known, who holds knowledge, what type of knowledge gets admitted to decisionmaking deliberations, etc. In short, knowledge is power.

Adaptive management has attracted attention in part because of its apparent capacity to deal with the complex, ambiguous world as it really is, rather than what it might have been or as we might wish it to be. However, it is critical that adaptive management offer a substantive alternative to traditional, technical-rational approaches rather than simply a rhetorical variant. There is a danger this could be

Today, there is a growing openness to acknowledge the value-laden nature of knowledge; what is known, who holds knowledge, what type of knowledge gets admitted to decisionmaking deliberations, etc. In short, knowledge is power.

the case; Lee (1999: 9) has noted (referring to the Plan) that "the Forest Service's definition of adaptive management does not emphasize experimentation but rather rational planning coupled with trial and error learning. Here 'adaptive' management has become a buzzword, a fashionable label that means less than it seems to promise." His comment again manifests the underlying concern regarding the definition of adaptive management: Is it simply a reaffirmation of a long-standing practice of incremental management through trial and error, or does it reflect a fundamentally different approach focused on formal experimentation?

The past decade has seen a struggle within the natural resource profession in general, and forestry in particular, to find a unifying framework around which to organize. This struggle reflects concerns about the utility of the time-honored concept of multiple use and a growing sense that it lacks applicability in a world of increasing complexity and pluralism. Since 1990, and parallel to the various assessments described earlier in this chapter, we have seen the idea of "New Perspectives" appear—a different way of thinking about managing the national forests and grasslands, emphasizing ecological principles, to sustain their many values and uses. Less than 2 years later, New Perspectives was replaced by the concept of ecosystem management; Forest Service chief Robertson wrote "we must blend the needs of people and environmental values in such a way that the national forests and grasslands represent diverse, healthy, productive, and sustainable ecosystems" (Robertson 1992). Ecosystem management, in turn, as a management framework, seemingly gave way to the idea of ecological stewardship (Johnson and Herring 1999).

It is tempting to treat this swirl of slogans as rhetorical and cosmetic in nature, with none of them representing a paradigmatic change or any change at all (Fairfax 2005). This leads to the concern that adaptive management is simply the latest rhetoric in a chain of slogans that lack substance or an organizational capacity for, and commitment to, change.

At the same time, the concept of adaptive management, at its core, represents a fundamental change in the way management is undertaken and in the way knowledge about biophysical and socioeconomic systems and their interactions is acquired, tested, and validated. The potential of adaptive management is therefore considerable (Stankey and Shindler 1997). Moreover, there exists a considerable body of experience with regard to its application; as noted in chapter 1, adaptive management has attracted serious academic and professional attention tracing into the 1970s. This experience derives from a variety of resource sectors, such as agriculture and water resource management. It also can be traced to a variety of sociopolitical settings, including overseas. This offers a potentially rich source of understanding as to its utility as well as to the kinds of constraints and barriers that have been encountered. In chapter 3, we turn to a summary of the key findings of that review.

Chapter 3: The Adaptive Management Literature: A Summary of Key Findings

George H. Stankey, Roger N. Clark, and Bernard T. Bormann

Key Findings

- The concept of adaptive management is found in a range of disciplines and sectors, from business and operations research to agriculture and fisheries management.

- Interest in adaptive management in resource management is driven by what Holling (1995) hypothesized as a "puzzle"—less resilient and more vulnerable ecosystems, more rigid and unresponsive management agencies, and more dependent societies.

- In contemporary conceptions, adaptive management treats policies as hypotheses and evaluates them through processes that mimic the scientific method.

- Adaptive management treats learning as a specific, desired outcome of policy implementation and uses it to inform subsequent applications.

- Experimentation is essential for adaptive management, because it provides a process through which the effects of policies can be determined and adjustments, as appropriate, made.

- Although risk and uncertainty are inevitable realities, there must be both political permission and organizational willingness to engage them explicitly. However, the literature suggests this seldom occurs; risk-aversion is more typical.

- Barriers to adaptive management implementation are primarily institutional in nature, including statutory and political constraints and risk-averse organizational cultures.

- Effective adaptive institutions facilitate knowledge acquisition, enhance information flow within and outside the organization, and work to create shared understandings of this knowledge and its implications.

- Leadership is essential to successful implementation of adaptive management; it establishes direction, contributes resources, and aligns, motivates, and inspires people. Leadership must occur throughout an organization; e.g., advocates at field levels are as essential as progressive agency heads.

Introduction

The concept of adaptive management has attracted scholarly attention for many years. Haber (1964), for example, traces its origins to the ideas of scientific management that took root at the turn of the century. The idea also is relevant to disciplines outside natural resource management; for example, it, or closely related notions, are found in business (total quality management and learning organizations [Senge 1990]), experimental science (hypothesis testing [Kuhn 1970]), systems theory (feedback control [Ashworth 1982]), industrial ecology (Allenby and Richards 1994), social learning (Korten and Klauss 1984), and others (Bormann et al. 1999).

However, the concept has drawn particular attention in natural resource management. In 1978, with publication of Holling's *Adaptive Environmental Assessment and Management*, its potential as a framework for dealing with complex environmental management problems was clearly articulated. The subsequent publication of *Adaptive Management of Renewable Resources* (Walters 1986), *Compass and Gyroscope: Integrating Science and Politics for the Environment* (Lee 1993), and *Barriers & Bridges to the Renewal of Ecosystems and Institutions* (Gunderson et al. 1995) added increasing sophistication and elaboration to the concept. These books also offered important discussions regarding the key elements upon which adaptive management is built; e.g., the importance of design and experimentation, the crucial role of learning from policy experiments, the iterative link between knowledge and action, the integration and legitimacy of knowledge from various sources, and the need for responsive institutions. Building from these texts, a growing literature, reflecting a diverse body of interest and experience in application of adaptive management, has developed, ranging from agriculture (Röling and Wagemakers 1998, marine fisheries (Pinkerton 1999), waterfowl hunting (Johnson and Williams 1999), riparian and coastal zone management (Walters 1997), water resource management (Walters et al. 1992), and forestry (Taylor et al. 1997). Adaptive management has been applied in areas managed for commodity values (Baskerville 1995) as well as areas where the preservation of natural processes and conditions is primary (Colfer et al. 2001).

Efforts to implement adaptive approaches have occurred throughout the world, from the United States and Canada to Australia (Allan and Curtis 2002), the Baltic region (Jansson and Velner 1995), and The Philippines (Guerrero and Pinto 2001). The concept has found its way into a variety of resource sectors and biophysical and sociopolitical settings and has been the focus of a growing literature. For example, in a literature search of the Cambridge Scientific Abstracts and SciSearch for 1997-98, Johnson (1999) found 65 papers that used "adaptive management" in their title, abstract, or key words, covering topics from wildlife management to wetland and coastal restoration, to public involvement.

This expanding interest in adaptive management is driven, Holling (1995: 8) hypothesized, by a "puzzle":

> The very success in managing a target variable for sustained production of food or fiber apparently leads inevitably to an ultimate pathology of **less resilient and more vulnerable ecosystems, more rigid and unresponsive management agencies, and more dependent societies.** This seems to define the conditions for gridlock and irretrievable resource collapse [emphasis added].

The notions of gridlock and resource collapse command attention in the media; scarcely a day passes when headlines do not call attention to the latest impending crisis. Yet, the process of discovery, exploitation, and collapse is a recurring cycle. History reveals how societies have struggled with balancing demands for the goods and services produced by natural systems with the long-term sustained capacity of those systems. However, Holling's puzzle suggests that as we succeed in capturing the benefits of these systems, we simultaneously sow the seeds of destruction.

Societies long have sought strategies to better confront this puzzle. Although scholarly attention to adaptive management is relatively recent, it has a long history in practice. McLain and Lee (1996) argued that ethnographic evidence indicates that humans long have relied upon ad hoc hypothesis testing as a means of learning from surprise and increasing the stock of knowledge upon which future decisions to use environmental resources are made. For example, Falanruw (1984) described how the Yap of Micronesia for generations sustained high population densities in the face of resource scarcity by using adaptive management techniques. Such techniques resulted in the production of termite-resistant wood and the creation and maintenance of coastal mangrove depressions and seagrass meadows to support fishing. The Yap altered their environment by using adaptive management processes; they undertook actions, observed and recorded results through story and songs, and codified practices through rituals and taboos.

However, despite examples as to the potential of an adaptive approach, contemporary implementation efforts have been disappointing. In many ways, this seems paradoxical. On the one hand, adaptive management presents an intuitive, compelling framework; i.e., learn from what you do and change practices accordingly.

Yet, the literature and experience reveal a consistent conclusion; although adaptive management might be full of promise, it has generally fallen short on delivery. The dilemma is widely discussed (e.g., Halbert 1993, McLain and Lee 1996, Roe 1996, Stankey and Shindler 1997, Walters 1997). Lee (1999: 1) concluded "adaptive management has been more influential, so far, as an idea than as a practical means of gaining insight into the behavior of ecosystems utilized and inhabited by humans." Walters (1997), as noted in chapter 1, is particularly critical, reporting that few adaptive management experiments he has examined have been grounded in a statistical design that permits well-founded conclusions.

Walters' critique rises, in part, from the question of what constitutes an experiment. As used here, we see it "…loosely as an action whose outcome we cannot predict completely in advance or specific beforehand" (Bernstein and Zalinski 1986: 1024). To Lee (1999), experimentation has three components: (1) a clear hypothesis, (2) control over factors extraneous to the hypothesis, and (3) opportunities to replicate the experiment to test reliability. However, the general disappointment about the effectiveness of implementing adaptive management derives from more than a definitional conundrum. There is a growing appreciation of the various cultural, institutional, sociopsychological, and political-legal challenges confronting adaptive management (Miller 1999). But although there are challenges, there is also a growing body of experience and scholarly commentary reporting alternatives for addressing them. Moreover, it is the crises and controversies challenging society that often provide the conditions under which science has the opportunity to affect public policy (Clark et al. 1998).

Key Conclusions of the Adaptive Management Literature

A review of this extensive literature, including a variety of cognate areas, was undertaken in support of this evaluation and is reported elsewhere (Stankey et al. 2005). Based on that review, a number of key findings emerged, and those are summarized in the following discussion. In some cases, findings are characterized by a consistency across sectoral or geographic contexts, whereas in other situations, results are mixed or inconclusive. Yet, patterns emerge from the literature that should enable us to better assess the performance of adaptive management in the Plan and identify the steps needed to increase the effectiveness of adaptive approaches.

- **Although the concept of adaptive management has an appealing simplicity and is widely cited in the literature, it remains primarily an ideal rather than a demonstrated reality.** In a review of bioregional assessments, Johnson and Herring (1999: 361) concluded "adaptive management is more of an abstraction than an acceptable enterprise, and institutions still do not allow managers to risk failure." Similarly, Lee (1999: 2) concluded "adaptive management has been much more influential as an idea than as a way of doing conservation." Although ideas are important and can serve as the basis for change and innovation, major challenges remain in translating adaptive management from rhetoric to reality. An important first step is to acknowledge that much remains to be done and that past experiences in incremental adjustments in light of new information typically do not meet the rigorous standards implied by contemporary notions of adaptive management.

- **There are many definitions of adaptive management. Often, the term includes any process in which incremental adjustments occur. Typically, however, these do not involve the core characteristics of an adaptive approach as envisioned in the Plan or as discussed in the contemporary literature.** Although organizations long have relied on experience as a source of information to change subsequent policies and actions, such efforts generally lack the explicit hypothesis-testing, monitoring, and evaluation that characterize contemporary definitions of adaptive management. In essence, adaptive management, as a process to accelerate and enhance learning based on the results of policy implementation, mimics the scientific method. Successful implementation of experimentally driven adaptive management requires incorporation of these characteristics, as opposed to simply a continuation of learning by incrementalism and trial and error. As Van Cleve et al. (2003: 21) noted "adaptive management is a very powerful, yet poorly understood natural resource management tool…but (it) must be understood by those who use, support, fund, and challenge it." The literature reports few examples of formal structures and processes for implementing adaptive management, although there are exceptions (e.g., the Grand Canyon [National Research Council 1999]). In the worst case, adaptive management has become a code phrase for "we'll make it up as we go." One outcome of these disparate conceptions is that they confound efforts to undertake a comprehensive appraisal and evaluation of progress in implementing adaptive management.

Although organizations long have relied on experience as a source of information to change subsequent policies and actions, such efforts generally lack the explicit hypothesis-testing, monitoring, and evaluation that characterize contemporary definitions of adaptive management.

Photo 1 An adaptive management project on the Colorado River focuses on the impacts of alterna tive low flow releases through Glen Canyon Dam on ecological conditions in Grand Canyon National Park. *Credit: National Park Service.*

- **Experimentation is the core of adaptive management, involving hypotheses, controls, and replication.** Although experiments involving tests of alternative resource management policies and institutional arrangements are possible, it is rare to find examples where such experiments have occurred, particularly involving controls and replication. Such characteristics are difficult to impose in the complex, interjurisdictional settings found at the landscape level; moreover, there has been reluctance, even resistance to experimenting with alternative institutional structures and processes, such as integrating local knowledge into decisionmaking processes.

- **Adaptive management requires explicit designs that specify problem-framing and -solving processes; documentation and monitoring protocols, roles, relationships, and responsibilities; and assessment and evaluation processes.** This suggests that various ways to implement adaptive approaches exist, varying by context, organizational capacity, resources, etc. However, clear documentation protocols prescribing the details of the experimentation process often fail to be undertaken, thereby diminishing the potential for feedback and learning. Guidelines and protocols to aid managers and policymakers in fashioning useful adaptive management models generally are lacking (an exception is Salafsky et al. 2001).

- **Adaptive management is irreducibly sociopolitical in nature.** Effective implementation must involve the active involvement and support of the full set of partners and stakeholders. Such an inclusive approach is required not only to build understanding, support, credibility, and trust among constituent groups (Van Cleve et al. 2003), but also to ensure adequate problem-framing and access to the knowledge, experience, and skills held by these groups. Because natural resource management problems are social in origin and any potential solutions are framed in a social context, effective management programs must embrace both biophysical and social elements. Agee (1999: 292) argued adaptive management can only work "if simultaneously adopted in the sociopolitical world" and while "the political world does not have to embrace uncertainty itself...it must fund activities that reduce or define uncertainty...." However, this has proven difficult to achieve because of the reluctance of parties to work collaboratively and because organizational and professional biases continue to define problems in technical, scientific terms (Miller 1999). In some cases, adaptive management is framed simply as a variant of traditional scientific-rational inquiry.

- **An adaptive management approach is grounded in a recognition and acceptance of risk and uncertainty.** When working in a complex and chaotic world, characterized by imperfect knowledge and unpredictability, improved management and policymaking is dependent on a learning process undertaken in a deliberate, thoughtful and self-reflective manner (Buck et al. 2001). A key element of this is explicit acknowledgment and acceptance of the limits of understanding and the risks that accompany decisions undertaken in the face of such uncertainty. Yet, most management organizations have been reluctant to do this; concerns with political and legal criticism and sanctions often lead to a denial of uncertainty and an unfounded confidence in the tentative, provisional nature of most policies (e.g., the standards and guidelines).

- **Managerial decisions to undertake actions involving risk are influenced by a complex web of incentives and disincentives, both formal and informal.** To encourage risk-taking behavior and to foster development of learning organizations, rewards and reinforcements (i.e., sources of positive feedback) are needed. Unfortunately, such feedback is often lacking or is no different for behaviors that maintain the status quo. Conversely, risky endeavors that fail to work out as intended can lead to sanctions, penalties, or other disincentives that clearly communicate, to individuals and organizations, that such efforts lead to little in the way of rewards but can trigger significant penalties.

- **Adaptive management focuses attention on the meaning and significance of learning.** Despite the importance of learning, it remains fundamentally inferential in nature; i.e., it must be inferred based on observations of behavior or communications that suggest learning. Parson and Clark (1995) suggest four useful questions to facilitate the determination of whether learning has occurred: (1) Who or what learns; i.e., where does learning reside in an organization? (2) What kinds of things are learned; i.e., does learning manifest as more data, improved understanding, wisdom, etc.? (3) What counts as learning; i.e. does learning occur at the cognitive or behavioral level or both? What criteria, established through what processes, help identify whether the outcomes of an adaptive management approach constitute an adequate basis for changing or maintaining a policy or management strategy? and (4) Why bother asking; i.e., are the results merely interesting or do they have manifest consequences for organizational behavior?

- **Adaptive management is open to many forms and sources of knowledge.** This requires processes and structures that enable forms of knowledge in addition to scientific—personal, experiential, traditional ecological—to be obtained and incorporated into the decisionmaking process. However, the record of achievement is spotty, with public involvement venues and processes geared primarily to informing citizens of organizational intent or of obtaining some sense of public support or opposition to potential plans or policies.

- **In the presence of risk and uncertainty, the adaptive management process provides a capacity to recognize and accommodate surprise.** This involves an acknowledgment that mistakes and failures are normal when working in uncertain and chaotic situations, rather than unwanted feedback deriving from incompetence or inability (Schelhas et al. 2001). It highlights the importance of documentation, which provides a basis for examining differences between predicted and actual outcomes. All too often, negative outcomes are viewed as liabilities or even denied, rather than being seen as a source of learning and insight that could inform and improve subsequent decisionmaking.

- **Various institutional barriers constrain effective implementation of adaptive management.** These include legal and political constraints (e.g.,

Endangered Species Act), socio-psychological barriers (e.g., risk-aversion; Miller 1999), and technical-scientific constraints (e.g., lack of adequate knowledge bases or appropriate monitoring protocols) (Stankey et al. 2003). It is unclear which institutional structures and processes are best suited to facilitating adaptive management. McLain and Lee (1996: 446) noted that "the adaptive management literature pays little attention to the question of what types of institutional structures and processes are required for the approach to work on a large-scale basis."

- **Effective implementation of adaptive management requires organizational leadership and political support, coupled with skilled advocates and champions at the field level.** A sustained commitment to adaptive management requires ongoing capacity-building efforts by organizations. Such commitment must be present at all organizational levels. Creation of the adaptive management area (AMA) coordinators and lead scientists was an important action in efforts to implement an adaptive approach in the Plan and the loss of organizational commitment, and support for these positions seriously constrains the future of adaptive management in the Plan.

- **A commitment to adaptive management requires transition strategies that enable the transformation from a command-control system to one built upon learning, collaboration, and integrative management.** Ongoing assessments of needed changes in organizational structures and processes are essential. However, there are strong legal, organizational, and socio-psychological forces at play that sustain the status quo and resist efforts to change (Miller 1999). The ability of agencies to implement the systemic changes required in reframing existing conceptions of resource management—the role of citizens, managers, and scientists; the reality of dealing with a world characterized by chaos, complexity, and uncertainty, rather than order and predictability, etc.—remains problematic.

Becoming an adaptive organization will not be simple. The challenges to organizational change and the transitions that organizational members must undertake are formidable but essential. What is involved here is a need for **transformation**, a process with which the private and corporate sector is well-acquainted (Blumenthal and Haspeslagh 1994, Kotter 1995). These transformations often involve strong tensions among competing interests both internal as well as external to the organization. Bridges (1991) defined change as an objective and observable state that differs from the way things previously were. But the potential effectiveness of

Although barriers continue to face implementation of adaptive management, the concept remains an important even essential, component of efforts to deal more effectively with today's complex, uncertain world.

a change depends on the way individuals in the organization work through the transition from one state of conditions to another.

Transition is a psychological process; it begins with an ending. Traditional ways of operating within the organization have changed and members must come to grips with that fact. This is never easy, but it is an essential first step. Bridges (1991: 4) noted "nothing so undermines organizational change as the failure to think through who will have to let go of what when change occurs." Bridges described the second step in transition as negotiating the neutral zone, a time and place of instability, ambiguity, and uncertainty. This can be threatening; what used to work no longer does; the rules that used to apply no longer fit. During this period, "anxiety rises and motivation falls," polarization can increase, and the entire organization can become vulnerable to outside attack (Bridges 1991: 35-36). But it is also a creative period; because old ways no longer work, there is a need to find new ways that do and these provide organizational members with productive opportunities for creativity, innovation, and reinvention. Finally, the third step involves arrival at a new state of affairs. And the cycle begins again.

Although barriers continue to face implementation of adaptive management, the concept remains an important even essential, component of efforts to deal more effectively with today's complex, uncertain world. In the absence of an adaptive-grounded approach, rule-based planning—administrative or legal—will continue to dominate management, with a further diminution of the ability of managers to modify actions and policies in light of new knowledge and experience. To avoid this will call for renewed innovation and leadership from all interested parties: managers, policymakers, scientists, and citizens.

Chapter 4: The Adaptive Management Areas: Description, Structure, and Processes

George H. Stankey and Roger N. Clark

Key Findings

- The Northwest Forest Plan (the Plan) established 10 adaptive management areas (AMAs) across the three-state region of California, Oregon, and Washington, embracing a diverse range of biophysical and socioeconomic conditions.

- The technical objective of the AMAs was to improve understanding of the dynamics of the region's biophysical systems and provide locations where the Plan's assumptions, standards, and guidelines (S&Gs) could be tested and validated. What was learned would form the basis for adjusting the S&Gs consistent with local conditions.

- The social objective of the AMAs was to explore opportunities to cultivate creative and innovative partnerships among communities, interests, and management agencies.

- To provide leadership, AMAs were assigned coordinator(s) from the management agencies and, in Oregon and Washington, a lead scientist from research.

- Although initial financial support existed to support management and research activities within the AMAs, this declined sharply in the face of competing demands and reduced budgets. The AMAs were seen as a low priority, and funding was cut by both management and research.

- Although the AMAs continue to exist, their contribution to successful implementation of the Plan has fallen short of expectations.

Introduction

The adaptive management areas (AMAs) were a key allocation in the Northwest Forest Plan (the Plan) because they represented sites where the experimentation and learning required to facilitate the long-term implementation of ecosystem management as envisioned in the Forest Ecosystem Management Assessment Team (FEMAT) would occur. This chapter provides a basic description of the intent of the AMAs, as defined in FEMAT and the record of decision (ROD); much of the following discussion derives from the description of AMAs contained in section D of the ROD. The organizational structures that have been developed to make the AMAs work are also described; both the management and the research organizations took steps to alter their operations to accommodate the AMAs.

Creation of the AMAs

The FEMAT recommended creation of a set of 10 AMAs across the three-state region; four each in Oregon and Washington and two in California. The 10 areas (fig. 1) range in size from slightly less than 100,000 acres (40 000 hectares) to nearly a half million acres (200 000 hectares); collectively, they represent 6 percent of the overall land allocation in the Plan.

The AMAs are designed to "encourage the development and testing of technical and social approaches to achieving desired ecological, economic, and other social objectives" (USDA and USDI 1994: D-1). They are distributed across the region's physiographic provinces to provide a diversity of biophysical conditions. They also are associated with regions and communities identified as bearing much of the social and economic impact associated with declining timber harvests from federal lands.

The overall objective of these areas is "to learn how to manage on an ecosystem basis in terms of both technical and social challenges...**consistent with applicable laws**" (USDA Forest Service 1994: D-1; emphasis added). The technical challenges involve "development, demonstration, implementation, and evaluation of monitoring programs and innovative management practices that integrate ecological and economic values"; the ROD acknowledges that "experiments, including some of large scale, are likely" (USDA and USDI 1994: D-3). It also noted that monitoring is "essential to the success of any plan and to an adaptive management plan. Hence, development and demonstration of monitoring...should be emphasized" (USDA and USDI 1994: D-3). "Technical topics requiring demonstration or investigation are a priority for Adaptive Management Areas...from organisms to species to landscapes. Included are development, demonstration, and testing of techniques for:

1. Creation and maintenance of a variety of forest structural conditions including late-successional forest conditions and desired riparian habitat conditions.

2. Integration of timber production with maintenance or restoration of fisheries habitat and water quality.

3. Restoration of structural complexity and biological diversity in forests and streams that have been degraded by past management activities and natural events.

4. Integration of the habitat needs of wildlife (particularly of sensitive and threatened species) with timber management.

5. Development of logging and transportation systems with low impact on soil stability and water quality.

6. Design and testing of effects of forest management activities at the landscape level.

7. Restoration and maintenance of forest health using controlled fire and silvicultural approaches." (USDA and USDI 1994: D-3-4)

The social objective of the AMAs is "the provision of flexible experimentation with policies and management." Such areas are to encourage innovative approaches that "include social learning and adaptation, which depend on local communities having sufficient political capacity, economic resources, and technical expertise to be full participants in ecosystem management" (USDA and USDI 1994: D-4). Because several AMAs involve multiple jurisdictions, coordination and collaboration are necessary to facilitate mediating across diverse interests, purposes, and uses. This ultimately proved difficult, even within individual agencies. For example, because the Snoqualmie Pass AMA was split between two national forests—the Mount Baker-Snoqualmie on the west side of the Cascades and the Wenatchee on the east side—managers initially proposed that the AMA be administratively divided along forest boundaries, rather than treating the area as a single unit requiring coordination and collaboration. Finally, the ROD described adaptive management as "by definition, information dependent" (USDA and USDI 1994: D-4); the AMAs are to be used not only to "learn to manage" but also to "manage to learn." (USDA Forest Service 1994: D-5).

As noted earlier, learning is a central element of adaptive management. This was reinforced in the discussion of adaptive management in FEMAT chapter 8. The chapter authors noted that although managers often assumed they possessed an adequate understanding of the implications of their actions, in fact, often this was not the case. Indeed, surprise, rather than certainty, is the norm (Lee 1993). Thus, "managers of public lands have no choice other than to try to learn from each management decision through a process of evaluation of the results. The

Managers of public lands have no choice other than to try to learn from each management decision through a process of evaluation of the results.

fastest way to learn is, philosophically, to consider all management as an experiment, remembering that much of the extant knowledge comes from just such an approach" (FEMAT 1993: VIII-21).

The FEMAT elaborated on the notion of learning and what it implies. It argued that learning involved implementing an array of practices, then "taking a scientific approach in describing anticipated outcomes of those practices and comparing them to actual monitored outcomes...(it) also includes society by identifying a range of treatments and practices based upon the needs of individual communities of interest ...this...allows different communities to participate and to evaluate...effectiveness" (FEMAT 1993: VIII-21-22). Following on this latter quote, chapter 8 in FEMAT clearly foreshadowed the notion that the scientific community would need to play a central, proactive role in the implementation of adaptive management, principally by contributing a deliberative, documented, and explicit approach to problem-framing and to the description and assessment of results of management actions and policies.

Finally, the FEMAT discussion of learning sounded a warning:

"we must be sure 'managing to learn' is not used as a license to implement a socially unacceptable agenda under the guise of 'research' ...Agencies should share decisions with the public, managers, and scientists...Together, these groups would gain the information needed to design the next experiment....Managers...must take the evaluation process seriously because it will probably lead to changes in the way they do business—the whole point of adaptive management" (FEMAT 1993: VIII-22).

This reference to a change in the way agencies do business will, as we turn to a discussion of the results of interviews with managers, citizens, and scientists, appear as a recurrent, if not agreed upon, theme.

The ROD (USDA and USDI 1994: D-7) directed all AMAs to prepare a plan, including:

- A shared vision of the AMA (e.g., the kind of knowledge the participants hope to gain). Identification of the desired future conditions may be developed in collaboration with communities, depending on the area.

- Learning that includes social and political knowledge, not just biological and physical information.

- A strategy to guide implementation, restoration, monitoring, and experimental activities.

- A short-term (3- to 5-year) timber sale plan and long-term yield projections.

- Education of participants.

- A list of communities influenced by the AMA projects and outputs.

- A list of community strategies, and resources and partners being used.

- Coordination with overall activities within the province.

- A funding strategy.

- Integration of the community strategies and technical objectives.

These 10 issues later were adopted as evaluative criteria by Regional Ecosystem Office (REO) officials, who review and approve AMA plans.

Each AMA was linked to a particular emphasis in the ROD (USDA and USDI 1994: D-12-16). These emphases derived from a variety of sources (see in chapter 1 table 1); past investigations and history, particular local circumstances, regional location, and connections with local communities (Franklin 1994). However, as evident from interviews with the authors of chapter 8 of FEMAT, these emphases were intended to be only broad approximations of the purposes for each area. What was intended was that each area would develop, through collaborative processes among managers, citizens, and scientists, a locally grounded vision of what the area might achieve through an adaptive approach. However, when these emphases were included in the ROD (a legally binding document), they acquired a codified status, negating the hoped for flexibility outlined in FEMAT. During discussions with AMA administrators, researchers, and authors of FEMAT chapter 8, we heard concerns that this has tended to stultify, rather than broaden, the subsequent search for direction, purpose, and vision for individual AMAs.

The vision of adaptive management and AMAs outlined in FEMAT provides the fundamental base from which any evaluation of their role and utility should be made. Although AMAs are only one land allocation in the Plan, it is critical to understand that FEMAT envisioned that adaptive management would extend across the entire region and affect management in both the matrix and reserves. In that vision, in the short term, the standards and guidelines (S&Gs) that mandate management across much of the region provide a consistent set of land management principles and approaches. However, in the long term, the S&Gs were not immutable but provisional, awaiting testing and validation and the formulation of well-grounded alternatives. The AMAs and the practice of adaptive management offer the responsibility and the opportunity to learn how to more effectively manage the regional landscape; as argued previously, creative, learning-based management of AMAs is essential to the long-term, successful implementation of the Plan. Whether this vision was impractical, naïve, or simply unachievable in the contentious political and legal environment or in a risk-averse administrative culture, it nonetheless represented a fundamental precept of the Plan.

In addition to this fundamental vision of AMAs, we have distilled the following key points from FEMAT chapter 8; we believe these are essential to understanding the intent of such areas. In many cases, these points constitute the vision underlying the adaptive management and AMA concepts expressed in FEMAT and the extent to which that vision has failed to be realized in implementation efforts:

- Establishment of the AMAs is a means to ensure that research focuses on management needs in both the short and long run, to overcome gaps in knowledge, and to ensure timely use of new scientific findings.

- The AMAs represent places that provide opportunities for ecological, social, and organizational innovation and learning.

- The AMAs provide opportunities where the assumptions underlying the plan and the prescriptive, uniform S&Gs can be tested through formal hypotheses and validated or modified accordingly, potentially leading to changes in their application in areas outside AMAs.

- The AMAs are to foster learning through new approaches to research, management, and public collaboration. They offer opportunities for people to develop and scientifically examine new ways of doing forest management and research. The AMAs are distinct from other land management allocations called for in the Plan (the reserves and matrix); within the AMAs, it is not only acceptable, but necessary, to take risks.

- Each AMA has a defined focus in FEMAT and reaffirmed in the ROD (see in chapter 1, table 1), but these foci were not intended to limit or constrain the kinds of projects or activities taken within any one area. Indeed, many issues transcend several or all of the AMAs, and as we learn about these issues in one area, findings likely have applicability elsewhere.

- The AMAs are discrete areas as well as components of a system. They are distributed throughout the region to provide diverse ecological, social, and organizational conditions. As elements of a system, they are intended to refocus learning from an individual area (e.g., national forest) to a wider ecosystem level, including biophysical and socioeconomic systems. Indeed, this is a fundamental component of the notion of ecosystem management (Robertson 1992). Learning is intended to occur within, as well as among, the AMAs; how this is best accomplished is a major challenge to AMA administrators, researchers, and citizens alike.

- The AMAs present researchers with an opportunity to ensure that scientific knowledge is used properly in developing responsive, state-of-the-art management strategies and techniques, to minimize gaps between research knowledge and management practices, and to test innovative science structures and processes.

- The AMAs represent places to demonstrate adaptive management in action through experimentation driven by carefully framed questions identified by citizens, managers, and scientists. Monitoring, evaluation, and shared learning are critical components of success.

The AMA Coordinators

Following creation of the AMAs, steps were taken to establish an organizational structure that provided direction for individual AMAs and linked them with one another and with other allocations and functions (e.g., timber, wildlife). The assignment of responsibility for the AMA was established at the managing unit levels (e.g., ranger district, resource area). There were no established guidelines for selection of individuals to these positions; in some cases, local rangers or other staff specialists undertook the job.

The model for the concept of a coordinator might have its roots in the Applegate Partnership in southern Oregon. Local citizens representing the partnership had approached the Bureau of Land Management and the Forest Service to ask that they establish an interagency position to facilitate communication. This request preceded publication of the FEMAT report and creation of the AMAs. The district ranger of the Applegate Ranger District was the choice of both the partnership and the agencies; this individual had served in a temporary detail as an interagency liaison between the agencies and the partnership prior to creation of the AMA.

We asked each AMA coordinator how he/she had come to be in the position. Some had volunteered, whereas others were assigned. In either case, all expressed a high level of interest, commitment, and enthusiasm for the job and the opportunities it offered. In most cases, the coordinator position has been added to a list of other responsibilities for the individual (only two coordinators, both from the Bureau of Land Management are full-time). As we shall discuss later, the failure to make the AMA coordinator a full-time assignment has meant that other assignments continually compete for the coordinators' time and energy, resulting in a gradual diminution in their ability to focus on AMA-related issues and opportunities. Among Bureau of Land Management and Forest Service coordinators, most estimate they are able to commit 20 to 25 percent of their time to AMA activities.

We also asked coordinators whether they were provided with training, orientation, or familiarization with the nature of their new job. Two concerns underlay this question; first, there is a literature on the concept of adaptive management and on the experiences gained in efforts to implement it. Second, as a core element of the plan, it is essential that those charged with its implementation have a solid grounding in the implications and consequences of adaptive approaches. This was especially true in the case of the Plan, as neither the FEMAT report nor the ROD contained much detail or elaboration about expectations, approaches, or strategies for implementing an adaptive approach.

However, there is little evidence that any formal training or orientation was made available to the coordinators. At best, coordinators had the applicable sections of the ROD to read; however, it is apparent that for most people, the assignment involved a complex planning arena for which they had little formal training or background.

Internal and External Outreach in the AMAs

In each AMA, efforts to inform both the public and other members of the management organizations (and other professionals, such as in the regulatory agencies) have been undertaken. These efforts include traditional tools such as public meetings, newsletters, and field trips. On the Applegate AMA, a series of Research & Monitoring Notes were published; in addition, local managers have encouraged publication of short (typically one-page) "learning summaries." A large number of field trips and information sessions also have been undertaken. These are intended to report on research and monitoring results, new procedures and techniques, and observations made in the field that have potential management implications; they also played a key role in building interpersonal relations between agency staff and local citizens.

The Central Cascades AMA also has been aggressive in promoting field trips for interested citizens and other resource management professionals. The AMAs coordinating committee has published the results of a "Brainstorming session on public involvement," containing a review of the role and function of the public in management of the AMA. This work derives both from published research on public involvement as well as from experiences gained by local managers in efforts to work with citizens.

At this time, seven of the AMAs have established Web sites (Snoqualmie Pass, Olympic, Cispus, North Coast, Central Cascades, Applegate, and Hayfork). Up-to-date maintenance of the individual sites remains spotty; it is also not possible to assess levels of use of any of the sites. In 2000, a cooperative research project was undertaken between the Forest Service and the Oregon Graduate Institute to develop a Web-based information portal that would provide ready access for any interested party to access information deriving from work on any of the AMAs. This project also is designed to serve as a prototype for better integrating information collected at the local, regional, national, and international levels and with information collected for other purposes.

The AMA Business Plan

In 1999, the Regional AMA coordinator, assisted by AMA coordinators and lead scientists, prepared a business plan. This plan, modeled on the growing interest in developing written statements of organizational purposes, direction, and strategy, contained various elements; a mission and vision statement, a statement of key values, and a set of goals and objectives, including an effort to identify key target audiences and specific action items. It also provided a discussion of the importance of the AMAs as an interlinked network. A short "strengths, weaknesses, opportunities, threats" discussion is included as a marketing plan.

Providing an explicit, documented outline of directions, strategies, and purposes is an important part of developing an identity for the AMAs, for creating a sense of community among them, and for identifying specific courses of actions required for effective long-term implementation. It does reinforce the importance of learning and the idea that the AMAs represent test beds where new approaches to meet the objectives of the Plan can be undertaken. It also emphasizes the idea that adaptive management involves not only the input of best knowledge to decisions, but also the idea of strengthening old, and establishing new, collaborative links with communities. However, it is unclear as to the extent to which non-AMA staffs are familiar with the business plan or how it has facilitated connections between the AMAs and other staff functions.

Providing an explicit, documented outline of directions, strategies, and purposes is an important part of developing an identity for the AMAs, for creating a sense of community among them, and for identifying specific courses of actions required for effective long-term implementation.

The AMAs, Research, and the Lead Scientists

Application of adaptive management concepts in AMAs is underlain by the vision described earlier. However, there was concern among management and research ranks that existing scientific knowledge was not being used effectively in policy and management. In part, this concern derived from rapid changes in understanding of complex systems; what once was clearly right can become equally wrong in the light of new understanding. However, this can also pit research against management, as evolving knowledge leads to conclusions contrary to existing policy, or conversely, as results of land management policies stand in contrast to findings from research. Further exacerbating the situation, outside interests often use emerging knowledge to challenge management decisions, leading to conflicts between management and research.

A common element shared by FEMAT and other regional assessments undertaken around the country is that they have demonstrated the limits of substantive scientific understanding of biophysical and socioeconomic systems and of nature-community interaction; even more fundamentally, these assessments reveal the limits of science in resolving the complex biophysical and sociopolitical problems facing natural resource managers (Johnson et al. 1999). One conclusion emerging from these assessments is that it will be increasingly necessary to develop management frameworks capable of operating under high levels of uncertainty. Yet, the demonstrated ability to operate under such conditions is meager. Although forest management has always displayed an adaptive quality, FEMAT called for a formal, rigorous adaptive management process to replace the anecdotal and idiosyncratic approaches of the past. The AMAs provide important opportunities for developing the skills, approaches, and thinking necessary to meet the challenges of tomorrow.

The AMAs, and the management and citizen clientele involved with them, provide real-world laboratories in which there are opportunities to test the validity, applicability, and utility of their concepts, data, and understanding. The AMAs represent settings in which formal mechanisms ensure that science becomes a requisite and essential component of the decisionmaking process. Concerns and skepticism that the AMAs remain nothing more than the old way of doing business in a new wrapper, are only valid if science is excluded, or scientists choose not to be involved, in administration of the areas.

However, the role of research in AMAs will necessitate new structures and processes as well as a new attitude on the part of scientists and research administrators. For example, it is key that scientists see as a fundamental responsibility that their work is used appropriately, that appropriate safeguards and processes are used in the design of management experiments, and that appropriate caveats are associated with conclusions derived from these experiments (Mills et al. 2001). At the same time, scientists need to understand the limitations under which they are working, such as the lack of control over factors that can influence outcomes (e.g., the political decision to list a species as threatened or endangered in an area where research is planned). The inevitable tension between formal scientific design and applications in the "real" world will be difficult to resolve. However, there are important benefits in the form of an opportunity to have immediate impacts on land management practices consistent with the state of knowledge.

The tension between management and research noted above and the need to develop appropriate, responsive institutional structures and processes for linking science, management, and communities posed challenges to how the Pacific Northwest Research Station (PNW Station) would respond to the AMA system. In 1996, a lead scientist was assigned to seven of the AMAs in Oregon and Washington, the exception being the Finney (the Pacific Southwest Research Station, with research oversight responsibilities over the two California AMAs — the Hayfork and the Goosenest—chose to maintain a more traditional link between research and the two areas). The roles these lead scientists would play in the AMAs were seen as evolving, but based on discussions among these scientists and between them and the Station, the following seemed key:

- **They were to serve as a "conduit" to facilitate exchange of information among BLM and FS managers, AMA coordinators, community members, and researchers.** In this capacity, they provided a point of contact for managers and others who have questions concerning research. This means they needed to be aware of the range of programs within the PNW; they also linked people to other research institutions, such as universities or the private sector.

- **They would provide leadership in implementing the AMA concept across both disciplinary and organizational boundaries.** In this role, they would become champions of the AMA concept and take a leadership role in encouraging and supporting research involvement in AMAs.

- **They would help coordinate the PNW Station's science program with respect to AMAs.** For example, they would work to link AMA research to the priorities identified by the Station. They also would seek opportunities that build on, or extend, ongoing research within the Station to both research and management actions undertaken within AMAs.

- **They would provide a link to local communities and other interested publics in scientific activities in AMAs.** A key role would be to foster understanding of the importance of science to AMA management and also to identify ways in which citizens could participate in research (e.g., helping define key questions, providing knowledge).

- **They would be a principal means to ensure quality control through appropriate technical review of research plans and results.** They also would help ensure that management plans are undertaken so as to maximize the rigor and conduct of ensuing actions to promote learning and understanding.

- **They would serve as sources of expertise and knowledge within and across the AMAs and other PNW Station research programs.** In treating individual AMAs as part of an integrated system, lead scientists would work to contribute their particular knowledge and skills to issues and problems in other AMAs. They would take leadership in seeking the input and advice of others in management and research issues in the specific AMA for which they had responsibility.

- **They would conduct research as the principal scientist or team member.** In this role, lead scientists would undertake activities in keeping with the traditional conception of science, as primary investigators seeking to improve understanding of some given phenomenon or process.

Lead scientists were not intended to be seen as extension agents, technology transfer specialists, or staff specialists to local managers, although their role would require them to engage in such activities from time to time. Their ultimate responsibility and accountability was to the PNW Station, and their activities and performance were to be evaluated against established research evaluation guidelines.

Organizational responsibility for AMA research in Oregon and Washington was assigned to the People and Natural Resources (PNR) Program of the PNW Station. This assignment of responsibility to a social science program recognized the core idea of adaptive management as a social process and the importance of collaboration and community participation in AMA planning and action. The PNR Program had responsibility for the design, implementation, and coordination of research within the AMAs; the focus of research was to improve understanding of the interrelationships among, as well as within, biological, socioeconomic, and physical systems. As noted earlier, because of their wide dispersal across the region, a variety of biophysical and social contexts, and land tenure, AMAs provided important opportunities to examine complex relationships at a range of scales from the site to the watershed and landscape.

In January 1996, the PNR Program hosted a 2-day workshop with lead scientists. The lead scientists had been selected based on their expressed interest in the AMA program and on the basis of their record of involvement. In some cases, there was a considerable history of such involvement; e.g., Fred Swanson, lead scientist for the Central Cascades AMA, had long been involved with work on the H.J. Andrews Experimental Forest immediately adjacent to the AMA, while in southern Oregon, Mike Amaranthus, lead scientist on the Applegate AMA, had been working closely with the Applegate Partnership. A decision was made to not appoint a lead scientist for the Finney AMA; there was no obvious candidate and little historical presence of research in that area (it was assumed that at a later date, this could change). The PNW Station Director also participated in the meeting.

The purpose of the meeting was to begin to build a community of scientists committed to the ideals of the AMA program. A memo to participants offered thoughts on what the meeting was "not to be":

- It was not a "normal" meeting, with a formal, fixed agenda; rather, it was a forum for discussing and agreeing on a philosophy regarding the AMAs and the PNW Station.

- It was not a presentation to the Station Director; he and the lead scientists would be learning from one another.

- It was not a task-oriented meeting, but an opportunity to reflect on where we (Research) had come from and where we might go with regard to the AMAs.

- It was not a meeting to defend what had been done in the past, but an opportunity to explore how we might learn from past actions and how we might better organize to embrace the ideals of adaptive management and the AMA program.

During the session, the group began to explore the implications of adopting an adaptive management approach and how Research might best organize to capture the opportunities provided by the AMAs. This involved an exchange of philosophies and perspectives about the role of research in general, the type of organizational environment required to facilitate an adaptive approach, and the juxtaposition between AMA research and ongoing PNW Station priorities. It also triggered a substantive discussion about specific issues and problems around which adaptive research might be undertaken. Based on these discussions, several key issues emerged:

- The importance of defining a strategy and process for improving inter-AMA research; two particular substantive areas were noted: natural disturbance processes and social acceptability.

- The need to incorporate work of other scientists/cooperators to facilitate and strengthen AMA work.

- The need for coordinating mechanisms for AMA work, including learning, coordination, and concerns regarding efficiency and cost-effectiveness.

- The need for financial support for AMA lead scientists was required in addition to any effort toward supporting their substantive involvement in specific research projects (e.g., to support the scientists in providing advice and counsel to AMA coordinators).

- Working with the various procedural requirements that would inevitably influence work (e.g., National Environmental Policy Act (NEPA) approval for manipulative studies).

- Assurances regarding long-term funding stability for multiyear studies.

- Balancing demands on lead scientists, including concerns with impacts of their involvement with the AMAs in terms of performance evaluation, expectations of clients and stakeholders, and competing demands for their time and resources.

Creation of the AMAs as venues where the role of an adaptive management approach in implementing the Plan might be tested held important implications for the research community.

Creation of the AMAs as venues where the role of an adaptive management approach in implementing the Plan might be tested held important implications for the research community. It created both a responsibility and an opportunity for improving integration of scientific knowledge into the management and policy process. However, it also challenged the conventional structures and processes through which research was undertaken; the widespread criticism that the Bureau of Land Management and National Forest Systems management organizations adopted a business-as-usual approach applied equally to Forest Service Research. Thus, not only were scientists faced with the challenge of assessing their substantive program of research priorities and activities, but also with examining how research structures and process either facilitated or thwarted an adaptive approach. The organizational challenge—how do we "best" organize to practice an adaptive approach—remains unanswered.

Funding of the AMA Program

In describing the AMA program, FEMAT noted "to achieve its multiple objectives, the AMA program will require substantial and stable funding" (FEMAT 1993: III-28). The report went on to suggest a variety of funding alternatives in addition to the regular appropriation process. Several of these proved impossible or illegal; e.g., dedicating monies from receipts from activities within the AMA to monitoring, research, retraining, and restoration within the same area. However, it was clear that the FEMAT discussion recognized the need to seek innovative, alternative sources of funding given concerns that the regular appropriation process was unlikely to be adequate for meeting the needs of the AMAs. At the same time, it also argued that such alternative sources should not be seen as a substitute for the regular appropriation process; it noted "rapid implementation of programs within AMA is essential to both their regional function and to the adjacent communities. In at least the short term, this implementation will only be possible through the regular appropriation process" (FEMAT 1993: III-29).

As noted earlier, lead scientists identified the question of funding, especially stable funding for long-term studies, as a key concern. But as suggested above, funding to support the overall AMA program had been a concern to policymakers since FEMAT (as had the question of funding to implement the plan). Given the inherent and inevitable uncertainty that accompanied an adaptive management strategy, the ability to specify the needed financial resources to accomplish any given task was problematic.

During the interviews, we attempted to determine if the costs of fully implementing the AMA program had been estimated. Although no documentation of such an estimate could be located, informal discussions during the preparation of FEMAT chapter 8 suggested a figure of $650,000 per area per year or $6.5 million annually. It is unclear what assumptions underlay this estimate. However, the reality was that no such funding eventuated. The AMAs began to receive financial support from the overall allocation made to the PNW Region and Station in 1994. In that year, a total of $400,000 in support of the AMAs was received. However, there was no decision process in place to guide the allocation of those funds; no specific criteria or guidelines were available to base a decision to support one project or one AMA as opposed to another. This situation prevailed for the following 2 years (1995 and 1996). It became clear that in order to bring visibility, transparency, and traceability to AMA budgeting, some type of criterion-based system was required. To ensure these qualities, a competitive proposal process was developed, through which funds would be allocated in support of research within the AMAs. Station scientists, with external cooperators, could submit proposals.

Working with AMA lead scientists, staff of the PNR Program formulated such a system. In developing a process to allocate scarce resources, several fundamental considerations were deemed important:

- It is important to not lose sight of the vision of adaptive management and the AMAs as described in FEMAT and the ROD.

- The research priorities undertaken within the AMAs must, in general, reflect overall PNW Station priorities.

- The specific research projects to be undertaken need to reflect the judgments of need and priority of those doing the work as well as those for whom it was undertaken; i.e., it was biased toward a "bottom-up" as opposed to a "top-down" approach.

- Consistent with the vision of the AMAs, there needed to be a concern with learning across the full system of AMAs, in both process as well as substantive terms.

Given these fundamental considerations, three premises were identified as crucial to the evaluation of AMA research proposals:

- Outcomes (e.g., research results, development of management protocols or frameworks) are the principal measure of performance and priority.

- The vision of AMAs as expressed in FEMAT and the ROD provide the basic framework within which judgments of research priority are made.

- There is a need for an evaluation process that reflects both the implications of the research for a specific AMA as well as its implications for learning across the AMA system and beyond.

Finally, a set of questions was developed to guide the assessment of research proposals:

- Was the proposal responsive to the call for ecological and social innovation?

- Did the proposal involve a new project? If not (i.e., if it was part of a continuing project), what was the projected timeline until completion, and what were the estimated annual and total costs?

- Could the proposal be undertaken in phases or could it be postponed without undue consequences?

- Did the proposal involve research issues or questions that could be addressed with less than a "full-scale" research project; e.g., could syntheses of existing literature contribute to understanding that could assist on-the-ground management?

- Did opportunities exist for efficiencies in the study; e.g., was it necessary that work on riparian buffer strips be undertaken in multiple areas or could a lead be taken in one area, with links to convey both protocols and results to other areas?

- Did the proposal provide an opportunity for testing S&Gs?

- Was the proposed research responsive to the PNW Station's priorities?

Discussions among the lead scientists provided a forum for clarification of the proposed funding levels. These discussions also provided an opportunity for discussion of the importance of cross-linking and transboundary projects. The importance of thinking of the AMAs as a system, rather than simply a collection of individual and largely unrelated entities, was continually emphasized. The notion of cross-linking and transboundary work was especially important for projects related to riparian management, silvicultural options for enhancing old-growth conditions, monitoring, and social acceptability of forest management practices and conditions.

To enhance learning and as a means of encouraging lead scientists to extend their expertise and experience outside the traditional geographic focus of their previous work, we added a "strings-attached" caveat to funding for several areas. Funds would be provided to a lead scientist with the proviso that the additional money would be used in supportive work with other AMAs and other lead scientists. This created a mechanism to encourage innovative learning, by providing support for scientists who had developed a body of expertise (either substantive, procedural, or both) to work with scientists and managers in other AMAs to translate and adapt that expertise.

It was agreed that lead scientists should work with the various stakeholders in the AMAs (managers, citizens) to broaden the search for, and utilization of, knowledge about the ecological and social systems with which they were working. Tapping into a broader base of knowledge about the AMAs was seen as having the dual benefits of improving the base of information with which to work and of enhancing the likelihood of adoption of, and support for, current scientific knowledge and its incorporation into management plans. It was also concurred that AMA funding would not be used to fund scientist's salaries unless there was to be direct, substantive involvement by the scientist in the research. In other words, support for solely occupying the position of lead scientist would not generally be done.

Beginning in 1997, AMA funds were allocated according to these criteria, in a competitive process. Short proposals were submitted to the PNR Program; tentative allocations were made but tabled for discussion pending a conference call involving all lead scientists. Lead scientists had the opportunity to describe their projects in greater detail; they also had the opportunity to look for collaborative connections with other scientists and other AMAs. Through such a process, it was intended that we would have a research effort more specifically linked to the vision and objectives of the AMAs and that we also would be moving toward the creation of a learning community among the scientists and, it was hoped over time, with managers and citizens in the individual AMAs.

Table 2—Allocation of Northwest Forest Plan funds, fiscal year 1997-98 for AMA research

Year	Disturb-ance processes	Late-succession and silviculture	Fire	Com-munity assess-ment	Monitor	Riparian management	Land-scape design	Other	Total
				Thousand dollars					
1997	40	72	54	56	47	157	196	132	754
1998	40	125	97	28	58	77	236	54	715
Total	80	197	151	84	105	234	432	186	1,469

This process was in place for 2 years (FY 1997 and 1998). During those 2 years, AMA funds were allocated for a variety of tasks, summarized in table 2:

The disturbance projects focused on the Snoqualmie Pass AMA and were designed to address the impact of the Interstate 90 corridor on the movement of threatened and endangered (T&E) species. Restoring habitat connectivity was a primary goal of the Snoqualmie Pass AMA, and work was intended to test assumptions used in development of the Connectivity Emphasis Areas and the selected alternative in the environmental impact statement (EIS). However, the disturbance theme is also imbedded in the work noted under "landscape design," particularly in the Central Cascades AMA. Scientists and managers on the Central Cascades were concerned with the impacts of the February 1996 floods on landslides, road drainage, and stream and riparian changes (and the aquatic biota effects in response to these changes). In addition, the role of disturbance processes and agents was a key element of the landscape design work undertaken on nearby Augusta Creek (Cissell et al. 1998), and there was interest in the extension of that work into the AMA. In discussions about disturbance work in the Central Cascades, we argued that this represented a major opportunity for the extension of concepts, approaches, and perspectives for scientists concerned with disturbance management in other AMAs, such as Snoqualmie Pass.

Restoration of old-growth conditions and structure was a major concern throughout FEMAT. Thus, several projects were proposed identifying opportunities for testing how various silvicultural techniques might be used to accomplish this objective. This work focused on testing key assumptions within FEMAT and the Plan as to how various management interventions would achieve their designed objective. For example, work proposed under this topic was designed to improve the information base regarding how late-successional forests evolved and how silvicultural treatments of younger stands could facilitate development of late-successional structure and habitat. It also examined the extent to which mortality rates of older trees exceeded the rate of replacement and, to the extent that mortality exceeded the rate of replacement, what management interventions might offset the resulting deficit. There was also interest in the extent to which existing work, grounded in empirical studies in the Cascade Range, might extend to areas in the Coast Range and Siskiyou Mountains. A more focused project on the Little River AMA sought to determine the causes of decline in sugar pine (*Pinus lambertiana* Dougl.) populations in that area, testing the effect of thinning alternatives as a means of reducing competition as well as increasing the vigor of the species to withstand insect and disease infestations.

The role of fire was a third research theme. On the Little River AMA, research was proposed to examine the extent to which fire, along with various silvicultural treatments, might be used to maintain vulnerable late-successional forests, particularly during the critical period in which late-successional conditions were evolving in nearby, less fire-prone areas over the next century or more. Such treatments were designed to test recommendations in the ROD to use underburning and thinnings to reduce fuel loadings in late-successional forest containing primary spotted owl (*Strix occidentalis caurina*) breeding habitat that would be prone to catastrophic wildfire. In the Applegate AMA, similar objectives motivated the work. There, concern existed about the potential impacts of wildfire on riparian values and survey and manage (S&M) species. There was a belief that these values and species were

Photo 2   Concerns among resource managers and many citizen groups regarding the role and impacts of fire in forest ecosystems has increased interest in how active interventions to reduce fuel loads can best be implemented. *Photo by Roger Ottmar.*

jeopardized by the long-term suppression of the frequent, low-intensity fires that historically had shaped area forests. Research was undertaken to determine how the large-scale reintroduction of such fires could be best accomplished.

In both the Little River and Applegate projects, there was recognition that for the successful use of fire to occur, community attitudes and concerns must also be addressed; the challenge of undertaking socially acceptable practices was recognized (Brunson et al. 1996). There was a legacy of public interaction on the Applegate, and researchers, along with their management colleagues, recognized the need to continue to build an effective link with community members. Close collaboration between the AMA coordinator and lead scientist on the Cispus AMA led to an extension of the foundations originally started in the Applegate. In particular, there was a major effort (on both AMAs) to involve local citizens in monitoring and evaluation projects and, on the Cispus, in preparation of a community self-assessment, a key recommendation in chapter 7 of FEMAT.

Monitoring is an essential element of adaptive management, and several specific projects across the AMAs were undertaken to improve this capacity. As noted above, the Applegate AMA had developed a close link with community members in undertaking key monitoring projects. On the Central Cascades, the focus was on streamflow response to changes in land use and vegetation succession. On the Cispus, projects focused on recreation and on the status of mushroom populations, a key species given the sharp rise in subsistence utilization. On the North Coast AMA, research attention focused on developing, in collaboration with managers, regulatory agencies, and the public, improved monitoring protocols regarding the effects of alternative forest thinning and riparian restoration efforts.

The protection and restoration of riparian areas is a key element of the Plan. For example, on the Little River AMA, an innovative project was undertaken to test alternative silvicultural treatments in the riparian zone (hence the description as a "zipper") as a means of examining the creation of snags, the input of dead wood into stream corridors, and impacts on water quality parameters (e.g., temperature, dissolved oxygen). Such a project would test S&Gs prohibiting timber harvesting in riparian reserves, unless those practices could be demonstrated as contributing to implementing the Aquatic Conservation Strategy. It also would provide new insight as to the efficacy of alternative riparian buffer widths.

Photo 3   A key concern in several adaptive management areas and in other allocations in the Northwest Forest Plan focuses on the quality of streams and riparian environments and management options for protecting these settings. *Photo by Paul Fusco, NRCS.*

A major focus of projects undertaken in the AMAs and supported by AMA funding was to test key assumptions and S&Gs contained in the Plan.

A major portion of AMA funds was used to support ongoing work on the Central Cascades AMA, extending the application of the Blue River Landscape Management Design work originally implemented on Augusta Creek. The intention was to carry this work into the AMA, focusing on the use of disturbance regimes as the core concept of the design. This work was defined as a challenge to the Plan's S&Gs, proposing an alternative conceptual framework to landscape management. The central idea was to test landscape designs based on the reserve-matrix approach to landscape management (i.e., the design promulgated in the Plan) with the ecosystem dynamics approach based on emulating natural (historical) disturbance regimes.

On the Olympic AMA, the Habitat Development study, originally undertaken through an earmark of Pacific Northwest Region funds on the Olympic National Forest, was designed to test the hypothesis that development of late-seral ecosystems could be accelerated by removal of wood products in variable-density thinning and that augmenting understory and coarse woody debris was necessary to accelerate ecosystem development. Particular attention was given to determining the effects of thinning on vascular plants, amphibians, and small mammals.

In summary, a major focus of projects undertaken in the AMAs and supported by AMA funding was to test key assumptions and S&Gs contained in the Plan. Although the primary focus was on investigating components of the biophysical system, there was also recognition that community relations and social acceptability were keys to successful implementation of any program. Moreover, relations with communities and people went beyond simply keeping them informed; it needed to embrace meaningful involvement related to specific activities, such as monitoring and data collection. The studies offered a series of rigorous scientific projects to test and validate specific assumptions and S&Gs; in the case of the Central Cascades, work there offered a fundamental alternative operational approach to that proposed in the Plan.

The above studies represented scientific projects, designed to contribute to the evolving notion of ecosystem management and consistent with the idea of adaptive management and the vision of the AMAs. However, results fell short of expectations. For example, studies on the Little River proposing silvicultural treatments in riparian zones as a means of recruiting large trees, snags, and downed wood were cancelled because of opposition from within both the managing agencies and the regulatory agencies over concerns the experiment might impact salmon. On the North Coast AMA, preliminary work on development of a landscape design study occurred, but this also came to a halt, largely from a lack of local interest (Gray 2000). Work on the Olympic AMA focused on landscape design largely has been terminated, owing to a lack of support and interest. Moreover, efforts to build a rigorous research program in support of the AMAs came to an abrupt end in 1998. With a decline in funds to support ecosystem management work in the Pacific Northwest Region, national forest administrators made the decision to terminate contributions to the AMA program, in order to adequately fund monitoring and the S&M program. In response, the PNW Station Director withdrew the research component of those funds as well, arguing that if the region did not see fit to fund the AMA program, there was little point in the Station doing so. Some of the specific projects noted above continue, funded with monies from a mix of sources (e.g., work on landscape design on the Central Cascades). However, as a specific entity and programmatic effort, the AMA research program no longer exists.

The AMAs, the Standards and Guidelines, and the Northwest Forest Plan

The AMAs were designed to foster scientific and technical innovation and experimentation (FEMAT 1993: III-26). Such innovation and experimentation were seen as difficult to achieve under traditional management schemes, and an adaptive approach was the apparent means through which changes could be made. However, despite the latitude accorded the AMAs, they were still bound to contribute to the overriding goals of option 9, which later became the selected alternative and the basis of the Plan.

During preparation of the ROD, the guiding principle of providing "freedom in forest management approaches" expressed in FEMAT (1993: III-26) was substantially compromised. The S&Gs promulgated in the ROD significantly constrained the exercise of discretion and individual choice in the AMAs. At the same time, agency innovation and experimentation remained central objectives of the AMA program. As a result, there has been confusion, tension, and conflict between these latter objectives and the need to satisfy requirements of the ROD, particularly with regard to implementing the S&Gs within the AMAs. In addition, because other land allocations (e.g., late-successional reserves, riparian reserves) overlap the AMAs, the management strictures governing these other allocations also came to be seen as in conflict with the objectives of innovation and experimentation.

In 1999, the REO developed a working paper to address this confusion. The paper (REO 2000) reaffirmed the importance of the AMAs as venues for innovation, new thinking, and experimentation with regard to the assumptions underlying the Plan and the specific S&Gs. It also acknowledged the tension between these elements and the need for AMA managers to take the S&Gs into account and noted that modifications in the S&Gs would require rigorous and scientifically valid research designs. But it also indicated that it was important to distinguish between **testing** and **changing** the S&Gs. It argued that "abundant latitude within the requirements of AMAs" (REO 2000: 3) existed to foster the search for new ways of doing business. It concluded "S&Gs can be changed through appropriate planning, testing, evaluation, and plan amendment. AMAs are in a unique and important position to systematically test most S&Gs, and alternatives to them, without need for formal amendment" (REO 2000: 3). It also recognized that the existing S&Gs might be appropriate, but that there might be alternative means through which they could be achieved.

The REO report organized the S&Gs, and their application within the AMAs, into four categories (see box 1). First, there were those S&Gs for which the "Intent must be met." For these, a variety of specific land management measures could be taken, as long as the underlying objectives of the S&G were met. Second, there were several specific S&Gs in which "Changes are allowed" according to specific directions described in the REO report. Third, there were S&Gs where it was necessary to "Meet the specific S&G;" here the S&G must be applied similarly within an AMA as in any other land allocation, unless the activity under consideration involves a research, monitoring, or administrative study specifically designed to test the S&G or an alternative approach to achieving the underlying objective. Fourth, S&Gs applied to all late-successional reserves and to congressionally reserved areas within AMAs, unless amended on a site-specific basis, following procedures mandated by the Federal Land Policy and Management Act, National Forest Management Act (NFMA), and other relevant statutory requirements.

In effect, the REO report affirmed the use of the AMAs as venues for testing, validating, and, at least potentially, changing the S&Gs. There was a hierarchy of requirements and procedures to guide such activities, some clearly easier to do than others. But in the final analysis, AMA managers had direction to test and validate the S&Gs.

However, in October 2003, at the request of the Regional Interagency Executive Committee (RIEC), a staff and legal review of the ROD, S&Gs, and other pertinent documents was undertaken to determine the extent to which there was latitude for using the AMAs to meet Plan objectives. This analysis concluded, contrary to the 2000 REO report, that there was no basis for exemptions, exceptions, or other flexibilities owing solely to the fact that an activity was proposed within an AMA. In short, the Plan contained no provisions for exempting proposed

Box One

Applicability of standards and guidelines (S&Gs) in the Adaptive management areas (AMAs) (Adopted from Standards and Guidelines and the Adaptive Management Area System, Regional Ecosystem Office, Adaptive Management Area Work Group Paper Number 1, 2000: 4-5).

- **Intent Must Be Met**
  - The intent of matrix coarse woody debris, snag, and green-tree retention is to be met, but specific standards and guidelines are not prescribed.
  - Having less than 15 percent of federal forest land in a 5th-field watershed in late-successional forest should be considered as a threshold for analysis of effects of proposed activities rather than a strict S&G.
  - Riparian protection in AMAs should be comparable to that prescribed for other federal land areas.

- **Changes Are Allowed as Specifically Indicated**
  - Interim riparian reserve boundaries in AMA and non-AMA watersheds can change based on watershed analysis, site analysis, and appropriate National Environmental Protection Act (NEPA) decisionmaking process. See also: Riparian Reserve Evaluation Techniques and Synthesis Module (REO memo, March 17, 1997).
  - S&Gs in existing plans, where they were not amended by the Northwest Forest Plan, can be modified in AMA plans based on site-specific analysis.
  - Within the Finney and Northern Coast Range AMAs, the late-successional reserve designations may be changed by AMA plans.

- **Meet the Specific S&G. Temporary Deviations May Be Allowed if Part of Approved Research, Monitoring, or Administrative Study Specifically Designed to Test a S&G.**
  - Meet S&Gs to minimize soil and litter disturbances.
  - Meet S&Gs to survey and manage.
  - Meet S&Gs to manage recreation areas to minimize disturbance to species.
  - Meet S&Gs to protect sites from grazing.
  - Meet S&Gs to protection of roost sites for bats.

- **Meet the Specific S&G. Any Deviation Requires Site-Specific Plan Amendments.**
  - Congressionally reserved area S&Gs apply where they occur in AMA; Aquatic Conservation Strategy objectives must be met.
  - Key watershed S&Gs overlay all land allocations.
  - Late-successional reserve S&Gs for mapped and unmapped LSRs apply where they occur in AMAs. Management of the AMA around these areas will be designed to reduce risk of natural disturbances.

- **In Addition, All Adaptive Management Areas Must:**
  - Develop an AMA plan.
  - Establish a technical advisory panel.
  - Conduct implementation evaluations of the S&Gs, including the requirement that an AMA plan be developed that established future desired conditions.
  - Monitor key items in AMAs, including the completion of AMA plans and measurement of conditions that have been agreed to in the AMA plan.

activities within AMAs from S&Gs where overlapping allocations occurred. In light of this, the RIEC instructed REO to identify options for improving AMA management to promote Plan goals.

The role of AMAs as venues for testing and validating S&Gs and for undertaking innovative experimentation remains uncertain. The questionable legal and policy basis for such work, coupled with a risk-averse management environment, compromises the value of AMAs and the objectives prescribed for them in the Plan. The situation remains uncertain; whether a satisfactory resolution is possible remains problematic.

Chapter 5: Evaluating Citizen-Agency Interactions at AMAs

Bruce Shindler[3]

Key Findings

- Results are based on a mail survey of over 400 "attentive public" (citizens who demonstrated interest in the adaptive management areas (AMAs) by direct involvement, such as attending meetings) as well as 105 managers with AMA responsibilities.

- Managers were divided (40 percent agreed, 41 percent disagreed) on how well agencies had defined the purposes of AMAs. Disagreements existed between managers and citizens on various issues; e.g., the extent to which agencies sought and used citizen input.

- There was little agreement between citizens and resource managers on the extent to which productive interactions between the parties occurred; 75 percent of managers believed that AMA management had shown concern for well-being of local communities, but fewer than half of the citizens concurred.

- Although managers rated themselves highly in terms of paying attention to local issues and following through on decisions, this view was not shared by citizens. Both groups gave low ratings regarding the extent to which citizens could trace how their input was used and in understanding AMA decision processes.

- Over 80 percent of managers agreed that the lack of public trust and credibility constrained efforts to implement an adaptive approach; 60 percent felt there was a lack of understanding among local citizens regarding the AMA concept.

- Perceptual gaps exist between attentive publics and AMA staff. Four areas of needed improvement were identified: make planning processes more inclusive, make procedural elements of public involvement process more efficient, improve delivery of on-the-ground results, and provide internal staff support to meet AMA program objectives.

---

[3] Bruce Shindler is a professor, College of Forestry, Oregon State University, Corvallis, OR 97331, Tel. 541 737 3299, e mail: Bruce.Shindler@oregonstate.edu.

Photo 4   The adaptive management areas provided an opportunity for interested citizens to work with area managers. Such close interaction also increased opportunities for mutual learning among group members. *Photo by Bruce Shindler.*

Introduction

Monitoring and evaluation are central elements of adaptive management. These activities not only apply to the ongoing management of biophysical resources, but they also are essential to learning about the interactions—or lack thereof—among citizens, managers, and scientists. In the Pacific Northwest, an important opportunity for assessing such interactions is found in the adaptive management areas (AMAs). As discussed earlier, the AMAs are places for ecological, social, and organizational learning: "These areas should provide opportunities for land managing and regulatory agencies, other government entities, nongovernmental organizations, local groups, land owners, communities, and citizens to work together to develop innovative management approaches" (FEMAT 1993: III-27). This chapter summarizes research undertaken to assess agency effectiveness for involving stakeholders at the 10 AMAs. It relies upon empirical data from mail surveys administered to agency personnel and citizen participants at each AMA, and it complements the qualitative assessment reported in chapter 6.

In 1998, the adaptive management experiment in the Pacific Northwest was 4 years old. To help determine program effectiveness—specifically the effectiveness of the Forest Service and the Bureau of Land Management in engaging the public in planning and implementation in the AMAs—citizens and federal forest agency personnel were surveyed about their experiences. The surveys were designed to help managers, researchers, and the public understand what citizens think is important in their interactions with AMA personnel and to assess the nature of those interactions from the public's perspective. The agency survey followed the same format; it was intended to assess progress from an internal point of view and to provide a means for comparing the opinions of resource professionals with those of citizens. Taken together, the data provide a report card on attempts to integrate communities and citizens into the AMA experiment and to establish a baseline for further monitoring and evaluation. Additionally, this analysis offers insight regarding the level of agreement among citizens and agency personnel about important aspects of program implementation.

The citizen survey sampled members of the attentive public in communities surrounding the 10 AMAs. "Attentive public" is a term used to describe individuals who have more than a passing interest in a particular topic; essentially, these are people who pay attention to a project, problem, or issue. Analysts often equate "attentiveness" with political involvement in the democratic process (Barber 1984, Lunch 1987). In this case, the sample derived from citizens who were involved with local AMAs. Names and addresses were obtained from AMA mailing lists from various activities. The 418 completed surveys—a 74-percent response rate— were dispersed across the 10 areas, indicating a representative sample of people who paid attention to the AMAs. For example, 73 percent had attended an information meeting or open house; 71 percent received an AMA newsletter; 66 percent had phoned, written, or visited agency personnel to discuss an idea or problem; and 53 percent had gone on an agency field trip. Three quarters of the surveyed individuals reported they give a great deal of attention to federal forest issues in their area.

The agency survey was completed by 105 managers (an 83-percent response rate) who had various levels of responsibility at the 10 AMAs. This sample derived from lists provided by AMA coordinators of members of AMA planning teams. It includes Forest Service ranger district staff, Bureau of Land Management district personnel, and a group of Pacific Northwest (PNW) scientists who had been assigned to each AMA. On balance, these were agency members best qualified to offer an assessment of public interaction on the AMAs. For example, the survey revealed these individuals averaged 10 years at their current assignment, 63 percent said their agency expected them to have frequent contact with the public, and 64 percent had received formal training from their agency in public interactions.

Table 3—Efficacy of adaptive management areas (AMAs)

Objectives	Citizens	Resource professionals	Significance level
		Percent agreement	
Scientific experimentation with forest ecosystems is appropriate on AMAs.	70	92	<.01
Forest agencies have clearly identified for the public what AMAs are intended to be.	40	36	NS
Agencies have clearly identified the role of citizens in AMAs.	34	29	NS
I feel that citizens can actually participate in planning and management activities at my AMA.	49	68	<.01
Forest Service and the Bureau of Land Management are open to public input and use it in making decisions.	41	73	<.01
Efforts by local forest managers to involve the public do not have full support of national agency leaders.	40	8	<.01

NS = not significant.

Four years after inception of the program, less than half of the citizens and even fewer resource professionals thought the agencies had either identified what AMAs are intended to be or the role citizens should play in their management.

Overall, 87 percent believe that involving the public is an effective method of resource management.

Efficacy of the AMAs

Initially, we wanted to know how people felt about the efficacy of agency efforts in implementation of AMA programs, particularly those that involved citizens. Table 3 reveals how respondents feel about the AMAs as places to conduct forestry research and how well the public is being incorporated into AMA activities. Although a large majority of citizens (70 percent) and agency personnel (92 percent) agree that the AMAs are appropriate places for scientific experimentation, the public's ability to be part of the adaptive management experiment appears problematic. Four years after inception of the program, less than half of the citizens and even fewer resource professionals thought the agencies had either identified what AMAs are intended to be or the role citizens should play in their management. Previously,

Stankey and Shindler (1997) cautioned agencies over the need for clear purpose statements about AMAs and that leadership would be required to eliminate public confusion about the agency's intent for these sites. An assessment of public processes on the Central Cascades AMA by Shindler and Neburka (1997) found that citizens believed forest projects were more successful when the public's role was defined and a desired end product was identified at the outset. In addition, there is a need for clear, unambiguous processes and expectations. People must know when and where opportunities for involvement are to be found; the rules of engagement with managers, scientists, and other interests; and what type of input is sought by area administrators (e.g., commentary on proposed plans, citizen initiatives, and knowledge).

In the current survey, citizens generally felt their input was discounted; less than half believed they actually could participate in planning and even fewer believed agencies used their suggestions in making decisions. Equally distressing is that 40 percent thought that local managers did not have the full support of their national leaders. Throughout the region there is growing sentiment within many forest communities that local forest managers, in many cases individuals they have come to know and trust, are hindered from doing their jobs because of directives from Washington, D.C. or by pressure from national interests outside their local area (Shindler and Toman 2002, Shindler and Wright 2000). In contrast, most agency members responded just the opposite to the last three statements about citizen participation.

Several reasons account for these differences. First, agencies are having difficulty getting their message of open participation across to constituents. Second, the public does not believe that managers will, or perhaps even can, fulfill the promise of citizen participation. Such a belief is likely anchored in experiences that can trace back over 30 years. Third, there is simply no compelling evidence that managers are communicating with or involving the public. In this last instance, we find a common dilemma—sometimes the problem with evaluations is that there is little to evaluate.

However, a more basic, root cause might lie in fundamental differences in the way in which managers and citizens define the very concept of involvement. For managers, involvement is conceived of as an administrative and statutory requirement. Here, the core element of any measure of adequate public involvement is one that conforms to procedural compliance; i.e., does the program meet the requirements of the law and organizational policy? Citizens, on the other hand, see public involvement as a means of political empowerment, as a way of gaining access to, and becoming equal players in, forest management decisionmaking. Rather than simply commenting on the adequacies of proposed management actions, citizens become equal players at the table along with managers and scientists, helping frame problems, identifying strategies, and providing information and knowledge.

In the final analysis, for whatever reason, there seems to be a high degree of public cynicism about involvement and cooperation on the AMAs, a point also reflected in many citizen comments reported in chapter 6 by Ryan and Sturtevant.

Adaptive Management Area Implementation

In a framework developed for adaptive management situations, Shindler et al. (1999) identified two conceptual levels from which to monitor and evaluate citizen-agency interactions. The first involves the broad goals, or desired outcomes, of productive interactions. Several syntheses of public involvement research (Lawrence and Daniels 1996, Shands 1992, Shindler and Aldred-Cheek 1999) helped identify five essential goals for such programs. Public processes can be used to:

- Improve the quality of decisions.

- Reach decisions that enjoy increased public support.

- Contribute to the building of long-term relations.

- Incorporate citizen's ideas and knowledge in decisions.

- Learn, innovate, and share results with others.

Table 4—Agency goal achievement at adaptive management areas

Goal	Citizens	Resource professionals	Significance level
	Percent agreement		
Showing concern for local communities and their well-being	49	76	<.01
Contributing to good relationships with citizens	48	67	<.01
Contributing to public knowledge by educating communities about benefits and costs of proposed plans	44	49	NS
Incorporating citizens' ideas and knowledge in decisions	40	67	<.01
Increasing innovation and creativity in programs and projects	39	53	<.05
Improving the quality of decisions by effectively involving citizens	36	52	<.01
Building trust and cooperation with citizens	32	48	<.01
Reaching decisions that enjoy increased public support	25	42	<.01

NS = not significant.

To determine the extent to which these broad goals were being achieved on the AMAs, a set of eight related statements were evaluated by citizens and agency members (table 4).

Overall, findings indicate little agreement between the public and resource professionals on any item; in no case did a majority of citizens agree that goals were being met on the AMAs. Not surprisingly, agency members believed to a much greater extent that they were successful; strong majorities felt they were showing concern for communities, building good relationships, and using citizens' ideas in decisions (all indications "we are trying").

Responses are notable for the significant gap in the two group's perceptions. The collective data show a difference between how agency staff believe they are treating citizens and how citizens feel they are treated by staff, reflecting a substantial and fundamental disagreement over the quality of interactions. As a result, judgments about desired outcomes are low, especially among the public. For example, few citizens (36 percent) believed the quality of decisions was improved through citizen involvement or that public support for decisions had increased (25 percent). Perhaps the most distressing statistic, however, is the low number of citizens (32 percent) who thought that public trust and cooperation were being built on the AMAs.

The repercussions of such disagreement in views can go beyond the normal frustrations we might expect from either side in the search for collaboration. Although we have become familiar with the public's discontent, we often fail to recognize common reactions among personnel who believe they are doing a good job but find their efforts reap little success. In these situations, it is easy to point a finger at a public who "just doesn't get it" or conclude that "it's their problem." These are normal, legitimate reactions by individuals who might be doing the best they can under difficult circumstances. As we will discuss later, such situations call for a new approach and a different set of public communication tools.

The second conceptual level for evaluating citizen-agency interactions involves examining more specific attributes. Although examples of successful public involvement can be found in a variety of situations, there is general agreement among researchers about a number of common characteristics (Blahna and Yonts-Shepard 1989, Delli Priscoli and Homenuck 1990, Shindler and Neburka 1997, Wondolleck and Yaffee 1994). These interactions can be organized into four basic categories: (1) inclusive and interactive, (2) procedurally sound, (3) innovative and flexible, and (4) outcome oriented.

Table 5—Achieving specific public involvement objectives

Goal	Citizens	Resource professionals	Significance level
		Percent agreement	
Inclusive/interactive:			
All citizens are welcome at meetings or planning sessions.	63	71	NS
Public meetings are interactive and personal.	57	67	NS
Agency personnel are sincere, honest, and open to suggestions.	53	75	<.01
Citizen participants are shown consideration for their efforts.	49	75	<.01
Public deliberation is encouraged.	47	50	NS
Procedurally sound:			
Decisionmakers regularly attend and participate in public planning activities.	47	78	<.01
Efforts to involve citizens start early and continue through all stages of a project.	42	64	<.01
Agency information is current, reliable, and easily understood.	41	47	<.05
Controversial issues receive genuine attention and a sufficient response by agency personnel.	33	69	<.01
Innovative/flexible:			
Activities foster relationship building among group members.	36	54	<.01
Efforts to involve citizens are innovative and flexible.	33	43	NS
Agency personnel and citizens analyze information together to build a collective pool of knowledge.	29	21	NS
When new information arises or a surprise occurs, it is usually factored into subsequent decisions.	27	72	<.01
Outcome/results oriented			
Local forest issues are given greater attention than national interests.	43	65	<.01
Projects/plans are carefully designed, with purposes and end products clearly identified at the outset.	40	44	NS
Agency personnel follow through on decisions.	35	64	<.01
Citizens can see how their contributions are used in decisions.	23	31	<.05
Citizens understand how decisions are made and which information is used.	22	18	NS

NS = not significant.

Shindler et al. (1999) developed a framework for monitoring and evaluating these interactions in adaptive management settings by using a set of core attributes for measuring whether certain objectives were being achieved. The resulting 18 objectives (see table 5) were used in the current survey to determine the extent to which interactions on the AMAs were inclusive and interactive, procedurally sound, innovative or flexible, and results oriented. However, prior to asking citizens if these objectives were being achieved, we also asked them (on a four-point scale) **how important** each objective was. For simplicity, these results are not reported in table 5, but for all 18 objectives more than 80 percent of the respondents rated these attributes as either important or very important. Many items received importance ratings over 90 percent.

The general pattern revealed in table 5 is that, in most cases, citizens did not think the objectives were being met, while agency members had a higher opinion about the level of success. The only area where a majority of citizens believe achievement has occurred is in the **inclusive/interactive** category. It is clear (and consistent with the interview data in chapter 6) that many citizens believe the agency is making an honest effort to create additional opportunities for interaction. Results indicate that most people felt welcome at meetings, that meetings are interactive and personal, and that AMA personnel are sincere, honest, and open to suggestions. Fewer believed they were shown consideration for their efforts and that public deliberation was encouraged. As mentioned, managers generally gave higher ratings to their performance on these objectives, but only 50 percent could say that deliberation is encouraged. For resource managers, demonstrating good interpersonal skills is critical to the success of public engagement activities (Shindler et al. 1999); however, proficiency in this area continues to be a stumbling block (Cortner et al. 1996). Whether the modest ratings reported here indicate that AMA personnel have improved outreach skills cannot be assessed from this one-time study; however, the findings suggest room for improvement.

There is little evidence from the three other major categories to suggest that citizens see a high degree of success in agency public involvement efforts. It is worth noting that one category—making sure agency efforts are **procedurally sound**—is part of the public process equation that does not necessarily require a high degree of interpersonal skill to accomplish. Instead, this set of objectives requires that AMA personnel take public outreach seriously and attend to procedural tasks simply because they are important and legally required. Although agency members believed they were following through on these responsibilities, their view was not universally shared by the public. For example, most citizens did not see line officers and senior decisionmakers participating in public planning activities, an important element because it provides stakeholders some assurance that leadership is being exercised and that their concerns have been heard by the individual who ultimately will make the decision (Shindler and Neburka 1997).

Similarly, citizens want to be involved early instead of being asked to come in "after the decision has already been made." They also have an expectation that agency information is current and easy to understand. Neither of these procedural functions was rated very high by citizens nor by agency members. In fairness to public outreach personnel, it can be difficult for citizens to accurately assess each

Results indicate that most people felt welcome at meetings, that meetings are interactive and personal, and that AMA personnel are sincere, honest, and open to suggestions. Fewer believed they were shown consideration for their efforts and that public deliberation was encouraged.

of these elements. For example, it is logical that agency members are better at recognizing when decisionmakers attend meetings and in judging the reliability of their information. But the point should not be missed that many citizens see these areas as agency shortcomings, and perception can be the reality. Opportunities exist in these cases to improve public understanding. However, from the low level of agreement (33 percent) about agency response to controversial issues, there is clear indication that citizens feel shortchanged in the amount and type of attention given to issues they view as important. It might be there is lack of agreement among citizens and agencies on what constitutes a controversial decision. In these instances, greater sensitivity to public concerns becomes the real issue.

Overall achievement ratings in the **innovative/flexible** category were less than satisfactory, even among agency members. This is problematic, given the central role that innovation and flexibility have in adaptive management. Only about one-third of the citizens believed that relationship-building had occurred or that public involvement activities were innovative and flexible. Resource professionals rated themselves higher in the first area, but tended to agree with the public regarding innovation. As before, it can be difficult for citizens to accurately judge certain objectives; for example, whether citizens and agencies have analyzed information together or if new information was factored into decisions. But public ratings of these items are sufficiently low to indicate this as an area of concern. Because agency members agree that joint analysis of information is not occurring, it probably is a case where this type of innovation has not been introduced to any degree on the AMAs. One reason is the difficulty in doing so. This activity requires a substantial commitment of time as well as an ability to get beyond the common belief that the public lacks the background to evaluate such information. As for using new information in decisions, the high level of agreement among agency members suggests this might be more of a communication gap with the public than a lack of followthrough on incorporating new data. Collectively, this set of responses reflects the public's general dissatisfaction with agency performance and responsiveness (Cortner et al. 1996)—developed over years of interactions—rather than citizens' ability to objectively rate accomplishments on the AMAs.

Ratings of objectives in the final category—**outcome/results oriented**—were also low, especially among citizens. A majority of agency members gave themselves high marks for paying attention to local forest issues and following through on decisions. These are likely two areas in which agency personnel can more accurately judge their own actions. It is apparent, however, that the public does not share this view. Also of importance is the low level of agreement by both groups about the statement that projected plans are designed so that purposes and products are clearly identified. This objective is critical to the success of any planning process (Delli Priscoli and Homenuck 1990), but effective execution is lacking. Another point shared by both citizens and resource professionals is that the public does not understand AMA decision processes. However, this might reflect the absence of decisions being made—a common complaint reported in chapter 6— thus, the public's inability to evaluate them.

Among the 18 objectives, the two lowest ratings from both groups concerned how citizen contributions were used and understanding how decisions are made. The first is a shortcoming of the public process and falls to managers for remedy. Tracking public suggestions, particularly on smaller AMA projects, seems straight- forward. However, understanding how decisions are made is more complicated. Among citizens, this can stem from various reasons (e.g., lack of information, poor communication), any of which are frustrating for both public and agency partici- pants. From a managerial standpoint, for example, some agency personnel might still be influenced by beliefs such as "the public just doesn't understand forest management" or that citizens should not have a role in the decisionmaking process. Either situation has ramifications for reaching productive interactions. Evidence of this tension was reflected in that 21 percent of agency respondents agreed that local publics possess insufficient knowledge to engage adequately in planning discussions about ecosystem management. In any case, decision processes that are not "trans- parent" and readily understood by citizens are a problem, and it is up to agency managers to address these shortcomings.

Photo 5 Efforts to build effective public participation programs must move beyond merely listening sessions to venues that facilitate mutual learning and bring citizens more directly into the decisionmaking process. *Photo by Bruce Shindler.*

Table 6—Agency members assessments of adaptive management area (AMA) public involvement efforts

Regarding my experiences with the AMA	Agree	Disagree
	Percent	
General observations:		
Involving the public in planning and projects is worthwhile and should be part of how we do business.	93	1
I feel comfortable working with the public.	81	5
We have a successful public involvement program on our AMA.	44	23
I am frustrated with our attempts to involve the public.	33	36
Organizational support:		
My agency has clearly defined for personnel what AMAs are intended to be.	40	41
I have received adequate training to fulfill the public contact part of my job.	63	20
I receive adequate support from my work unit for the public involvement aspects of my job.	61	20
I receive adequate support from administrative levels above my work unit for the public involvement aspects of my job.	48	26
Action/achievements:		
Our AMA is linked to wider community social and economic concerns.	72	11
We have identified who our publics are and how to reach them.	64	16
We have established demonstration projects where we can actually obtain feedback from our publics.	54	21
I have seen new or creative ways of involving the public on our AMA.	47	24
We have tried to find out what local people know about forestry.	37	25
Potential barriers:		
Agency trust/credibility issues are major constraints among our local publics.	81	7
Most local citizens do not understand the concept behind the AMA.	57	17
The agency timeframe for producing results is unrealistically short.	46	26
I am hindered in my activities with local publics because of their perception that decisions are really made on a regional or national level.	39	37
Our local publics do not have sufficient knowledge about ecosystem management to adequately participate in planning discussions.	21	50

In any case, there seems to be a need for development of formal, well-defined processes that accommodate the public and their concerns. This would extend the conception of public involvement beyond merely listening sessions that permit expressions of preference regarding agency proposals, replacing it with venues that facilitate mutual learning and bring citizens more directly into the decisionmaking process.

Internal Operations

Finally, it was important to understand more about internal agency operations on the AMAs. For this perspective, we asked agency personnel about their general observations of public involvement and their specific experiences regarding the type of internal support they receive, their evaluation of the success of attempted actions, and potential barriers associated with their AMA. Results are categorized under these same headings and reported in table 6.

In their **general observations**, almost everyone (93 percent) saw value in involving the public. This might only reflect that individuals feel it is the right thing to do or to say; on the other hand, they might have learned over time that public involvement is a useful and necessary step to reach more lasting decisions. Regardless, inclusiveness is a cornerstone of decisionmaking and most AMA personnel report feeling comfortable working in this public setting. On the other hand, fewer (44 percent) felt their programs were successful and about one-third voiced frustration regarding attempts to involve the public.

Regarding **organizational support**, only 40 percent agreed their agency had defined what AMAs are intended to be. It is likely these opinions are linked with frustrations about attempts to involve the public, but this also could reflect inadequate leadership for the public outreach job. In any case, a majority of personnel believe they are getting adequate training (63 percent) and support (61 percent) from their local administrative unit to carry out public interactions on the AMA. Somewhat fewer (48 percent) see this type of support from higher levels within the agency.

In the **action and achievement** category, findings are mixed. Substantial majorities believed their AMAs were linked to broader social concerns of the community and that agency staff had identified who their "publics" are. A smaller majority (54 percent) agreed that demonstration projects are in place to gain public feedback. However, less than half (47 percent) saw new or creative public involvement activities occurring. Only about one-third think AMA personnel have attempted to find out what local people know.

Finally, three problems appear critical as **potential barriers** to progress on the AMAs. Almost all personnel (81 percent) agree that trust and credibility are major constraints among local publics. This is not surprising given the rancor that surrounds many federal forest management issues. On AMAs, where some agency members have worked hard to develop positive relations with communities—and in many cases well before creation of the AMAs—this is no doubt frustrating for those involved. It is likely that other barriers contribute to the lack of trustworthiness in relations; noteworthy is the significant percentage (57 percent) who thought that most local citizens do not understand the AMA concept—an interesting point, given how few agency personnel (40 percent) understand it themselves. There is

The most striking features of these data are the perceptual gaps that exist between citizens and resource professionals and the demonstrated need for improved interactions among participants on the AMAs.

little doubt that the lack of clear objectives about AMA designation and implementation is a frustration for both agency and citizen participants.

Another important barrier is concern that the timeframe for demonstrating results on AMAs is unrealistically short. Stankey and Shindler (1997) argued successful implementation of adaptive management in the AMAs would take time. Specifically, they noted that pressures for quick results characterize the current culture in the forest agencies, a mentality that works to the detriment of the AMAs. Given the distrust of the agencies among stakeholders, sufficient time must be invested for mutual respect to develop. A third concern is that many managers (39 percent) believed their local publics think decisions are not made locally; i.e., at a regional or national level. Studies in Oregon (Shindler and Toman 2002, Williams 2001) provide growing evidence of this sentiment, a point of view that could scuttle many AMA programs. As noted earlier, a small percentage of agency personnel (21 percent) felt local citizens lacked sufficient knowledge to participate in planning for ecosystem management. Although this sentiment represents a minority opinion, such views still reflect a "we know best" attitude that can be particularly detrimental to public planning processes, especially in areas where mutual learning is deemed an essential feature of the underlying adaptive approach.

Conclusion

The most striking features of these data are the perceptual gaps that exist between citizens and resource professionals and the demonstrated need for improved interactions among participants on the AMAs. In the first case, a principal issue raised by these ratings is not whether citizens or agency personnel are "right," but why their perceptions differ so widely. Answers to this can involve obvious explanations; for example, because of their day-to-day involvement and level of personal commitment, agency members feel strongly they are achieving many aspects of the public outreach job, whereas citizens do not share this perspective. However, other explanations involve more complex ideas, such as differences in the scope of projects that various AMAs have attempted, the degree of trust that exists in these communities, and the quality of leadership evident among agencies and citizens groups. For example, it probably is easier for citizens and the agency to reach agreement about a Jobs-in-the-Woods Program that provides local employment than it is to reach consensus on how much timber to harvest. In other situations, the level of trust among participants might be so eroded that no amount of infor-mation or encouragement will remedy the current situation.

In addition, the context in which judgments are made is important (Brunson et al. 1996). Each public process is situationally dependent on a number of factors, many of which are local. More indepth qualitative analysis can help reveal the influence of contextual factors on these interactions (the following chapter provides insight to some of these factors). In any case, the most promising finding here might be the level of importance given to public involvement activities; both citizens and resource professionals agree that effective, high-quality interactions are essential to AMA success. Ultimately, however, demonstrable results will be necessary before any real long-term gains accrue.

There is also substantial evidence from these findings that improvements are necessary if the AMA experiment is to continue. Many of these ideas are reflected in the notion of civic science put forth by Lee (1993) in his observations of adaptive management. He argued that the challenge for agencies in effectively managing large ecosystems is to build community relationships that incorporate both science and politics. At its most basic level, adaptive management must be a public activity, open not only to the participants who must exercise responsibility but also to those who value and depend upon these resources. We cover these ideas in some depth in our concluding chapter, but the data reported here make them especially evident.

First is the extent to which citizens are being included in planning and decision processes. The data suggest that, at least for the attentive public, agencies are making gains in this area—particularly in the quality of personal interactions with citizens. The public responds best to sincerity, honesty, and genuine effort. However, it would be a mistake to take the level of public agreement reported in these tables (simple majorities at best) to mean that planning processes are highly inclusive or that the public participation part of the job is complete. Even among those individuals who pay attention and are actively engaged, many citizens still are not convinced that public deliberation is encouraged.

The second general area for improvement involves procedural functions. We point this out because these often are easier to implement than other more complicated components of public involvement. Some immediate gains can be made in this area by recognizing the importance of these tasks and making them a priority. For example, current and reliable project information is often available; providing timely documents in a clear, understandable format is usually achievable on most forest units. Also, making a commitment to engage citizens early in project discussions seems reasonable as long as agency personnel themselves have a clear idea about what they hope to achieve. And although attendance at public planning sessions might in some cases be an added responsibility, visible participation by decision-makers is an important symbol of organizational commitment and a sign that meetings merit their attention and participation; this could help reinforce the idea that they also are worth citizens' time and that their input is likely to be taken seriously.

Third is the degree to which public involvement activities on the AMAs are any different from previous attempts and will result in outcomes that are recognizable by the public. An expectation has been created by the record of decision, and in many cases by individual AMA planning teams, that the agencies will be more flexible and more creative in getting projects accomplished. Thus far, our survey shows, few people could describe what has actually occurred as innovative. Innovation usually involves some risk, but the adaptive management philosophy—as practiced on the AMAs—has not supported a risk-taking environment (Stankey and Shindler 1997). Learning from the failures that engaging in risky enterprises will inevitably lead to on occasion is a central component of adaptive management; learning from errors and factoring this new information into subsequent attempts is what makes adaptive management **adaptive** (Lee 1993). Yet, the findings here suggest that little failure has occurred—probably because few new activities have been implemented—and thus, little learning has been achieved. The upshot of agency efforts thus far is the lack of progress for getting things accomplished "out on the ground" where citizens can see, feel, and react to the results.

The fourth area is probably the major stumbling block for successful public interactions, particularly if responses from resource professionals are any indication. This involves the internal operations of the management agencies and their inability to come to agreement on what the AMAs are supposed to be. The low level of organizational support for personnel in adaptive management functions is directly related to the lack of results observed by the public and the barriers identified by AMA personnel. Wondolleck and Yaffee (2000) reported that a key reason for declining public support of agency programs has been the failure of agency staff to do what they said they would do. Little progress will be made with citizens —especially those who think local managers are unable to make decisions on their own—until internal problems and politics are resolved in substantive measure. As we discuss in the concluding chapter, this is an agencywide dilemma that is not likely to be settled on individual AMAs.

Chapter 6: Citizen and Manager Views of Adaptive Management and the AMAs: A Qualitative Assessment

Clare Ryan and Victoria Sturtevant[4]

Key Findings

Five basic themes emerged:

- The concept of adaptive management. There is confusion over the meaning of adaptive management; there was a belief that agencies always have been adaptive.

- Institutions and processes to facilitate adaptive management. There is a lack of documentation processes to support adaptive experiments, little evidence of communication among AMAs, and an absence of criteria to determine how and when learning would lead to changes in policies.

- Achievements and accomplishments of the adaptive management program. Positive developments related to improved interaction with citizens were reported. However, communication and collaboration with other agencies, especially regulatory bodies, was poor. There was concern about the lack of on-the-ground projects.

- Internal and external barriers to adaptive management. The statutory and regulatory environment, combined with a risk-averse management culture, constrain experimentation and risk-taking. Agency personnel reported that skills, commitment, and capacity to follow through with citizens were inadequate. There was limited organizational support for adaptive management.

- What's necessary for adaptive management to succeed? There must be clear definitions, goals, and objectives for adaptive management along with organizational commitment and support, capacity building, and leadership. Public involvement must be meaningful and effective, with visible progress and on-the-ground results.

---

[4] Clare Ryan is an associate professor, College of Forest Resources, University of Washington, Seattle, WA 98105, Tel. 206 616 3987, e mail: cmryan@u.washington.edu; Victoria Sturtevant is a professor, Department of Sociology and Anthropology, Southern Oregon University, Ashland, OR 97520 Tel. 541 552 6762, e mail: Sturtevant@sou.edu.

Introduction

This chapter reports on the results of the interviews and surveys with agency staff and citizens regarding their assessment of the implementation of an adaptive approach in the Northwest Forest Plan (the Plan) and, more specifically, the performance of the Adaptive Management Areas (AMAs). We explore how various organizational personnel—staff and line, research and management, and implementation and oversight—assessed adaptive management and AMA efforts, based on interviews with the evaluation team. Particular interest centers on their evaluation of the extent to which the objectives of adaptive management and the AMAs have been achieved, the factors and forces that shaped and influenced implementation efforts, and ideas regarding the future of adaptive management and the AMAs. We also assess citizen views on the same subjects, as revealed in qualitative, extemporaneous comments derived from both the surveys and interviews with citizens described in chapter 5.

Study Design and Methods

As noted earlier, this evaluation of adaptive management and the AMAs is based on several information sources. A key purpose underlying the literature review was to provide a grounded basis regarding key issues and elements of adaptive management the interview needed to address; e.g., the role of risk and uncertainty. Working from these issues, the evaluation team developed an interview guide (box 2) which, in turn, provided the structure for interviews with participants involved in efforts to implement an adaptive approach. We also reviewed agency documents, such as AMA plans and guides and the AMA business plan, prepared for implementing an adaptive approach; such written records provided additional details to supplement the oral records obtained through the interviews. Finally, we undertook additional analyses of surveys of citizens involved in the AMAs, conducted by Shindler (chapter 5), which generated a large number of unsolicited comments by respondents. This information (often lengthy written comments, either following on from a specific item contained within the questionnaire or from a more general observation on the part of the respondent) was reviewed and summarized, providing additional qualitative information regarding citizen perspectives on adaptive management and the AMAs.

Box 2

Adaptive Management Area (AMA) interview question guide

- Give me some idea of how it was you came to be involved in the AMA. For example, were you assigned or did you volunteer? Were any of your previous duties/responsibilities dropped? Did you have any opportunity for training, orientation, etc. w/regard to adaptive management?

- Has your involvement in the AMA effort led to any changes in the way you "do business"? If so, examples?

- As you think about your involvement in the AMA, what would you cite as the best example of what you think of as an adaptive management project?

- What would you see as the major things that have helped you practice/implement adaptive management?

- Conversely, what are the major barriers that have gotten in the way of practicing adaptive management?

- In your experience, what has been the role that line officers have played in implementing adaptive management; think about both the local, forest/area, region/state levels? How about the role of technical specialists, such as fishery biologists, others?

- What about the role of citizens: have you taken, or have they sought, opportunities for increased involvement? If so, examples? What is the nature of this involvement (e.g., informed, providing data, doing work, establishing priorities/problems, etc.)?

- The idea of learning is a big part of adaptive management. First, what do you think are some of the major things you've learned (either about process or substance)? Second, do you have a process in place for documenting what and why you've done things, what you've learned, what lessons emerged ("good or bad")? Or, how do you document learning?

- How do you share what you've learned with others; in the community, elsewhere in the organization, in other AMAs, etc.?

- Think about this statement (from the Regional Ecosystem Office report on AMAs and the standards and guidelines [S&Gs]): "Deviating from S&Gs for the purpose of funding new approaches to meeting the Northwest Forest Plan objectives is not only appropriate in AMAs, but is a specific responsibility of the AMA program." How would you describe efforts on your AMA in terms of this responsibility?

- How do you evaluate progress with regard to the AMA?

- What recommendations would you make to change the AMA to make it more effective? In other words, what do you see as necessary to making this experiment in land management really effective?

- In your estimation, has the AMA led to an improvement in the number and nature of working relations with other organizations, groups, citizens, etc.? If yes, in what ways? If no, why not?

The Interviews

Qualitative methods are an important tool for social science researchers (Rubin and Rubin 1995) and typically are used to explore issues that cannot be adequately addressed through quantitative survey techniques. Qualitative research allows investigators to gain the perspective of the interview subjects, to understand their experiences, in their terms, without imposing judgments by the investigator on their responses (Kvale 1996).

In a qualitative study, research begins with a **what** or **how** question. A qualitative approach is useful in situations where variables are not clearly identified, theories need to be developed, a detailed view of a topic is needed, or the study requires that individuals be studied in a "natural" setting (Creswell 1998). This study was driven primarily by an interest in how adaptive management and the AMAs have been implemented, the factors that facilitated or constrained implementation, and the perceptions of individuals involved in implementation as to needed changes. Because these interviews are a key source of data for this evaluation, further details about the interview process and the procedures we took to collect and analyze information derived from them are appropriate.

An interview is an interactive research tool that involves "a conversation between two partners about a theme of mutual interest" (Kvale 1996: 125). In this study, we used a semistructured interview format; this means the interview had:

> A sequence of themes to be covered, as well as suggested questions.
> Yet at the same time there is an openness to changes of sequence and
> forms of questions in order to follow up the answers given and the
> stories told by the subjects (Kvale 1996: 124).

In other words, although a predetermined set of questions had been prepared (based on themes from the literature review), neither the specific sequence of those questions or the way in which they were posed to respondents were always the same. Depending on the flow of the conversation, or the specific responses given by the respondent, different questions might be asked, certain questions dropped, or the way in which a question was asked could be changed.

The questions developed constitute a conversational or interview guide (see box 2). As noted above, the questions were based on recurring concepts derived from the literature (e.g., role of organizational commitment and resources, development of monitoring and evaluation protocols) as well as specific aspects of AMA

Table 7—Adaptive management interview sample

Interviewee category	Number of interviews	Percent
Adaptive management area (AMA) coordinator	19	38
AMA lead scientists	8	16
Policymakers	5	10
Line officers	7	14
Forest Ecosystem Management Assessment Team chapter 8 authors	3	6
Regional ecosystem office	2	4
Other (citizens, academics)	6	12
Total	50	100

management (e.g., training received, budgetary support). Questions were open-ended because this helps "establish the territory to be explored while allowing the participant to take any direction he or she wants. It does not presume an answer" (Seidman 1998: 133).

Sample Selection

Because the objective of this evaluation was to assess efforts to implement an adaptive management approach in the Plan, we focused interview efforts on those individuals most responsible for putting the approach into practice. Fifty individuals were interviewed (table 7). They included the AMA coordinators and lead scientists, selected line officers (forest supervisors, area managers, and district rangers), policymakers (e.g., regional forester, station director), authors of the Forest Ecosystem Management Assessment Team (FEMAT) report chapter 8, and staff from the Regional Ecosystem Office. A small number of citizens involved with adaptive management and the AMAs also were interviewed.

Interviews ranged from half an hour to 3 hours. Respondents could decline to answer specific questions and could end the interview at any time during the interview process (none did). Interviews in Washington, southern Oregon, and northern California were audiotaped with respondent approval; the remaining interviews were documented by extensive written notes. Interviewees were assured they would not be linked with their responses, but that specific quotes might be used anonymously to illustrate certain issues.

Data Analysis

Interview data were analyzed by using qualitative analysis techniques. Rubin and Rubin (1995: 229) noted:

> The purpose of data analysis is to organize the interviews to present
> a narrative that explains what happened or provide a description of
> the norms and values that underlie cultural behavior.

The audiotapes were transcribed verbatim. Interview notes were also transcribed, and transcripts were reviewed thoroughly until themes became apparent and easily identifiable (e.g., impact of risk and uncertainty, importance of organizational support and commitment). Analysis consisted of coding data from individual interviews and grouping themes and ideas from the interviews into categories (Rubin and Rubin 1995). After coding was completed, similar themes were grouped together from all the interviews. We have used quotes and anecdotes from the interviews to illustrate individual themes.

Additional Information Sources

In addition to the interview data and results from the literature review, the study also benefited from the direct involvement of some of the authors in various aspects of efforts to incorporate and implement an adaptive approach into the Plan. For example, authors Clark and Stankey participated in discussions with the authors of FEMAT, chapter 8. They also oversaw creation of the lead scientist program at the Pacific Northwest (PNW) Research Station (the Pacific Southwest Research Station did not assign lead scientists, but individual scientists did work with managers in the Goosenest and Hayfork AMAs and were included in our interviews). Since establishment of the AMA program, several of the authors participated regularly in meetings of the AMA coordinators and collaborated with individual coordinators and scientists. Authors have also been involved with previous efforts to assess AMA performance (e.g., Shannon et al. 1995, see footnote 1) and in research projects, particularly focused on citizen-AMA relationships (Shindler 2003, Shindler and Aldred-Cheek 1999, Shindler et al. 1996). These various experiences provided the evaluation team with a rich, experiential body of knowledge, insight, and perspectives on the adaptive management experiment in the Pacific Northwest.

Other Key Themes

Based on the literature review, five key thematic areas were identified; these, in turn, were used to organize analysis of the interview data. The five areas include:
- Adaptive management in concept
- Institutions and processes to facilitate adaptive management
- Public involvement and communication

- Internal and external barriers to adaptive practices
- What is needed for adaptive management to succeed

Thematic Area 1: Adaptive Management in Concept

As reported in chapter 3, there is disagreement about what the notion of adaptive management embraces. On the one hand, an incrementalist view argues that constant modification in response to change is a classic form of adaptive management. On the other hand, more recent adaptive management theorists (e.g., Walters 1986) argue for an approach that "mimics" the scientific process. These views are also found commonly in discussions with resource managers. Some argue that resource agencies long have practiced an adaptive approach and that the recent attention given to the concept ignores this long-term management tradition. Others contend that an adaptive approach embraces a fundamentally different management strategy. There is also concern that although adaptive management has gained recent interest on the part of resource management agencies, this attention has been limited to the ideal and rhetorical level, rather than being translated into on-the-ground management practices. Thus, this theme focuses particularly on how agency personnel and citizens defined the adaptive management concept, what they saw as the goals and objectives of such an approach, and whether adaptive management had changed how business is conducted.

Agency respondents acknowledged there is confusion surrounding the adaptive management concept, both generally and in terms of its role in the Plan. Among the respondents, definitions of adaptive management differed considerably, ranging from ideas such as "getting the agencies to work together," to "involving the public more," to "I think it's supposed to help us learn something." Other agency respondents alluded to the idea that AMAs were designed to help local economies, a view also espoused by some citizens. Contributing to the confusion is that little effort was devoted to developing an agreed-upon language and set of definitions; additionally, no formal training relative to adaptive management and its role in the Plan was made available. For example, among the coordinators, none received any training or orientation prior to taking on their new role. Although many reasons might account for this, a prevailing belief that the agencies had always "been adaptive," and thus had no need for any specialized abilities or skills, seems a likely explanation. As one resource manager interviewee commented "I think it's (adaptive management) a buzzword. I think we have already been doing adaptive management."

A heavy emphasis on the public involvement aspects of adaptive management also was notable. Certainly, this is an important aspect; the social objective for the

Among the respondents, definitions of adaptive management differed considerably, ranging from ideas such as "getting the agencies to work together," to "involving the public more," to "I think it's supposed to help us learn something."

AMAs embraces the idea that such areas "should provide opportunities for land managing and regulatory agencies, other government entities, nongovernmental organizations, local groups, landowners, communities, and citizens to work together" (USDA and USDI 1994: D-4). However, the record of decision (ROD) also lists a technical objective for such areas, noting the importance of "development, demonstration, implementation, and evaluation of monitoring programs and innovative management practices that integrate ecological and economic values" and acknowledges that "experiments, including some of large scale, are likely" (USDA and USDI 1994: D-3). Despite the parallel importance of this experimental, action-oriented objective, little attention was given to it in the definitions offered by agency interviewees.

Citizen comments were concerned with the absence of clear and explicit criteria upon which it would be possible to judge the success of adaptive management or the AMAs:

> I feel the agency has not identified for itself either the intent of the AMA or the role of citizens in it.

> Goals for AMAs expressed in the Plan were indistinct at best.

The objectives and guidelines for AMAs are still too vague to determine success.

Such comments reflect the search for better goal definitions and a set of objectives with which citizens could identify. In general, citizens recognized the need for objectives for their AMA, but went further in identifying some central concerns over operating without an expressed common direction:

> The AMA is in its early stage and no one is really clear on how it should be.

> Not much AMA activity yet to judge…. It remains to be seen if genuine experimentation will occur or if this will be an excuse to harvest.

Such quotes suggest the absence of an aggressive, substantive effort on the part of the management agencies to inform the wider community about the role of adaptive management and the AMAs in achieving Plan objectives. They also reflect a lack of clarity and specificity regarding the processes and procedures for improved citizen engagement in AMA management. This might simply reflect the lack of a fundamental grasp of this issue among the management agencies; i.e., it was not clear to them what these roles might or should be. The latter quote is particularly interesting because it reflects an undercurrent of cynicism and distrust about the Plan in general and the role of AMAs in particular; i.e., that the AMAs were intended to be places where the influence of the standards and guidelines (S&Gs) and other restrictive prescriptions would be relaxed or dropped altogether, permitting expanded timber harvesting.

These quotes introduce another element typically lacking in discussions of what adaptive management was or what role the AMAs might have—the role of **action** or **implementation**. Although adaptive management commonly was defined as "learn by doing," more emphasis was given to learning than to acting. In our literature review, for example, the emphasis of adaptive approaches has been on the outcome of better informed actions or policies; learning is a means to that end, not an end itself (Stankey et al. 2005). However, the limited evidence uncovered in our review of on-the-ground experimentation or of designs to facilitate learning-driven actions suggests a breakdown of the learning-action link.

Agency respondent opinion was split regarding whether adaptive management has changed what they do. Of those who did think it had changed the way they did things, the principal changes cited were in the ways that public involvement was conducted. Among respondents who saw the primary mission of AMAs as one of conducting community involvement efforts, there was a conviction that adaptive management had resulted in changes in the way in which resource management was conducted. An agency respondent noted that the adaptive management concept and the AMAs represented opportunities to convince people that the agency was not just doing business as usual, but this required the agency to build confidence and trust, qualities which, unfortunately, the agencies had not been very successful at accomplishing. The challenge, this manager believed, was to show that adaptive management is different, and on-the-ground action, rather than rhetoric, was a key in doing this.

Thematic Area 2: Institutions and Processes to Facilitate Adaptive Management

Adaptive management, as defined by Holling (1978), Walters (1986), or Lee (1993), differs from traditional management or research in a variety of ways. Compared to traditional management approaches, adaptive management requires a high level of formal documentation and explicit hypothesis testing in how management programs are framed and conducted. The emphasis is on designing management programs and policies to expedite the creation of knowledge that will either validate existing actions or provide insight as to what changes are appropriate or needed to

Compared to traditional management approaches, adaptive management requires a high level of formal documentation and explicit hypothesis testing in how management programs are framed and conducted. The emphasis is on designing management programs and policies to expedite the creation of knowledge that will either validate existing actions or provide insight as to what changes are appropriate or needed to achieve some particular objective. In this sense, adaptive management attempts to mimic the scientific method.

achieve some particular objective. In this sense, adaptive management attempts to mimic the scientific method.

In terms of a comparison with traditional research, an adaptive approach differs by who leads the projects (managers vs. scientists), the scale of the projects (routine operations in the field vs. lab or small plot experiments), the rigor of the design (adaptive management projects are often less controlled and replicated than research experiments), and the intensity of measurements (a few key response indicators are measured rather than several researchers measuring several variables) (Nyberg and Taylor 1995, Taylor et al. 1997). As the literature review suggested, adaptive management is especially valuable when significant uncertainty surrounds the potential outcomes of management actions. It differs from the more common trial-and-error approaches by deliberately designing management to enhance **learning** while requiring **documentation throughout the learning process** in order to increase the chances that knowledge gained through experience will be passed on to others (Taylor et al.1997). Thus, we were interested in the extent to which activities such as documentation, information sharing and provision, and learning were valued and implemented. We were also interested in clarifying how various institutional structures and processes facilitated or constrained such activities. In particular, we were interested in the extent to which traditional management culture either sustained, or conflicted with, such formal learning processes.

In general, agency respondents noted there was little or no documentation of activities, or that a concern with documentation was premature because they had not yet undertaken any experiments. Others mentioned AMA plans, National Environmental Policy Act (NEPA) documents (including Environmental Impact Statement (EIS) reports), and revisions of watershed analyses as examples of documentation. Despite the claim that few experiments were being undertaken, and thus documentation was not needed, a number of respondents mentioned various forms of public engagements (e.g., field trips); apparently these are not seen as experiments in public policy; and documentation of their purpose, how they were conducted, or the outcomes associated with them generally were not available.

One objective of the AMAs was to create new and creative mechanisms that treated the AMAs as a system and encouraged close interaction and information sharing among areas. However, our interviews revealed mixed opinions regarding the extent to which information sharing took place—some respondents reported little interaction with other AMAs or even within the agencies, while others reported extensive interaction. The AMA coordinators met once or twice annually for several years, and some cited this meeting as a way of sharing information. However, there was also an undercurrent of resistance, or at least reluctance, to attempt to use these meetings as the principal venue within which information sharing occurred. One AMA coordinator, when asked about attending an upcoming meeting, commented, "No. With such a limited budget, I figure one [meeting] a year is enough." The constraints of money and available time interact to limit achievements on this aspect of AMA management. However, several agency interviewees noted that email has improved the level and timeliness of communication and information sharing with one another.

A major argument for including documentation as a part of adaptive efforts is to provide a transparent record of what was planned or intended, which can then be used to evaluate and provide feedback (Walters 1986). Through the feedback process and subsequent adjustment, learning—a key element of adaptive management—can occur. Several agency respondents thought there had been more learning about process than substance. For example, one manager mentioned that the importance of bringing all agency players together at the beginning was something learned on the AMA, a tactic now used on another project. Another manager thought they learned how to do public involvement in better ways, in that they tried several approaches simultaneously and learned and have abandoned one way of doing public involvement (a good example of the Bormann et al. [1999] notion of multiple pathways). The example this manager provided was augmenting traditional public meetings with an open house format that provided an opportunity for small groups to break off into interest areas.

Citizens assessed attempts at providing information—in its various forms—as the most positive of all AMA-related programs. Many citizens recognized and appreciated the increased effort made to help people become aware of activities:

> There has been considerable effort to inform and include the public—newsletters, educational events, newspaper articles.

> I am impressed with information sent to me and efforts to include me in the planning and discussion.

Other citizens noted the usefulness of field visits with agency personnel to discuss projects or problems onsite. Many felt these trips helped them make better judgments about the issues:

> The field trips have been very informative and more than worthwhile.... the exposure to experts in many fields is a great opportunity.

Photo 6   Adaptive management areas present an opportunity for resource managers to work closely with interested citizens, but significant challenges remain. *Photo by Dot Paul, NRCS.*

Such comments highlight a positive outcome associated with the AMAs and with the efforts of AMA staff to better connect with citizens. It suggests the AMAs have the potential, as suggested by Stankey and Shindler (1997), to serve as "venues for working through" (Yankelovich 1991); places where the public and resource managers have an opportunity to thoroughly explore the dimensions and complexities of issues facing them in a way that increases the likelihood of arriving at thoughtful, reasoned choices and where trust between and among competing interests can be fostered.

Yet, there are problems, although they are not unique to the AMA situation. For example, several citizens acknowledged the difficulty in reaching people or getting them to participate:

> Good information was provided at the meetings, questions were answered,
> but too few people attended.

> Rural citizens are difficult to reach. One always sees the same faces
> at meetings, so innovative ways of reaching populations of interest
> (e.g., specific issues) need to be developed.

Still, conceptions of what learning is and how it relates to management actions and policies seem confused. For example, some agency respondents mentioned that learning had occurred on their AMA, citing creation of a Web site as evidence of that learning—a seeming confusion between means (a Web site) and ends (learning). However, most echoed this manager's view:

> We have yet to set measurable criteria or even specific goals for public involvement. We have few examples of incorporating ideas and changing outcomes as a result of new information.

This is an astute observation, in light of the litigious, contentious environment within which the Plan operates. For examples, although a key objective of the AMAs and the strategy of adaptive management was to provide a means and place to test and validate the S&Gs, it is clear that neither the regulatory agencies nor environmental interest groups will accept recommended changes in those rules without rigorous, well-grounded scientific support. Yet, there has been little debate, by management, research, or regulatory agencies, as to what criteria would be used to evaluate the results of adaptive experiments in such a manner so as to warrant changes in S&Gs.

The interviews revealed an ambivalence and confusion about the role of learning in resource management in general, and in implementation of the Plan in specific. Comments from agency participants suggested a confusion regarding exactly what the goals of the AMAs were. Despite rhetoric in the Plan about the importance of learning, for example, one manager argued that the idea of "learning goals" conflicted with both traditional, commodity management objectives and emerging public demands for other goods and services:

> If Congress is still funding timber sales and the public is telling us they want recreation and other things, then there's a disconnect somewhere…we end up with a lot of our direction now seeming to come out of court cases.

Other managers commented that the Forest Service held little interest in becoming, or understanding what it means to be, a learning organization. A manager stated:

> We don't know what we have learned, because we do not have the time for those who are doing the learning to sit back and reflect. Need to remove yourself or bring in a third party.

Such concerns mirror reports from other organizations (Michael 1995, Senge 1990). The challenge of creating and sustaining an organizational environment

For examples, although a key objective of the AMAs and the strategy of adaptive management was to provide a means and place to test and validate the S&Gs, it is clear that neither the regulatory agencies nor environmental interest groups will accept recommended changes in those rules without rigorous, well-grounded scientific support.

within which learning is embraced as an essential part of decisionmaking is formidable. The influence of public pressures, judicial decisions, and the inertia of, and continued reliance on, traditional decisionmaking processes remain barriers to creation of a learning organization.

Thematic Area 3: Public Involvement and Communication

We asked respondents to describe what they saw as examples of accomplishments resulting from adaptive management and the AMAs. At the time of the interviews, the Plan had been in effect for only about 6 years, and this relatively short history probably limits opportunities for demonstrated implementation. Nonetheless, we were interested in the extent to which interviewees perceived results that could be attributed to the adaptive management program in the Plan. Most of their comments related to public involvement and communication.

Agency participants consistently described aspects of public involvement as major accomplishments associated with adaptive management and the AMAs. This included an increased emphasis on public involvement, regular and varied forms of contact, and improved connections with established groups.

> Public involvement has been extensive, active, highly visible, and has enabled us to reach a large portion of the population.
>
> Efforts by AMA personnel to genuinely seek public involvement have been above and beyond the call of duty.

There was widespread belief that public participation in the AMAs had resulted in an improved ability of the agencies to deliver information to citizens. One manager mentioned that a major accomplishment was getting outside parties to understand the Forest Service better:

> (The) subcommittee sees the hurdles we have to go through as an agency and they can take that information back to their coffee clubs and it starts making more sense why the Forest Service operates the way it does. The first couple of meetings explained the NEPA process, which was totally new to them. They thought we could go out there and just cut any 10 acres and now they realize they cannot do it.

Many agency respondents noted the positive outcomes of increased participation and in the ability to get things done through improved relationships with local communities and subsequent support for projects:

Public involvement was a critical component in the development of two important planning processes in the AMA.

Among the different ways of communicating and interacting with citizens, contacts at the personal level were cited as the most satisfying—and most productive—for agency members. Building meaningful relationships, partnerships, and teamwork were commonly cited:

> Success stems from our desire to meet people at their level and not facilitate them to death with B.S. public meetings.

> Meeting people "one on one" to discuss issues... people regularly call to discuss topics now that they know who is at the Forest Service end of the phone line.

Agency personnel repeatedly mentioned the importance of field trips and small group meetings. Many reported these forums are the most effective means for communication, collaboration, and an exchange of ideas between agency personnel and residents:

> Field trips to view alternative harvest treatments are very rewarding.... Once people see the "science in action," they seem to get interested.

> When planning projects, field reviews are the best way to foster interaction and understanding.

However, in noting the effectiveness of face-to-face contacts, agency staff also acknowledged the level of commitment such interactions required:

> It takes years and requires the agency to recognize the need to not constantly move good people on.

> What's different is the sheer numbers of those interactions.... A single timber sale could have as many as 15 to 30 separate meetings and field trips!

Despite the costs and time involved, however, there was a general belief that the public responded positively to these efforts:

> The interest of the local public in managing our AMA has been impressive.... It's been a result of extensive collaboration from meetings, questionnaires, surveys, and field trips.

Comments contained in citizen surveys agreed that agencies were attempting to communicate and connect better with citizens. Respondents from 9 of the 10 AMAs said they believed that local staffs were striving to conduct better public participation processes than they had in the past. Specific improvements mentioned were providing information (e.g., mailings, newsletters) and creating opportunities where information could be exchanged. Other specific actions included:

> They supply good information about plans, have good notification about upcoming events, and provide opportunities such as meetings, presentations, and field trips in which residents can get involved.

> The Forest Service has made a reasonable effort at public involvement and providing notice of planning processes and projects. Some new and innovative approaches to forest management are evident along with learning opportunities.

In the same way, many citizens noted that agency staff were more responsive to their concerns and did a better job of listening:

> The AMA Forest Service team is by far the most on the ball of any personnel I've talked with in the 8 to 10 years of inquiries about projects, plans, etc.

> The responsiveness of these good folks—I have come to see them all as people doing their best.

Agency respondents noted that some of the most positive interactions resulted from working with established groups such as watershed councils and advisory committees:

> We are working with other agencies and private industry as well as the school system and volunteers.

> The AMA has improved our working relationship with other agencies since it brought us all together.

However, although there was an indication of improved linkages with other organizational groups at the local level, there was less evidence of efforts to build interagency understanding and support with other governmental agencies, either at the state or federal level. In particular, the absence of efforts to improve communications and interactions with the regulatory bodies, such as the National Marine

Fisheries Service or Fish and Wildlife Service has come to haunt the management agencies (both Forest Service and Bureau of Land Management [BLM]). Although we will discuss this issue in more detail later, the failure to open a dialog with the regulatory agencies has contributed to the difficulty in gaining their support for approval of experiments that have the potential to test and validate the S&Gs or to initiate other management programs involving threatened and endangered (T&E) species.

In summary, the AMA program has provided a mechanism that has facilitated public involvement efforts, and the benefits of such programs are recognized by both citizens and managers. What is not clear is the extent to which these are dependent upon the existence of the AMAs; in other words, could such programs have been undertaken outside the AMAs (in management of the matrix or the reserves) and, if not, what particular features of the AMAs facilitated public participation efforts? One answer might be that the AMAs are seen as areas where options and choices are still available, as opposed to reserves (where active management is restricted) or the matrix (where the emphasis is presumed to be timber harvesting). Alternatively, the AMA program might benefit from the leadership of coordinators who have a personal investment in, and commitment to, a collaborative management model.

Notwithstanding this last comment, it is interesting to reflect on what was absent in the commentary about the benefits of increased public participation. First, comments from both agency personnel and citizens focus primarily on efforts to better inform the public; provision of information, field trips, open houses, etc. These are important efforts, but they are primarily unidirectional; from the agency to the citizen. However, there was virtually no evidence of efforts to actively seek public knowledge and information about resource systems or places; there was little evidence of efforts to actively integrate citizens into planning or decisionmaking systems in a manner consistent with Lee's (1993) concept of civic science. These latter actions are more reflective of a social learning model, in which all participants are acknowledged to hold knowledge and where active efforts are made to solicit such knowledge and bring it to bear on the problems at hand; in other words, efforts to facilitate mutual learning.

Second, the description of achievements reported during the interviews predominantly focus on only one objective of the AMA program; i.e., the social objective of interacting with other parties to develop innovative management approaches. There were few comments about efforts to achieve the technical objectives of the AMAs, focused on development, implementation, and evaluation of innovative

The AMA program has provided a mechanism that has facilitated public involvement efforts, and the benefits of such programs are recognized by both citizens and managers.

management practices, including testing and validation of S&Gs and on-the-ground experimentation.

Moreover, it was citizens, rather than agency respondents, who cited concerns with a lack of demonstrable evidence of visible progress or results. A key citizen concern across all AMAs was whether tangible on-the-ground results would take place. Citizens were interested in seeing achievements, and this was particularly important among those who repeatedly asked to participate by reviewing plans, attending meetings, or providing input. A frequent complaint among citizens was that the AMAs rarely complete any tasks, although agency staff spent much time on public participation. One result is that many people are disenchanted with the lack of progress:

> Overall, the Forest Service has worked hard to make the … AMA work, especially on public outreach. However, it does not seem that the economic well-being of the community is the driving force. Instead they are concerned about public impressions, involving people, and having meetings instead of getting anything done. In my mind they have accomplished very little and interest is waning.

Another citizen concern was whether the agencies are working to improve and maintain healthy forest systems. For many, the AMAs are viewed as places to practice ecosystem management and restore natural conditions, and citizen judgments of success appear to rest ultimately on the ability of the agencies to make good on this promise:

> I want forest ecosystem health to improve in all areas of our national forest lands, but I am not convinced it will improve on the AMAs.

Given the extensive and public discussion of forestry throughout the Pacific Northwest, many citizens have become "science savvy," which was reflected in their expressions of the need for credible research in restoring healthy ecosystems. A number of citizens expressed concern about the outcomes:

> The AMAs were intended to be laboratories for trying new things…. Communication among research branches seems lacking.

> Staffs in charge of AMA implementation are not qualified; some have no experience with adaptive management, and few have experience with scientific method or experimental design.

Given the extensive and public discussion of forestry throughout the Pacific Northwest, many citizens have become "science savvy," which was reflected in their expressions of the need for credible research in restoring healthy ecosystems.

Other citizens questioned the extent of the bureaucracy and cost of the AMAs, particularly given limited on-the-ground accomplishments. Some saw the lack of funding for AMAs as the problem; most citizens were attempting to judge accomplishments by the number of projects completed, although these were often defined as timber sales or programs that generated revenue for local communities, rather than for projects related to improving management, validating S&Gs, or protecting endangered species.

Thematic Area 4: Internal and External Barriers to Adaptive Practices

As noted in the literature review, there are few examples of successful adaptive management. In response to interview questions concerning factors constraining efforts to implement an adaptive approach in the Plan, similar issues and factors emerged to explain limited success. The following discussion examines concerns about the lack of meaningful and effective public involvement processes, the absence of trust and collaborative attitudes, a lack of clarity about the goals and objectives of adaptive management and the AMAs, constraints on creativity and innovation, institutional and cultural limitations, and agency support and resources. Many of the responses in this area reflect findings from the wider literature, as well as the discussion of survey results in chapter 5.

Meaningful and effective public involvement processes—
Although public involvement was cited as a major accomplishment by both agency and citizen participants, ironically, many agency respondents contended that little public involvement was actually occurring. Some pointed the finger at their own inability or inattention to this aspect in their AMA:

> I'm least satisfied that we have done little in our AMA analysis or management plan to even get the public involved.

> We have not brought the public in on projects in any way that we had not done before the AMA designation.

Another concern with the public participation process was the agency's difficulty in engaging a broad public. Agency respondents acknowledged their public involvement efforts only reached a small percentage of the public and that meetings tended to be filled primarily with interest group members. Although some believed that the general public simply was not interested in the AMA, others believed that residents did not get involved owing to time constraints. The lack of compensation for their time and the personal costs involved in participation were seen as reasons why citizens were reluctant to become more involved. One agency participant commented:

> The only interested parties are ones that are "paid" to be in an interest group or agency/organization. We miss a whole section (majority) of our publics–especially the surrounding local communities.

Other agency participants recognized that engaging citizens was simply difficult—getting people involved and keeping them active is hard work. They also acknowledged it requires commitment and followthrough from their organization:

> I do not believe we have identified or engaged the full range of public interests. We are basically getting the self-motivated people, but we are missing the "lizards"… those who appear uninterested but may suddenly jump up and bite us because we took their lack of involvement for a lack of interest.

> There's a lack of public meetings, AMA updates/newsletters, and internal/interagency communication…. lack of a clear message to the public that we want and will use their input.

Similarly, although citizens felt that agency public participation efforts had improved, many distinguished between the improved efforts at citizen involvement and poor followthrough on using public input in the decisionmaking process. One citizen noted:

> There's lots of energetic ideas and plans, but a lot of in-house indecision as to what to do with public opinion.

Other citizens noted that agency members rarely contacted them after they had attended meetings:

> Successful initiation but little follow through, especially on projects. After survey information was gathered from local residents, that was about the last time we heard from them again. Plans were written, but no activities resulted from all the meetings and plans. We asked for experimentation in projects involving types of logging, artistic uses of trees, firewood for senior citizens, and tourism use in the AMA. We never heard from the AMA people again; no followup.

These concerns are similar to those reported elsewhere in programs designed to enhance citizen participation in local decisionmaking processes. For example, in a review of progress in implementation of the Landcare program in Victoria, Australia, Curtis et al. (1995) noted explicit and meaningful involvement of individuals in decisionmaking processes related to topics that directly affect them is a prerequisite for successful participation approaches. However, concerns with issues such as the representativeness of participation can effectively stymie such efforts.

The term "token public participation" appeared repeatedly in citizen responses, with the implication that decisions already had been made prior to seeking public input or that ideas provided by citizens were seldom used to make substantive changes in plans. Most respondents were unable to see any tangible differences in the way the agencies conducted themselves, including both the intent of how they do business and their ability to engage the public effectively:

> Workshops are mostly one-way communication with limited opportunity for questions.

> Some land managers have not bought into public involvement sincerely and seem to use public meetings merely to check off the public involvement box.

Another common expression, "business as usual," reflected a sentiment among citizens that agencies were using the public involvement process to continue extraction activities rather than try different management strategies:

> Although concerns are addressed, the final outcome still appears to be preconceived and heavily weighted toward maximum allowable timber extraction…. very frustrating. Ultimately, public input seems to be considered then ignored in favor of business as usual under a different heading. It may now be called "adaptive management" but its still "timber harvest planning" punctuated by public placation.

> Citizen involvement in planning is tolerated when it is confined to trivial issues, but when it focuses upon the central issue of logging, it is not acknowledged at all…. Citizen involvement is a disingenuous ploy to garner public support for predetermined Forest Service policies, while appearing to invite input that would modify or balance those policies.

A related issue involves how agencies communicated with their publics. Some citizens cited the lack of communication skills among agency personnel, particularly in the preparation of written materials for public consumption:

> All reports are written in "governmenteze" and are virtually impossible to understand. They may as well be written in Russian…. examples: "management prescription DM," "the VQO is retention," "matrix," and "activities should remain visually subordinate to the surrounding landscape."

Thus, the performance of public participation related to adaptive management and the AMAs is characterized by a contradiction. As discussed under "accomplishments," both managers and citizens cite progress in public involvement efforts, yet here, we find criticism of agency public involvement efforts. Three comments seem germane.

First, the problems and challenges associated with public participation efforts, while real and formidable, are not unique to efforts to act adaptively or to manage the AMAs. These issues are enduring and systemic and it is not a surprise that they would arise more specifically in the context of adaptive management. For example, concerns with the impacts of the Federal Advisory Committee Act (FACA) have had a major, and generally negative, effect on soliciting and integrating public participation in federal agency decisionmaking processes (e.g., Wondolleck and Yaffee 2000).

Second, agency concerns about their lack of ability to undertake effective public involvement might constitute an honest assessment, but nonetheless, it is something of a puzzle. The management agencies have been involved in public participation for many years and the resulting body of experience should be the source of important insight, approaches, and methods to enhance performance. The apparent lack of performance in this area raises disturbing questions. Perhaps, as noted in citizen criticisms, public involvement has been driven mainly by procedural compliance concerns (e.g., NEPA). Given the extensive experience, but the apparent failure to build on it, it does not seem to be inaccurate to argue that the idea of "learn by doing"—an element of adaptive management—has little evidence to support it.

Third, although a large literature on public participation exists, including efforts to formulate specific guidelines (Shindler and Neburka 1997), it appears this has had limited impact on organizational policies and procedures. This literature provides important insight into problems plaguing efforts to secure effective public participation (e.g., time impacts, incorporation into decisions); the problems reported by respondents in this evaluation are commonly cited elsewhere. The extent to which the failure to capitalize on this body of knowledge is a matter of unawareness, disinterest, or an inability to incorporate it into organizational culture and operations simply is not known. Public involvement in adaptive management seems crucial to its long-term success, but much remains to be done in integrating it in an effective manner.

Trust and collaborative attitudes—
Many agency personnel voiced dissatisfaction over the amount of opposition that continues to plague or disrupt their outreach efforts. This lack of collaboration was reported as occurring between the agency and the public, the agency and formal interest groups, and between the management and regulatory agencies. In the view of agency respondents, interest groups, particularly environmental groups and timber industry organizations, tended to dominate the agenda at meetings and displayed little inclination or interest in communicating and collaborating with others. Agency respondents mentioned how these interest groups (and occasionally other nonaffiliated members of the public) will often take a "no-compromise position" that effectively prevents the AMA from operating effectively. One agency participant commented:

> Environmental community cannot/will not move past status quo.
> If they would, their involvement would be more meaningful.

In addition, there was a perception amongst agency personnel that interest groups further hinder the AMA process by refusing to participate in the meetings when they felt that they could achieve their goals through other means. Such strategic behavior is common and predictable. For example, in the dispute-resolution literature, the strategy of "best alternative to a negotiated agreement" occurs commonly in efforts to implement collaborative designs (Wondolleck 1988). Simply put, people come to the table as long as they perceive the outcomes of those negotiations as favorable to their interest. Once they perceive this not to be the case, they withdraw, turning to other avenues, particularly political or statutory, to achieve their goals. In short, there is little or no incentive to engage in a collaborative process. For the manager interested in promoting collaboration and consensus building, this can be frustrating, and this was reflected in the comments made by agency personnel from all AMAs:

> It's hard…to get collaboration from the different entities or different groups that have interest in what happens in the forest, because those groups have found that they don't need to sit down at the table and work with us and come to some compromise or resolution on how we manage the area. If any group has a certain agenda, they can go to the courts and very likely get what they want through the court system, so there's no incentive again for people to work in a collaborative entity…

There was some frustration with local interest groups and the belief that their tactics detract from the agency's ability to involve the wider public. For example:

> Several local groups see all federally sponsored meetings as fair game for public "grand standing" and disruption…. this is not a fun place to attempt public involvement.

Many agency participants believe these attitudes and behaviors serve to further erode efforts to build trust with communities:

> Personal agendas still hinder the collaborative process…. Trust and credibility issues remain a constraint to education, collaboration, and implementation.

> Individual, well-managed projects establish trust, poorly managed projects break down trust previously built. The only way I have found to mitigate "damage control" is to establish a project team on a personal level so the community sees you as an individual, who just happens to work for the Forest Service.

For many citizens as well, the perceived undue influence of interest groups exacerbated feelings of powerlessness in local AMA decisions. They believed that special interest groups have more time and money to influence decisions than local citizens. In particular, respondents felt that local input was underrepresented:

> If you don't have a Ph.D. grant or are from an environmental organization, your views are dismissed…. A "smoke-filled back room" atmosphere prevails.

There were similar suspicions about industry groups and their influence on decisionmaking:

> I feel industry is listened to with greater interest than public…. they patronize the public as if we were fools.

> Not sure whether the AMA effort is the velvet glove to the industry's iron fist.

A predominant sentiment for many citizens who criticized public processes as too political was the high level of distrust in the motives of the natural resource agencies. Some cited the need for a more trustworthy environment, but suggested that watchdogs will be necessary until that condition exists. One citizen noted:

> It would be so much more effective for all parties if a true effort were made to include the public's concerns early on in establishing overall goals and objectives, and a level of trust established so that the public would not feel the need to monitor or influence each agency action. But the current rhetoric is not demonstrating an agency commitment to balanced activities.

The lack of trust seems to derive in part from what many citizens believe to be previous unsatisfactory public participation processes and subsequent decisions. Some citizens noted that agency members "double talk," lack honesty, or outright tell lies. In addition, the public's belief that their input is rarely used in the decisionmaking process often stems from the strongly held belief that plans come "from above" and the Forest Service is not acting in the public's interest:

> Trust and relationship building on local levels get undermined by higher up bureaucrats who continue to decide policy in their good-old-boy ways as ever before. This erodes public sense that our input counts and erodes perception that local agency folks hold any real control on local issues.

> Trust is in short supply. They lie about the reasons to cut timber and about lack of true scientific credibility…. The strategies of timber planners to get around the laws by withholding information or giving out misleading information.

At the same time, there is concern among some agency personnel that efforts to incorporate citizen views, knowledge, and perspectives into decisions somehow abrogates their professional training and responsibilities. In one of the stronger, more candid statements of this belief, one manager noted:

The potential the AMAs held as possible examples of a devolution of authority, with attendant benefits of improved citizen access to, and influence on decision-making at local levels, has been replaced by a conviction that business as usual prevails, with national or other nonlocal influences, predominating.

If the agencies just want to use the uneducated public's input for decisionmaking we should fire all our professionals and hire local folks to make decisions.

The comment reflects a strong undercurrent of suspicion and distrust facing efforts to incorporate citizen input into decisionmaking in support of adaptive management and the AMAs. For example, citizens might perceive that the personal knowledge they hold is not acknowledged or treated as legitimate or credible by agency personnel; unless one possesses the credentials of education or speaks on behalf of environmental or industry interests, one's views hold little merit. The commonly held idea that only industry and environmental interests are important imparts a sense of powerlessness, further discouraging active and broad citizen involvement. The potential the AMAs held as possible examples of a devolution of authority, with attendant benefits of improved citizen access to, and influence on decisionmaking at local levels, has been replaced by a conviction that business as usual prevails, with national or other nonlocal influences, predominating (Miller 1999).

Lack of clear goals and objectives—
Many agency members reported they felt uncertain about the mission and direction for the AMAs. They cited a lack of clear goals for their work and the existence of different expectations among the various players that collectively served to hinder public involvement efforts. There was also a sense that the AMAs might be ephemeral, existing only because of current political whims. One agency participant noted:

> The AMA is too vague and not "immediate" enough to interest most of our publics…. The concept and purpose of the AMA are difficult to communicate to the public since the agency itself isn't quite sure what to do with AMAs, or if they're going to last through the next political change or administration. This makes it difficult for staff to have a passion for the program—and I'm sure the publics sense this.

Some agency participants felt that developing appropriate management directions for the AMAs was handicapped by shortcomings in the rules and regulations:

> There's lack of clarity on the resource planning process required by law in terms of resource complexity, information, regulatory realities, and time required to fully implement a project.

Other agency participants saw the problems of an unclear vision of adaptive management and the AMAs as grounded in a lack of leadership:

> After public involvement, final approval of our AMA plan has taken too long! Forest leadership did not clearly set an expectation for what the decision space was, so the AMA plan is stalled.

Some saw this lack of clarity as detrimental for both citizens and agency interests:

> The AMA puts local folks into a false scenario that we are managing AMAs first for local interests.

To the extent that the lack of clarity contributes to confusion and ambiguity about the purpose of AMAs and the respective roles of agency staff and citizens, the potential for conflict increases, coupled with the likelihood that the respective parties hold the other responsible.

Citizens also cited the need for clear goals and objectives in order to evaluate success. There were a number of expressions of dissatisfaction with the agencies' lack of vision and a well-defined direction for the AMAs. Not only were citizen respondents unclear about the goals of their AMA, but many believed that agency members were also confused. As noted earlier, the lack of clarity about the definitions of adaptive management helped foster unrealistic or inappropriate expectations that, in turn, make efforts to implement innovative management strategies problematic.

Creativity and innovation—

Several agency respondents mentioned a lack of creativity as a major barrier to adaptive processes. A common expression was that if adaptive management was to succeed, it would be necessary to "think outside the box." In short, given their understanding of what adaptive management is, respondents thought that one had to be creative to be able to implement it (which seemingly stands in contrast to the earlier notion that the agency had always been adaptive). Several managers mentioned they thought the intent of adaptive management was to be more creative, and have the "harness off" when it came to AMAs, but for some reason have not been able to implement it as they envisioned. One manager identified what he thought was the biggest barrier to implementation of adaptive management

Creativity. Lack of creativity. How do you like that answer? I think we can meet our objectives, make this group happy, get some forest products out of the woods, if we're creative. Tell people to get out of their box. I think an obvious answer is lack of money, but I think with creativity you can come up with ways to get around that.

Another manager mentioned that in addition to a lack of creative thinking on the agency's part, there was a lack of **managing for** innovation and creativity. The respondent qualified this by saying that it might be an outright impossibility to manage creatively in the face of litigation and lawsuits regarding endangered species. We shall address this in more detail later, but it implies that efforts to create a supportive institutional environment are dependent on both internal (e.g., organizational leadership) and external (e.g., laws) factors.

Another respondent mentioned that adaptive management is not a standard on which they are evaluated, implying a lack of organizational incentives in place to help implement adaptive management. Similarly, one manager commented:

> Funding would help, but how do you give people license to take risks? If you are within an agency that doesn't support risk takers, how do you encourage it? There's no process to evaluate the type of risks people are taking or to reward them.

Other agency participants voiced dissatisfaction with their organization's inability or unwillingness to consider new ideas on the AMAs. Despite the rhetoric of adaptive management representing a "new way of doing business," they found the treatment of AMAs differed little from traditional management:

> The original approach to AMA public involvement in the NW Forest Plan was one of collaboration and shared decisionmaking. The ROD modified this approach and reestablished the traditional agency role.... I am most disappointed the new social approach was not tried in the AMA.

Agency participants mentioned the desire on the part of many of their colleagues to find **a single best way** and go with that. "People are still stuck on hard numbers," commented one manager. The idea that adaptive management could be undertaken through a variety of approaches and techniques seemed to stand in contradiction to the organization's traditional dependence on standardization and uniformity.

The idea that adaptive management could be undertaken through a variety of approaches and techniques seemed to stand in contradiction to the organization's traditional dependence on standardization and uniformity.

Institutional and cultural limitations—

Although many comments focused on the constraining effects of external laws and policies on efforts to practice adaptive management, there was the recognition that the internal culture and traditions of both the Bureau of Land Management and Forest Service also are sources of constraints. Agency respondents noted that the current agency culture and structure seeks to establish limits and rules and to create prescriptive approaches to solutions, typical characteristics of bureaucratic organizations. This effectively puts employees in positions where their roles and responsibilities are clearly prescribed and discourages efforts to be flexible and innovative. However, some agency respondents were concerned this traditional approach fostered and sustained their institution's inability to (and fear of) change, ironically at a time when change was essential for survival. They believed that organizations must learn how to move through periods of transition more effectively.

A risk-averse culture was cited as another major barrier to implementing adaptive management; as noted in chapter 3, this has been a consistent conclusion from other efforts to implement adaptive approaches. Agency respondents observed that the public, environmentalists, management agencies, and especially regulatory agencies all tend to disapprove of making decisions that include "high" risk. However, agency respondents noted that an avoidance of risk runs counter to the notion of adaptive management, which, through experimentation, necessarily includes some level of uncertainty and risk associated with any project. Agency participants also described how the burden of proof has shifted from being able to operate until a project has been shown to have an adverse effect to not being able to operate without prior evidence of a lack of adverse effects. Under these conditions, many concluded that it is nearly impossible to conduct experimental adaptive management; again, the literature review reports similar conclusions in other resource management contexts.

Because of their risk-averse nature, regulatory agencies (and their regulations) were seen as major barriers to adaptive management. Agency participants noted that regulatory agencies have become quite conservative owing to the constant threat of litigation. As a result, this makes it difficult to conduct the experimentation associated with adaptive management. It was acknowledged that the Forest Service and the Bureau of Land Management need to work more closely with regulatory agencies to better understand the respective responsibilities and the limitations under which they must work. However, as noted earlier, we found little evidence of efforts to undertake such interagency communication, coordination, and education.

Photo 7   The challenges of working closely with regulatory agencies with respon
sibility for enforcing the Endangered Species Act to protect species such as salmon
posed a major challenge to efforts to implement adaptive management. *Photo by
Gary Kramer, NRCS.*

Regulations—either statutory or administrative—were cited as another barrier
to achieving success. The need to strictly follow regulations (e.g., FACA or NEPA)
was discussed as effectively limiting the ability to conduct adaptive management:

> Agency regulations and laws regarding T&E species are pitted against
> experimentation and inclusion of social/economic elements.

However, there was little recognition of the possibility that definitions of what
constituted "strict compliance" with these regulations might be influenced by the

previously cited risk-averse attitudes and concerns; i.e., conservative interpretations of what NEPA or FACA require limit an organization's exposure to potential legal or political risks (Caldwell 1998).

Some respondents noted that many citizens are unaware of the limitations on AMA projects set by law, and thus have unrealistic expectations about the agency's ability to accomplish certain tasks on the AMA. Again, the extent to which the public's lack of understanding of various organizational and statutory constraints represents a means of justifying the lack of innovation or experimentation is unclear.

Organizational barriers to adaptive management were not cited by citizens, save for one, who noted an important cultural barrier, but also acknowledged the key role of local advocates of adaptive management:

> There's systemwide resistance to change of any sort. We are getting some change because a few committed individuals are willing to take risks.

Agency support, funding and other resources—
Agency respondents frequently noted that neither adequate funding nor nonmonetary support was available for the AMAs. The lack of funding has contributed to high workloads placed on existing staff and frequent burnout and turnover of employees. Another frequently cited concern related to conflicts arising from competing agency programs and priorities (e.g., monitoring, survey and management requirements). In particular, agency respondents noted a lack of support in the form of time, money, skilled employees, and overall encouragement for public participation. Because of this, AMAs do not have adequate resources to conduct effective public participation.

Several agency comments related to the specific resources needed to conduct appropriate analyses to implement adaptive management. The example was given several times of how much it cost to do a watershed analysis ($60,000 to $90,000 per watershed) and that the money just wasn't there anymore. When multiple watersheds are located in an AMA, the potential costs could be very large. The nature of the responses indicated a perception that because adaptive management was not a high priority, staff spends time on projects that have more pressing targets. One agency participant said:

> The money will go where we absolutely cannot let things slide, and rarely is that an AMA.

At least one agency respondent mentioned they thought that doing business on an AMA was more expensive, or substantially higher than in other areas, a comment reminiscent of Walters' (1997) observation that despite the belief that adaptive management is easy and cheap, the opposite is more often the case. This respondent mentioned the cost of doing more public processes as part of the additional cost. Respondents from both the Bureau of Land Management and the Forest Service were also worried that organizational capacity to undertake adaptive management was low and that they were only "one person deep." They noted difficulties transferring knowledge and experience to upcoming staff to ensure continuity in agency work. Contributing to the lack of continuity is the high turnover in these AMA positions. In sum, we found little evidence in terms of capacity building or the development of career paths to build and sustain an adaptive capacity.

Agency respondents expressed concern over the lack of time to effectively accomplish adaptive management projects. As a result, AMA responsibilities have been seen as "add-on" work to an already busy schedule and can become hidden under other duties, especially because the agencies have given the general impression (e.g., through the reduction in funding) that the implementation of AMAs is not a high priority. Agency participants consistently echoed concerns about spreading people thin and simply adding on to the duties already assigned. One respondent mentioned that as new priorities and demands come along, adaptive management is pushed to the side. During one coordinator's meeting, participants were asked to indicate what proportion of their time was spent on adaptive management and AMA-related tasks; the responses ranged from 10 to 25 percent, except for two Bureau of Land Management coordinators, who serve full time. One forest supervisor said that "the AMAs are on a starvation diet." One manager described how much time was allocated for AMA activities:

> I think right now if you look at the funding, we have about 261 days
> in the year. I have 9 days for doing something with the AMA. Not a
> whole lot.

Agency respondents also noted that although they need more time to complete tasks, they are expected to produce results quickly, and time was a major barrier to successful public involvement efforts on the AMA. Because timelines for completion of AMA activities were so short, there was insufficient time to conduct effective and innovative involvement efforts. Such short timelines are often simply inappropriate and inadequate for seeing significant effects, either in sociopolitical or biophysical systems. For example, agency respondents noted that many necessary public involvement processes, such as opening lines of communication and establishing trust, only occur over extended periods. Most frequently mentioned was the lack of time given to produce results, but budget and sufficient training also were noted:

> Too short a timeframe in AMA planning to develop meaningful relationships with [people of] differing views.

> Extremely short timeline in the early stages…. Directive was to be innovative, yet with short timeline all we could do was the "regular" modes of public involvement.

> Biggest problem is impatience…. Managers expect immediate results, people need time to process new ideas.

Related to these concerns was the perceived clash between the prevailing short-term mentality in management agencies and the need for long-term thinking and for dealing with long-term processes. For instance, one respondent noted that learning is a long-term goal usually associated with costs that come immediately but that benefits are accrued after a long period. Moreover, this contributes to the asymmetry between the costs and benefits of an adaptive approach; the economic, personal, and political costs are incurred in the short run, whereas any benefits do not accrue until much later. As Messick and Bazerman (1996: 11) have noted "the consequences that we face tomorrow are more compelling than those we must address next week or next year." Learning becomes more difficult when operating under a short timeframe and expectations that expect quick results. The challenge is exacerbated when there are high levels of staff turnover or when there is a lack of permanence and continuity. Meeting long-term management and research objectives requires at least some stability and continuity in the workforce.

Many agency personnel were candid about the lack of support from within the agency as well as the lack of resources for conducting public involvement work. Their comments are indicative that unrealistic expectations have been placed on field staff to do the AMA job; as a consequence, some reported a sense of abandonment:

> Lack of support from the SO to assign people to this process. District personnel are woefully understaffed to work on these issues; highest priority is always planning sales, restoration, or involvement with research. AMA Coordinator has a full-time job supervising a dozen employees and planning timber sales in addition to coordinator role…. Where is the time for community involvement?

There is little support for public involvement from the rank and file of the organization. Most see it as a waste of time, and some think we should just forget about it.

Funding, staff stretched too thin. Forest has had higher priorities in completing other AMA analysis and little has been done with the Finney AMA. Since nothing has been done at the AMA, my local feedback from the public is that the AMA is a "cruel hoax."

Thematic Area 5: What Is Necessary for Adaptive Management to Succeed?

Findings from the literature, as well as information contained in interviews, paint a pessimistic picture of efforts to implement an adaptive management strategy and the AMAs in the Plan. Are there realistic opportunities for revitalizing these elements of the Plan? In this final thematic area, we examine comments and suggestions about needed changes in the definition, goals, and objectives of the AMAs; organizational commitment and leadership; meaningful and effective public involvement; resources; visible progress and results; and appropriate scale for decisionmaking. What steps to incorporate designs for learning might be undertaken? What are the roles and responsibilities of the research community in the adaptive management program? Suggestions with regard to these ideas might hold important insight as to needed future strategies.

Agency participants in particular were strong in voicing a desire for education and training on adaptive management concepts and implementation, despite how this position stands in contrast to the prevalent view that the agencies "had always been adaptive."

Clear definition, goals, and objectives for adaptive management—
Both agency and citizen respondents suggested increasing efforts to explain the adaptive management concept, rationale, and mission to promote an improved common understanding. Several managers mentioned that they felt hung out to dry and did not know what they were supposed to do with adaptive management, and had asked for help and gotten no response. As a result, agency participants in particular were strong in voicing a desire for education and training on adaptive management concepts and implementation, despite how this position stands in contrast to the prevalent view that the agencies "had always been adaptive." Other agency respondents suggested creating new hiring criteria to obtain employees who can help the organization change and move forward (e.g., innovators, individuals with people and management skills, individuals who can span the boundaries of different disciplines).

Organizational commitment, capacity, and leadership—
The most frequently mentioned recommendation for improving the effectiveness

of AMAs was increasing organizational commitment to AMAs and internalizing adaptive management in the organization. Currently, adaptive management is tied to particular individuals and thus organizational capacity is low. Agency respondents remarked that the Forest Service and Bureau of Land Management need to show that AMAs are a priority to their organizations by embedding the concept into the organizational structure. Similarly, the organizations need to take a long-term view of their role in adaptive management. One respondent suggested that problems arise when adaptive management is viewed as a short-term "initiative" which might or might not be successful, and might or might not be continued in the future. As discussed in chapter 2, many employees are familiar with the "rise and fall" of new management initiatives, and that has bred skepticism about any new program.

Managers and coordinators often mentioned the importance of having key individuals (both inside and outside the agency) who were motivated, enthusiastic, took initiative, and were supporters and advocates of AMAs. In the absence of such key individuals, little appears to get accomplished. On a similar note, there was some discussion about the benefits of top-down versus bottom-up management. Agency respondents who addressed this issue felt that the lack of top-down direction for AMAs has resulted in a loss of direction for those implementing adaptive management and is interpreted as a lack of agency leadership and support for adaptive management. Immediately following creation of the Plan, a decision was made at the Forest Service regional office to not dictate or impose a policy to guide the adaptive management and AMA effort. This was grounded in a belief that such policies and directions should be of a "bottom-up" origin. Ironically, however, the failure to provide such direction at the regional level (i.e., "top-down") led many field people to treat it as evidence of a lack of priority. Other agency participants commented on the lack of leadership within as well as outside the agencies. This latter comment was directed primarily at environmental groups and their lack of willingness to support experimentation efforts by the Bureau of Land Management or Forest Service.

Agency respondents also mentioned that they lack funds to hire staff that have the necessary skills and capacity for working with the public. Because of the lack of time given to accomplish AMA tasks, agency members felt strongly that placing more staff time into public involvement efforts was necessary to achieve better public participation processes. They suggested hiring more employees who could focus on public participation efforts on the AMA. However, many agency respondents were adamant that these employees must already be skilled in communication and public involvement efforts. Such skills clearly could facilitate improved performance in achieving the social objectives of the AMAs.

Notably absent in comments regarding needed staff and expertise was a call for increased capacity in the design and implementation of experiments and other skills required in meeting the technical objectives of the AMAs. A couple of alternatives appear possible. One is to recruit and incorporate these abilities and skills within the management structure of the agencies. A second alternative would be to explore opportunities for improved integration of Forest Service Research into efforts to implement adaptive management.

A number of AMA personnel called for better leadership and a genuine commitment from their agency; their frustration is characterized by these sentiments:

> More inventiveness on agency's part and same for our partners…. We are still working with some narrow traditional ideas.

> Just do something! Quit sitting around! Use the resources/personnel that have the skills to get good public involvement programs organized and implemented.

> Try some new ideas and see successes…. Realize that some risk is inevitable, and we may have some failures.

Some citizens viewed the AMAs as places where new things could be attempted, but thought the agencies were slow in responding to this opportunity. Many wanted to see staff provide better leadership that included more risk-taking.

> Forest Service professionals and managers are not very creative, way too conservative, incredibly slow at planning efforts, and ever slower at getting projects underway.

> The AMA has limited success based on the willingness of certain managers to take risks and do some experimentation. Others are not innovative or interested, and it often seems like business as usual. The AMA is a great opportunity to do business a different way, but the agencies in general are not staffed with risk-takers. Much more could be done.

More aggressively managing risk and encouraging an increased willingness to engage it remain a major challenge, in part because much of the source of risk is external, such as the Endangered Species Act, the regulatory agencies, and political scrutiny.

Organizational resources—

The need for additional resources to do the job adequately was a priority for most AMA participants. Better funding and more training for personnel were mentioned frequently, but adequate time led the list. Realistic timeframes were seen as particularly important to project implementation and building more effective relations with citizens. Moreover, many respondents noted that time was required both to plan and undertake thoughtful work and to let results play out in such a fashion that learning could occur. Many agency respondents believed there was insufficient time to achieve any measurable results on the AMA, and noted their inability to achieve results has likely dampened citizen participation because people need to see the benefits of their efforts in order to commit to further involvement:

> Time for publics to see that the AMA is a meaningful endeavor for them…. we need some tangible projects that the public can see will benefit them.

Citizens also cited the lack of funds going to AMAs as a problem. Without additional funding, citizen respondents recognize there is little hope that AMAs will be able to complete needed projects.

Meaningful and effective public involvement and communication—

Despite barriers to effective public involvement that exist for AMA personnel, many called for renewed efforts to involve the public. Based on their experiences, they identified several factors necessary for successful interactions. Among these were the needs to involve a broader base of citizens, to establish more regular contact, to communicate more effectively, and to improve internal attitudes about public participation.

> We need to make more of an effort to educate the public on established land management planning process and which elements are likely to be inflexible before asking them to develop alternatives.

> Need to learn to listen to the public, not just well-organized environmental groups.

Many also saw the benefit of getting things done in ways where community members could feel ownership in agency activities.

> Projects that people can grab onto and be involved in…. Ways we can personalize what we do.

Implement actual projects in the AMAs—citizens will get involved if we are acting and learning new things.

Citizens also cited a desire for what they termed "legitimate" public involvement and communication and meaningful involvement in decisionmaking. As mentioned earlier, many citizens were concerned that agencies simply were conducting a token public participation process, with the decision having been previously decided. Some citizens expressed the need for open participation that allowed for citizen input, but generally described their particular experience as positive:

More input is needed and issues should be talked over more often….
[thus far] meetings have been open and honest; local concerned citizens
have been involved.

Public involvement was the focus of a large number of citizen respondents, but here the overriding sentiment was one of skepticism:

I have been heavily involved with our AMA. I attended two open
houses, submitted comments on the options, attended three meetings,
and helped draft the plan that was adopted by the Provincial Advisory
Committee. The AMA team certainly solicited public opinion, but as
evidenced by the new timber sales advertised, they have been very
careful in not letting public opinion affect their decisions.

There seems to be a difference between what they tell the public and what
is actually done on the ground.

**Aggressive efforts
to overcome citizen
suspicions and
skepticism about
adaptive manage-
ment and the AMAs
are called for...
a distinguishing
feature of such
efforts must be
demonstrable
evidence of a change
in organization
behavior.**

A related theme involves the extent to which agency personnel actually listen to community ideas and concerns. Citizens generally recognized that AMAs are places where the agency could potentially provide leadership and respond to local needs and concerns. However, many expressed skepticism that the AMAs will be different from previous attempts at involving communities:

I'll be listening to the rhetoric and promises, observing the results.

Citizen involvement has "bottomed out".… I keep getting involved out
of hope for what was once the best agency in the federal government.

Such comments suggest that aggressive efforts to overcome citizen suspicions and skepticism about adaptive management and the AMAs are called for and that a distinguishing feature of such efforts must be demonstrable evidence of a change in organization behavior. In a recent review of factors associated with making collaborative efforts work, Wondolleck and Yaffee (2000) concluded that the major factor in successful enterprises is simply that resource agencies did what they said they would do. This seems an appropriate conclusion for those charged with adaptive management responsibilities to consider.

Another concern about public involvement involves how much the agencies will be influenced by "interest groups" (often the term used for industry groups) over listening to regular citizens. People on all sides of the debate expressed frustration with organized groups having the ear of land managers.

> The Forest Service could be more effective if it were not for the
> constant pressure from special interest groups.

However, the key role of interest groups is a reality that both citizens and resource managers must accommodate. Such groups have a long and important role in American society, and it is unlikely we will see any significant change in this. An important lesson here is the need to recognize that the lack of affiliation with such groups is perceived as a liability by many people. This, in turn, might have detrimental effects on their decision to participate in the public debate about natural resource management issues, because they believe their views will not be acknowledged or given credibility. In the public discourse about resource management in general, or in regard to adaptive management and the AMAs in particular, resource managers should make it unequivocally clear that the lack of membership in a formal interest group, of whatever persuasion, in no way precludes or diminishes the importance or relevance of what someone has to say.

The issue of trust is a recurring element in much of the debate about natural resource management today (Wondolleck 1988). This held true during our interviews; an underlying theme in agency interactions with citizens continues to be the extent to which people trust each other. In the case of the AMAs, this concern now goes well beyond the relationship of local communities with the Forest Service personnel with whom they deal on a regular basis to questions about the ability of these individuals, operating in a larger bureaucratic framework, to make good on agreements:

> I trust our local district ranger to do the right thing, but I don't trust
> the Forest Service to let him do it.

This quote offers important insight as to two important elements of trust. First, trust develops at an interpersonal level, characterized by three attributes: honesty (believing what someone says), benevolence (having an interest in another's welfare to the point of working cooperatively with them), and reciprocity (when one receives benefits, one is motivated to reciprocate) (Moore 1995). Second, trust also develops at the organizational level; here, the emphasis is on the belief that processes are fair (Lawrence et al. 1997). Both are important, but the belief that those individuals whom one trusts work in an untrustworthy organizational environment means that deliberations between interests always will be dominated by a lack of confidence and trust. Trust building is a time-consuming process, so once again, we see that adaptive processes must have adequate time to proceed, not only for building under-standing of complex sociopolitical and biophysical systems, but also for building and sustaining trust among participants.

Visible progress and results—
A frequently mentioned comment from citizens was that rarely are any tasks com-pleted on the AMAs, although much effort is devoted to public participation pro-grams. This belief particularly has frustrated locals used to getting things done on the ground and not prepared for the slow process of the federal bureaucracy. Some respondents believed that the extent of the bureaucracy and cost of the AMA were wholly out of proportion to the accomplishments to date. Lack of progress was a major problem many citizens noted about public involvement and meetings, but the high number of responses in this area suggests it also describes widespread dissat-isfaction with general conditions on the AMAs.

> Meetings are not the problem, but the fruitlessness of them! Locals are doers, not all talk and no show.

> The information distributed to the public so far has been all about process and nothing about product.

Two important lessons are imbedded in this issue. First, there is a question of managing expectations. As discussed earlier, many processes that might be assessed through adaptive processes—sociopolitical or biophysical—often involve lengthy periods before it is possible to assess the effects and consequences of some action. Moreover, it is unlikely that the investigation of these processes can be short-cut or accelerated. Thus, it is important that realistic expectations be cultivated, and adap-tive management proponents need to play a proactive role in this. Second, we pre-viously noted the emphasis that has been given to learning, but, learning is only a means to the end state of better informed action. To gain the necessary political understanding and support of adaptive approaches, it is clear that greater emphasis needs to be given to on-the-ground evidence of work. This is not inconsistent with our first point; the key will be in developing an appreciation of the fact that actions taken today might require significant time before the consequences and implications of such actions become apparent.

Appropriate scale for decisionmaking—
It was the perception of many citizen respondents that federal forest management is one long, frustrating, political process, with decisions made at administrative levels well above the AMA. Overall, discontent with the decision system under which resource agencies currently operate was high:

> Involves national politics and not what is the right management for this area.

> The planning process is so heavily political that agency people cave in and professionalism goes out the window.

An important concern to some citizen respondents was that AMAs are not centered on community needs and interests. These citizens argue that the problem is with federal managers who want to implement "answers" that are not well-suited for local forests and do not want to listen to concerns of residents:

> Local ideas about forest practices are dead on arrival.

To the extent such concerns are valid, they reflect a lack of responsiveness to the social objectives of the AMAs. Clearly, increased emphasis needs to be given to developing venues and mechanisms for soliciting and incorporating local knowledge, needs, and concerns in adaptive management and the AMAs.

Some citizens had hoped that the AMAs would generate jobs in the form of harvesting or thinning contracts (an idea given credence in the discussion of AMAs contained in FEMAT). The lack of progress has created disappointment and a growing sense of impatience:

> It doesn't seem that the economic well-being of the community is the driving force. The AMA is concerned about public impressions, involving people, and having meetings instead of getting anything done.

Again, it seems important to manage the expectations held for the AMAs. The belief that the AMAs were primarily some kind of "economic enterprise" zone is

Photo 8   Some citizens saw adaptive management areas as places where commodity production could take place, thereby ensuring economic support for rural communities. *Photo by Lynn Betts, NRCS.*

not without at least some foundation; as envisioned in FEMAT, there was a recognition of the ability to derive commodity values from these areas, with the benefits largely accruing to local people. However, there were other important purposes, particularly with regard to their role as venues for experimentation, testing, and the validity and the priority of these purposes vis a vis economic outputs needs clarification.

Another issue for citizens stemmed from concerns that what is best for the environment is not adequately being addressed. Many citizens noted that AMAs were designated for experimentation with ecosystem management, but thought this too has largely failed to materialize. There was a feeling that managers might simply not know how to practice more diversified forest management or that they only continue to do what they already know very well. As a result, citizens were skeptical of agency motives:

> AMA activities get sidelined while salvage logging takes precedence...
> emphasizing resource extraction over ecosystem management.

> With respect to the central issue of preserving the forest ecosystem,
> federal forest managers are simply disinterested.

Citizens also recognized the need for better science and for resource organizations to share information about local forests. Among these were people who were concerned that ecosystem management was just another agency "smoke-screen."

> The whole idea of adaptive management at the face sounds good…
> I'm afraid however that some decisions that are being made are too
> drastic and have little hard science to support even trying.
>
> Little attempt to incorporate anything but the standard "get-the-cut-out-
> in-the-name-of- ecosystem-health" mentality…. So far the agencies
> have shown little interest in community directives or scientific challenges.
>
> Decisionmakers (the forest supervisor) ignore public input and their
> own science…. ecosystem management is not happening.

These remarks suggest recognition among many citizens as to the role of adaptive management and AMAs in improving understanding of complex ecosystems and their relation with the social, economic, and political systems within which they are located. There is concern that appropriate scientific input is lacking and that there is a lack of will, possibly even ability, to implement a more rigorous, scientifically grounded approach to management, by using adaptive processes to determine appropriate management strategies. These concerns hold important implications for the need for an overt role of research and science involvement in organizational efforts to implement an adaptive approach.

A recurring theme in the comments received from citizens focused on the legitimacy of the adaptive management initiative. Many citizens expressed a clear message that the success of adaptive management and the AMAs depends on an agency commitment to following the spirit and intent on which they were founded. Several comments questioned both the will and ability of resource managers to implement adaptive management on local federal lands:

> Are the AMAs a legitimate attempt to create long-term national forest
> policy or are they a public relations gimmick to appease the public,
> while "who knows" set the real national forest policies?
>
> I feel AMA decisions are being driven by goals and pressures that are
> beyond the scope of local planners.

In questioning the legitimacy of AMAs, many citizen respondents referred to a long history of experience with agency initiatives and projects—often characterized as frustrating. Although people agreed that adaptive management sounds like a good idea, many seem to be waiting to see if it will materialize in new or different programs. For some, there was a sense of disenchantment, disappointment, and abandonment as the agencies seemingly moved away from their earlier commitment to an adaptive approach.

There is concern that appropriate scientific input is lacking and that there is a lack of will, possibly even ability, to implement a more rigorous, scientifically grounded approach to management, by using adaptive processes to determine appropriate management strategies.

Conclusion

Although many themes and issues emerged from both the questionnaire data and the interviews, the items discussed under thematic area 5 capture the major concerns and issues regarding effective implementation of adaptive management. Clearly, there is confusion over what adaptive management means and whether it represents a "new" way of doing business. If adaptive management processes are to succeed, training regarding the concept (both in theory and in practice) is necessary. This would facilitate a more unified vision of the concept to develop within the agency, and perhaps alleviate the confusion expressed by many agency participants as well as citizens. Closely linked with this is the need for organizational commitment to, and leadership for, adaptive management. This commitment is reflected in the more obvious signals—which are often resource and personnel related—but perhaps more importantly, in the need to create an organizational culture that supports and rewards the risk-taking and creativity necessary to effectively implement adaptive management.

A large number of comments addressed public involvement and participation. Public involvement is simultaneously offered as one of the major accomplishments as well as one of the greatest challenges of adaptive management. Although the gap in perceptions might be due to trust and any number of other factors, clearly there is a need to bridge this gap. This could involve work to clarify or change the expectations of both agency and citizen participants about what goals public involvement processes can serve. In the same way, further inquiry is needed to clarify what effective and legitimate public involvement might look like and whether it can be achieved within existing organizational contexts and constraints.

Finally, in terms of program evaluation, it likely is too early to evaluate whether adaptive management has been a success or failure in the forestry realm. Evaluation is an area that elicited a number of suggestions regarding the need for additional thinking around defining and establishing credible criteria for measuring success in achieving program goals. Additional discussion is needed in relation to when it might be appropriate to begin to evaluate such programs. Many participants (both agency and citizen) stated that timeframes for evaluation stand in sharp contrast to physical and administrative realities. Frustration centers around a situation in which many of the management experiments will need years or even decades before they can be evaluated, yet political and administrative pressures continue to lead to premature claims of success or failure.

Chapter 7: Adaptive Management: Facing Up to the Challenges

George H. Stankey and Roger N. Clark

Introduction

We start with a proposition: if the agencies responsible for implementing adaptive management (including adaptive management areas (AMAs) continue on their present course, adaptive management will fail. In this chapter, we discuss some of the critical problems and choices to be made that will determine if this will be the outcome.

The performance of adaptive management and the AMAs must be evaluated within the context of the rapid and dramatic changes in forest management proposed by the Northwest Forest Plan (the Plan). The Plan called for changes to forest management processes, it assigned new roles and responsibilities to managers, it redirected the historical focus of forest management, and it imposed added institutional complexity. In short, if implemented as intended, it involved fundamental reform in forest management.

Yet, the Plan created demands and pressures in areas where little precedent existed, substantial organizational resources would be required, and significant political support was needed. For example, requirements to complete watershed assessments and to satisfy survey and management requirements absorbed (and continue to do so) large amounts of time, energy, and money. Continued regulatory scrutiny and the need for management agencies to satisfy requirements of the Endangered Species Act (ESA) has increased competition for time and money, and these demands have been exacerbated by declining organizational resources, both in personnel and budgets.

In the midst of these changes, adaptive management and the AMAs are among many competing demands for attention and resources. Although these ideas are critical elements for the Plan's successful implementation, neither adequate preparation, training, resources, leadership, nor direction has been put in place to capitalize on the opportunity they present.

This raises the question as to whether our evaluation reflects a general problem of the Plan itself or only a failure to implement the adaptive component. More than a decade after its creation, the Plan faces continuing challenges and criticisms including inadequate monitoring, questions as to its efficacy in protecting endangered species, particularly the northern spotted owl (*Strix occidentalis caurina*), the

Given the problems reported herein we have been asked if our evaluation should be taken as an obituary for adaptive management and the AMA program. The answer to this question is both yes and no. Yes if the future sees more of the same. No if substantial and systemic changes are put in place to demonstrate the potential of adaptive management.

failure to deliver promised timber volumes, and so forth. Adaptive management, as one element of the Plan, is entangled in such criticisms.

However, the problems identified in our evaluation are not unique to the Plan, but are consistent with those identified in the wider literature (see chapter 3). As a strategy, adaptive management could have been undertaken without the Plan in place. Indeed, in the discussion of the various options outlined in the Forest Ecosystem Management Team (FEMAT) report, it was noted that adaptive management could have been an element in any of them. However, contrary to recent assertions, fundamental and systemic shortcomings in current organizational structures and processes constitute major barriers to an adaptive approach and transcend any particular features of the Plan itself.

Yet, consistent with adaptive management's fundamental premise—policies are a source of learning—the experience to date provides insight as to the kinds of actions that might be undertaken and areas where improvements are needed. Although adaptive management and the AMAs represent innovative strategies for resolving complex natural resource management issues, they will take time. New ideas, no matter how compelling and appealing, always face the challenge of replacing the status quo. Given the problems reported herein we have been asked if our evaluation should be taken as an obituary for adaptive management and the

Photo 9 The challenges of improving management in the face of complexity and uncertainty make an adaptive management approach critical. However, without substantive changes in organizational structures, processes, and beliefs, this might prove impossible. *PNW photo.*

AMA program. The answer to this question is both yes and no. Yes if the future sees more of the same. No if substantial and systemic changes are put in place to demonstrate the potential of adaptive management.

A core asset at the agencies' disposal in fashioning an effective response is found among those individuals who took on the fledgling roles of AMA coordinators and lead scientists. Interviews with these people revealed that the ideas of adaptive management and the AMAs held great appeal: the opportunities for establishing new links between management and research, with local communities, and for seeking innovative ways of doing business, based on learning and adaptation. As a consequence, the coordinators and lead scientists brought enthusiasm and energy to the program. Similarly, the idea of an adaptive approach stimulated interest and enthusiasm among many publics, although ironically, the resulting expectations possibly exacerbated the level of disappointment and disenchantment revealed by the citizen surveys (see chapter 6).

Nonetheless, the extent to which adaptive management has become a central element in the Plan's implementation and how the situation is perceived by agency personnel and the public remains problematic. Similarly, it is questionable how effective the AMAs have proven in providing a setting in which the technical and social objectives assigned them have been met.

In short, and notwithstanding our remarks regarding agency staff committed to adaptive management and the AMAs, this assessment concludes that many serious problems confront the agencies. Some of these problems likely represent fatal flaws if they are not resolved. Some result from fundamental organizational limitations; that is, they stem from forces (both internal and external) that will require time and expanded political commitment to overcome. Others are operational in nature; there are internal organizational policies and practices that require attention, but are no less challenging. Some barriers are reported in the adaptive management literature, whereas others are linked to specific elements of the Plan.

It might be tempting to see the focus on barriers as unnecessarily pessimistic and discouraging, particularly in a profession that has long embodied the "can do" mentality. It might also be tempting to "slay the messengers"—a comment to the senior author of a Journal of Forestry paper (Stankey et al. 2003) reporting on this project was that "what happens next, now that you've killed the AMAs?"—or ignore or dismiss our findings and conclusions. We can only stress that it has been the intention of this review to openly and honestly present findings—indeed, we were impressed with the openness and honesty that characterized discussions with those we interviewed—and much of what we report is mirrored in the wider adaptive management literature. In other words, many of the issues, problems, and barriers uncovered in our evaluation appear grounded in systems that transcend resource sectors and cultural, legal, and political systems.

We believe that the basic precept of adaptive management—learning from outcomes and then adjusting subsequent behavior—is the key to fashioning innovative management alternatives. However, we also believe, as Kotter (1995: 60) has noted, that successful efforts in organizational change must start with a frank discussion of potentially unpleasant facts, the purpose of which is "to make the status quo seem more dangerous than launching into the unknown."

In this chapter, we focus on two major topics. First we summarize the major findings that emerge from this evaluation of adaptive management. Then we address a number of challenges facing agencies as they attempt to make adaptive management a viable enterprise.

Major Findings About the Status of Adaptive Management in the Plan

The findings reported in this section derive from the literature and from the efforts described in chapters 5 and 6.

Problems in Implementing Adaptive Management in the Plan Began at the Beginning

> It is conceivable that the process used to craft the Plan created a major barrier to implementation of adaptive management. The scientific foundation for the Plan was built by FEMAT in isolation from managers. Their report (FEMAT 1993) was then handed to managers and political leaders to craft a Plan and record of decision (ROD USDA and USDI 1994). Somewhere along the way in the handoff of science to policy and management the centrality and vision for adaptive management didn't make it intact though the words seemed to survive in the record of decision (Salwasser 2004: 12).

The FEMAT envisioned adaptive management as a core strategy for implementing an ecosystem approach to management (see FEMAT Table VIII-2: VIII-30, for details on how adaptive management would facilitate adjustments in the selected option over time). Chapter 8 in FEMAT outlined the role and purpose of adaptive management and the AMAs, particularly to evaluate the assumptions of the Plan and to test and validate and adjust the standards and guidelines (S&Gs). It also featured the social objectives of adaptive management and the AMAs and focused on opportunities for innovative partnerships among citizens, managers, and scientists.

Although some ideas presented in FEMAT in support of adaptive management and the AMAs proved untenable or illegal (e.g., earmarking revenue from commodity sales to local communities), the discussion offered an innovative vision for management. It anticipated the need for new organizational structures and processes, it acknowledged the key role of organizational leadership, and it envisioned a new working relationship among citizens, managers, and scientists.

However, during preparation of the record of decision (ROD), much of this vision and innovativeness was lost. It is difficult to determine exactly why this happened. In interviews with individuals involved in preparing FEMAT and the ROD, Schmucker (1996) reported responses to this question. They ranged from that it was simply the result of the normal revision involved in translating a scientific report to policy to an alternative view that the problem was a result of the exclusion of land managers in the FEMAT process, and/or an ineffective or incomplete handoff/transition from FEMAT to the ROD and to the managers and staff expected to implement it.

Although the core technical and social objectives of adaptive management remained, neither the ROD nor subsequent organizational initiatives engaged the significant challenges of what it meant to be an adaptive organization. For instance, questions regarding appropriate organizational structures, requisite budget and training, or frameworks and protocols to facilitate adaptive management received little attention. The inevitable internal and external challenges certain to confront a management approach explicitly designed to engage risk and uncertainty in an organizational, political, and legal environment attuned to risk aversion were not acknowledged, let alone addressed. One result of this, as Lee (1999) noted, is that adaptive management efforts in the Plan remained dependent on a conventional technical-rational planning mode, with limited accommodation for trial-and-error learning and efforts to improve links with citizens and communities.

There is probably an inevitable narrowing of scope and vision in moving from the creative context within which FEMAT was framed and the legally and organizationally bounded document that an environmental impact statement or ROD constitutes. This likely was exacerbated by the fact that the documents were written by different people. The result was that the premises, assumptions, and experiences upon which the FEMAT discussion was grounded failed to be communicated effec-

> **Moreover, it is essential that the organizations charged with administration of an adaptive management program must be the primary source of assertive and aggressive leadership.**

tively to those responsible for preparing the ROD. The disconnect between those framing the vision and those framing the implementation served as the initial source of breakdown constraining efforts to initiate substantive policy change.

Organizational Leadership, Willingness, and Capacity to Implement Adaptive Management Remain Problematic

Leadership, as a source of vision, support, energy, and motivation, emerges from the literature as a key element associated with productive applications of adaptive management. However, interviews with field managers, scientists, and specialists revealed a lack of leadership within both the management and research organizations, with a consequent debilitating effect on implementation efforts.

There were important exceptions. In the Central Cascades AMA, both management and research leadership is notable, promoting a strong link between the two. In the Applegate and Hayfork AMAs, leadership from local citizens complemented agency leadership. The capacity of local citizens to sustain their level of leadership, however, is problematic. Moreover, it is essential that the organizations charged with administration of an adaptive management program must be the primary source of assertive and aggressive leadership. Their command of resources, their legally defined stewardship responsibilities, and the compelling need to find better, more effective ways of managing the land should be primary motivators (Westley 1995). The presence of local champions who provide both leadership and capacity is a recurrent quality cited in the adaptive management literature related to successful implementation. Such individuals can be found among managers, scientists, or citizens, or a combination. They provide the motivation, energy, enthusiasm, and ideas that can spark implementation.

However, there can be tensions between the efforts of these local champions to set up innovative programs and efforts to provide regional direction and support. Our interviews reveal an interesting problem; on the one hand, many locals favor that the impetus and energy for adaptive management arise at that level and that the regional or national level not interfere. At the same time, the lack of regional or national direction, support, or other involvement is interpreted as prima facie evidence of a lack of understanding and commitment on the part of organizational leadership.

> Within the management agencies, there is a sense that adaptive management is "not on the radar screen." Former Forest Service Chief Jack Ward

Thomas reported during his interview that he found little or no interest at the WO level in adaptive management, a situation he attributed to concerns among some staff that adaptive management might erode their power, influence, or budget control. The National Coordinator of Adaptive Management took the view that because adaptive management was not an organizational priority, local advocates were best advised to focus locally because efforts to raise its prominence had little likelihood of success and could even lead to adverse consequences.

Burnout was identified as a problem among the coordinators, contributing to the challenges of developing sustained organizational capacity in adaptive management. At the time of our interviews, two coordinators had resigned their positions because of burnout. In part, stress on coordinators derives from the ongoing assignment of duties in addition to their AMA responsibilities. Some coordinators also reported the belief that their assignment was pro forma (i.e., we have to have someone in the job), rather than an organizational recognition of an opportunity to be supported. The stress of continuous interaction with interest groups, coupled with the frustration of attempting to follow through on the potential of adaptive management in organizations less than fully committed also took its toll. There is a tension between any program largely vested in an individual or small group and the need for developing enduring organizational capacity. Although both are important, in the case of the AMAs, much of the progress and learning that occurred derived from the former situation (i.e., grounded in individuals); there is little evidence of a developing organizational capacity.

Building Adaptive Organizations: Easy to Say, Hard to Do

If adaptive management is central to Plan implementation, how adequate are current processes and structures for achieving this? To address this question, it seems important that a thoughtful, deliberative assessment of current organizational capacity and a frank assessment of needed changes (resources, skills, legal requirements) be undertaken. This would involve questions such as what an adaptive approach implies for day-to-day management, how various organizational structures and processes facilitate or constrain an adaptive approach (e.g., budgeting, research-management links), what skills are required and how they are acquired when absent, the impact of the external political and legal environment (e.g., links with regulatory agencies, impacts of legislation such as National Environmental Policy Act [NEPA] and Endangered Species Act [ESA]), and relationships with the public (e.g., roles, trust building). Such issues are neither simple nor easily resolved,

and resolving them will not be inexpensive. For example, the Glen Canyon evaluation team concluded "It is important to recognize that the fiscal and human
resources needed to manage a newly formed and evolving institution (i.e., adaptive
management) are probably greater than those required to manage a decades-old,
established program" (National Research Council 1999: 61).

However, in the case of the Plan, this type of reflective and deliberative analysis has not occurred. Neither management, research, nor regulatory organizations
responsible for the Plan's implementation engaged in an indepth, critical assessment of how to make an adaptive management strategy work. One explanation for
this is the belief that the concept represented nothing fundamentally new; the
notion that "we've always been adaptive" was heard repeatedly during interviews
with agency personnel. If such an assertion is true, the case for organizational
reform would have little to recommend it. Although the extent to which natural
resource management agencies have, in fact, been adaptive in a manner consistent
with that discussed in the contemporary literature is arguable, a more important
issue concerns the basic issue of what it means to be adaptive and what an adaptive
management approach implies. In evaluating adaptive approaches to assessing the
effects of alternative flow regimes on the Colorado River ecosystem, the National
Research Council review team (1999) concluded that a lack of clarity about the
definition of adaptive management among stakeholders and scientists constrained
implementation and recommended that stakeholders work toward a common definition of the concept.

However, the issue is more complex than simply a disagreement or lack of
common understanding as to what adaptive management means. The conflict is
also shaped by differing beliefs as to the desirability and appropriateness of an
adaptive approach (Rayner 1996). For example, although scientists and specialists
might see it as necessary, other stakeholders might see it as a threat to their strategic interests.

Learning occurs at the individual level as well as within groups (Parson and
Clark 1995). However, even at the individual level, the larger social system within
which individuals exist is important in influencing what is studied, what is learned,
and what is done. Institutional structures and processes can do much to promote
conditions that encourage, reward, and sustain learning by individuals. This
includes providing time for individuals to learn, providing the skills and techniques
for learning (training, protocols), and facilitating and supporting networks with others. However, as our review revealed, the highly motivated coordinators were not
provided training; little was done to equip them with the concepts, techniques, and

processes that would facilitate learning; and most reported that the time they could devote to adaptive management and AMA-related issues steadily diminished as competing demands for their time escalated.

Erosion of the time and energy that could be devoted to adaptive management was particularly serious because it diminished the ability of the coordinators to act as advocates of adaptive management. The literature stresses the importance of such advocates. Information does not just flow to willing learners; it must be pushed by would-be teachers or sought by dissatisfied learners. As discussed above, we believe the coordinators and lead scientists were people who sought to achieve something different, but the crush of other demands and lack of support limited their ability to do this.

As we and others (e.g., Pipkin 1998) have argued, adaptive management is a central feature of the Plan. Moreover, although resource management agencies historically have shown an ability to make changes in practices and policies, often these have been driven by external interests or concerns with organizational survival (Clarke and McCool 1996). Taken together, however, these ideas suggest another fundamental shortcoming of efforts to implement an adaptive approach; namely, what does it mean to be adaptive?

The concepts of adaptive management and AMAs are rich, multifaceted notions, resistant to any standardized definition. Yet, the lack of shared understanding of what the concepts embrace confounds an ability to implement them in practice, to evaluate progress and effectiveness, and to facilitate the process of learning how to learn.

The problem manifests itself in different ways. For example, let us return to the contention that adaptive management is "nothing new; we've always been adaptive." In an interview with a senior policy advisor, it was noted "my assessment (of the assertion that adaptive management was nothing new) is that 'we learned something, so we adapted our management'...what I think of as the 2 X 4 finally got big enough...there was very little 'we need to learn something, so we set up actions to find out.'" In other words, management is conceived of as a stimulus-response approach, more akin to Lindblom's (1959) concept of disjointed incrementalism ("muddling through") than the deliberative, purposive, and explicit approach upon which experimental-based adaptive management rests. Many agency personnel likely consider that natural resource planning always has been grounded in the scientific method; for them, adaptive management is only the latest rhetoric describing the predominant management approach long followed by agencies. Yet there is little

The concepts of adaptive management and AMAs are rich, multifaceted notions, resistant to any standardized definition.

There is a persistent lack of clarity and consensus about the purposes of the AMAs among managers, scientists, and citizens.

evidence of any recognition of the role of experimentation and purposeful learning as key elements of an adaptive approach. In part, the statutory strictures noted above account for management reluctance to support field experimentation. In other cases, reluctance might trace to such causes as the potential need for changes in light of new information.

There is a persistent lack of clarity and consensus about the purposes of the AMAs among managers, scientists, and citizens. Among both scientists and managers, there was confusion about the differences between AMAs and experimental forests; this, in turn, led to views that either we have no need for the AMAs (i.e., they simply duplicate the purposes of one another) or that they are places for traditional scientific investigations, with no necessary linkage to management or ongoing, real-time learning.

Similarly, there was wide variation in public stakeholder's conceptions of the AMAs. For example, some saw the primary purpose of AMAs as a source of support for local economic development and the creation of family-wage jobs. As Stankey and Shindler (1997: 6) warned, "if one conceives of landscapes as tracts containing social meaning and…if one envisions managing these with the active participation of managers and citizens…then it is essential that a sense of ownership and legitimacy be associated with these places." Shindler et al. (1996) reported that interest among members of local communities for using the concept of adaptive management was high (e.g., most agreed with the statement that "in general, adaptive management areas seem like a responsible approach"), but in a subsequent survey of area residents near the Central Cascades AMA, only 16 percent of those surveyed even knew the AMA existed.

Fashioning a common understanding about adaptive management, particularly in settings involving multiple stakeholders, is critical to effective implementation. In their evaluation of the Glen Canyon adaptive management project, the National Research Council (1999) noted it was not clear whether the definition and interpretation of adaptive management provided in the 1997 Grand Canyon Strategic Plan was shared among stakeholders. Their finding is reminiscent of efforts to implement the Plan; i.e., there is a lack of a shared understanding of the fundamental meaning and role of adaptive management as a strategy for achieving the Plan's long-term purposes. Because the AMAs are only one element of the Plan, they can become seen as yet another source of competition for support among competing priorities. The failure to treat adaptive management and the AMAs as fundamentally new conceptions of, and approaches to, resource management constrains efforts to implement them successfully.

The AMAs were intended to represent a regionwide system that offers venues for testing and validation of the S&Gs and for implementing innovative partnerships with local interests and communities (FEMAT 1993). However, corporate support (or perhaps even recognition) needed to achieve such objectives has not eventuated. In some cases, creation of the AMAs—essentially, special management entities—exacerbated conflict and competition both among individual AMAs and between AMAs and other management units. Some national forests without AMAs, for example, saw those with them as gaining favor in budgeting processes; within forests with AMAs, districts without AMAs saw those with them again as having an unfair advantage. Such internal conflicts contrasted sharply with the explicit objectives of the AMA program. The idea that individual AMAs would be able to learn from the experiences of others generally has not been realized; e.g., it proved difficult to get lead scientists from one AMA to engage with other AMAs to discuss experiences, lessons, and so forth. The idea of creating a learning-based and linked system remains largely an illusion.

This latter problem likely transcends the particular mandates of the Plan. In many corporate cultures, creation of special entities, with the intention of supporting pilot efforts, can awaken petty jealousies and conflicts that work against the original objectives. The creation of boundaries is often the first step to creating rivalries and conflicts. Coupled with the lack of effective corporate leadership in management and research that clarifies the purpose, priority, and importance of a system such as the AMAs, the natural tendencies of competition appear to dominate. In the case of the Plan, this might also have been exacerbated by increased work pressures and declining budgetary support that characterized the management environment.

Learning Is a Means to Ends

Although adaptive management theory is dominated by the notion of learning, the empirical literature acknowledges that examples of effective, formal, and rigorous learning are rare. Our interviews, and review of projects and plans for the AMAs, lead to a similar conclusion. In fact, in some cases, there was resistance to the idea of developing formal protocols for policy/management experiments; in one interview, the comment was made that if managers were "required to write everything down and get statistical approval," adaptive management would fail. The irony is that not to do so leads to that end.

The rhetorical attention given learning masks the fact that little effort has occurred to build a learning organization, which in many ways is what adaptive

> The AMAs were intended to represent a regionwide system that offers venues for testing and validation of the S&Gs and for implementing innovative partnerships with local interests and communities.

management means. Several reasons may account for this. Organizational inertia, internal and external pressures to maintain the status quo, and confusion about what adaptive management requires may explain some of the resistance to change. Learning can produce discomfort; it can reveal that some existing policy isn't working, is wrong, or is leading to different outcomes than imagined. Clark (2001) concluded that much learning is unwanted; organizations often are not interested in what they should do differently and their predominant activity is defending the status quo. Although conventional wisdom might suggest that more information makes decisionmaking more decisive, or that new information "speaks for itself," this is seldom the case (Michael 1995, Wondolleck 1988).

An important step in experimental adaptive management is a modeling phase in which current knowledge (scientific, personal, managerial experience) is assessed, questions framed, and the search for alternatives begun (Holling 1978). As Michael (1973: 125) noted, "to learn requires recognizing what one wants to learn, and that means recognizing what one doesn't know." In short, there must be explicit and public acknowledgment of ignorance. Modeling facilitates this process. However, the literature also concludes that all too often, processes become paralyzed at the modeling stage or modeling becomes an end in itself (Walters 1997).

In the case of the Plan and the AMAs, with the exception of work on the Central Cascades (where, as noted in chapter 4, 1,700 silvicultural prescriptions were analyzed in modeling exercises to identify alternatives for meeting the landscape plan objectives), we found no examples of any effort to undertake a modeling approach. Although this might be seen as a benefit (i.e., the organization has not gotten "locked up" in model-building exercises), the more critical assessment is that there has been a general lack of attention to processes for comprehensive problem identification.

Despite the importance assigned to learning in the Bureau of Land Management and Forest Service's own rhetoric regarding adaptive management, virtually no attention addressed two critical questions regarding such learning. First, what, in fact, would constitute learning? Parson and Clark (1995: 456) noted that "short of calling any change learning, one might say that only change in response to identifiable stimuli or information is learning," but they acknowledge that others argue that "any cognitive change should be treated as learning," with questions of effectiveness or progress left to subsequent evaluation. However, in implementation of adaptive management in the Plan, the question of what standards, criteria, and processes would be used to assess learning escaped critical examination. This was a critical omission, given the objective of the AMAs to serve as test-beds for validation of the S&Gs. Second, even if learning were determined to occur, what processes for implementing change (e.g., in the S&Gs or in the allocations) would be required and by whom; what type, level, and specificity of learning would lead to a decision to modify them (Stankey et al. 2003)? This is a critical issue, given a situation where a number of stakeholders hold potential "veto power" over agency actions and also have varying interests that influence their decisions to facilitate or constrain change.

Moreover, given the political nature of the S&Gs (i.e., they represent policy controls favoring the precautionary principle) and because external agents (regulatory agencies, statutes) hold ultimate control over their application, it is doubtful that the managing agencies have the capacity to alter them, irrespective of the evidence. This is linked to earlier concerns regarding the loss of vision outlined in FEMAT; had a deliberative effort involving the relevant institutional actors to build understanding and support for adaptive management been undertaken early on, it might have been possible to create a policy environment more open to adaptive approaches and learning. In short, it is critical to recognize that any planning strategy ultimately involves a political activity (Friedmann 1987). Unfortunately, this reality was not recognized, and subsequent efforts to undertake experimentation—key to effective adaptive management—have faced opposition by regulators. As Tuchmann et al. (1996: 121) observed, "The regulatory and management agencies differ in their opinions about the extent of management and experimentation allowed within the (Adaptive Management) Areas." This opposition also stems from concerns regarding the treatment of risk and uncertainty.

Structuring a learning, adaptive organization has been handicapped by a pervasive belief that adaptive management did not constitute a significant departure from the past. Little attention was given to whether there was a need to alter organizational structures and processes, let alone in what ways, to accommodate an adaptive approach. It is difficult to assess why this is so. One explanation is that adaptive management was seen as marginal and did not represent a significant issue facing the management agencies and therefore did not warrant any special accommodation. On the other hand, the recurring sentiment that adaptive management was nothing new reinforced the idea that no changes in structures or processes were required: if "we've always been adaptive," what's the incentive for change? Alternatively, the types of organizational change required to incorporate adaptive management and a social learning approach might appear so formidable that little incentive exists to engage the issue in any substantive manner; as Lee (1995: 235)

> **Structuring a learning, adaptive organization has been handicapped by a pervasive belief that adaptive management did not constitute a significant departure from the past.**

noted "social learning entails wrenching changes in beliefs." This problem is as challenging today as it was a decade ago.

Adaptive Management Is a Risky Business

A challenge facing adaptive management and the AMAs derives from the problem of actively engaging risk and uncertainty in a risk-averse sociopolitical environment. Although "risk averse" is sometimes taken as a pejorative, it simply means that care is taken to prevent harm from occurring, whether to human health or in the management of endangered species. But such an approach has an important limit, namely that harm can only be prevented when one understands the origins of harm. In the case of uncertainty, where such understanding often is absent, it is difficult to prescribe what a risk-averse course of action should be. Under conditions of uncertainty, the notion that "no action" (i.e., little or no human intervention) is the safest course is unfounded; "no action" is an action, with the potential to trigger significant consequences. In such cases, a more fruitful strategy lies in efforts to build resiliency which, in turn, is best achieved through purposive experimentation (Wildavsky 1988). Based on the learning such experimentation provides, uncertainty can be reduced and policies and programs adapted to minimize the extent to which future harm occurs.

Experiments always introduce the possibility of error. Yet, one of the most significant sources of learning derives from what the operations research literature calls negative feedback (Dryzek 1987); in lay terms, mistakes. However, in risk-averse organizations, major efforts often are made to avoid making mistakes, primarily by minimizing risks. The perception that such risk taking leads to impacts on careers or incurring external sanctions lends credence to such avoidance behavior. A reluctance to engage risk and uncertainty, however, (and the possibility of mistakes) is effectively the death-knell of an adaptive management approach. Gunderson (1999: 35) noted "if the risk of failure during experimentation is not acceptable, then adaptive management is not possible." Similarly, Volkman and McConnaha (1993: 14) concluded that the "bold testing that was central to the original concept of adaptive management…is unlikely to fit comfortably in the endangered species era" because of the risks involved. Yet, this is largely what has happened in implementation of the Plan. "In many cases, managers simply gave up trying to make projects work or walked on eggshells to avoid legal trouble," Stokstad (2005: 690) wrote; he went on to quote Elaine Brong, Bureau of Land Management's director for Oregon and Washington as saying "Caution seems to have trumped creativity."

This issue is ironical. During our evaluation, we often encountered the presumption that a conservative, status quo-type approach was equivalent to minimizing risk; conversely, it was assumed that any human interventions would increase risk. In some cases, however, the restrictive S&Gs were founded on limited information, and there is little evidence to support the idea that their steadfast application is, in fact, the least risky approach. However, in the absence of a willingness and capacity to test and revise the S&Gs, we can become locked into a course of action that ultimately may prove detrimental to the very species and values they were designed to protect.

A crucial liability of the S&Gs is that they constitute "fixed" rules; i.e., they are standardized measures to be applied uniformly across a range of contexts. Such rules are highly subject to failure because they often place excessive confidence in the current state of knowledge and their applicability is particularly vulnerable to the idiosyncratic variations of complex ecosystems (Dietz et al. 2003). Although it might be argued that in the face of uncertainty, such rules are appropriate in the short term, and the Plan's longer term strategy called for their modification in the light of emerging knowledge, the reality is that such measures can take on a life of their own, proving resistant to efforts to alter them, irrespective of the evidence for change. In this sense, the S&Gs are examples of Socolow's (1976: 7) **golden numbers**; i.e., "a number that may once have been an effusion of a tentative model evolves into an immutable constraint." Although such prescriptions might seem to simplify the situation, ultimately they prevent acting on new knowledge and understanding.

> The Standards and Guidelines attached to the ROD [USDA and USDI] (1994) made the rules for reserve allocations binding on AMAs (section D-9), thereby constraining innovation and creative problem solving in AMAs before they ever got out of the starting block. Loading those standards and guidelines on to AMAs was not in FEMAT's vision and likely resulted from agency or political modifications made to change FEMAT Option 9 into the NWFP, which in operation has resembled FEMAT Option 1 (Salwasser 2004: 11).

The Asymmetry Between the Costs and Benefits of Adaptive Management Constrains Implementation

Asymmetry addresses the discrepancy in time between the costs and benefits associated with adaptive management. Managers considering some policy change weigh the costs and benefits associated with implementation. In many cases, the costs (e.g., the policy fails, anticipated outcomes are not readily apparent) become apparent relatively soon and can be attributed to a particular individual. The benefits (e.g., improved knowledge, understanding effects of policy shifts), on the other hand, given the long timeframes associated with many natural processes and systems, might not accrue for some time and attribution for them becomes diffuse. Thus, the tendency is to avoid actions that result in costs in the short term as opposed to adopting actions whose benefits, if any, lie in the future.

Walters (1997: 16) argued that "decisive action…has immediate and obvious costs…the costs of inaction are seldom so immediate. For many decision makers, even a short delay can be enough to ensure that someone else will have to make the decision." In such a context, inaction or delay becomes a rational choice; otherwise, to confront new knowledge might require a response on their part. As Michael (1973: 140) asked, "What is the incentive to take risks if you get rewarded whether you fail or succeed?"

Applying Evaluative Criteria to Adaptive Management in the Plan

In chapter 1, we described four criteria or dimensions that can be used to evaluate policy design:

* Conceptually sound: Is the idea sensible?
* Technical: Does adaptive management translate into practice well?
* Ethical: Who wins and who loses with adaptive management?
* Pragmatic: Does adaptive management make a difference?

Here we briefly describe efforts to date with respect to these criteria.

Conceptually sound: Is the idea sensible?—
Adaptive management has taken root in response to recognition that we do not know enough to manage complex biophysical and socioeconomic systems (Lee 1999). Moreover, there is general agreement that the rate of knowledge acquisition needed to deal effectively with this complexity through traditional scientific inquiry is inadequate. This is partly a result of inadequate resources devoted to research—people, money, and time. But constraints on the ability to manage complex systems derive from more than limited budgets or staffing; they also result from a particular form of inquiry, grounded in reductionism, disciplinary narrowness, and restricted conceptions of what constitutes knowledge and knowing. These qualities are important in dealing with certain kinds of problems and issues, but they become less useful at the interface of knowledge application, implementation, and policy.

Interest in adaptive management has grown from this context. Treating management policies as experiments and as the source of learning to inform understanding and subsequent action, is a powerful, compelling concept. In terms of this first criterion, we conclude that adaptive management is sensible; it represents a viable, productive complement (not a replacement) to traditional management approaches. Having said that, however, this question remains: Is adaptive management an academically and intellectually robust notion whose utility is profoundly diminished by political and legal realities making it impossible to implement?

Technical: Does adaptive management translate into practice well?—
Although adaptive management is conceptually sensible and logical, efforts to translate it into practice have fared poorly. Various problems and barriers (structural, organizational, sociopsychological, political, legal, value-based) stymie application. The inability or unwillingness to acknowledge the limits of knowledge and capacity, the inevitability of mistakes coupled with a lack of forbearance and tolerance, the difficulty in letting go of a way of doing business—combine to foster resistance to experimentation and implementing innovative structures and processes to better link learning and action.

Management agencies are challenged in how to overcome these barriers. This will require intentional action, leadership, and a willingness to confront risk. Until such steps are taken, adaptive management likely will languish as little more than rhetoric. In the case of the Plan, there are serious questions as to the extent to which there was common understanding of the goals and purposes of adaptive management among agency personnel. As the literature review suggests, this problem has plagued adaptive efforts elsewhere. Results from both the citizen surveys and interviews with agency personnel further confirm that a lack of clarity characterized implementation efforts. This lack of agreement confounds any efforts to gain a clear sense not only as to what the goals of the adaptive management and AMA programs were, but how we might evaluate whether in fact those goals had been attained.

This criterion also raises concerns about organizational capacity and the commitment of agencies to successfully implementing adaptive management. If adaptive management represented, as it was often characterized, "a new way of doing business," what evidence exists to suggest an organizational commitment to such a change? For example, the duties to promote adaptive approaches fell largely on the shoulders of the AMA coordinators, yet our interviews indicate these individuals were given no training, limited financial and logistical support, and often found themselves assigned other duties that inevitably drew time and energy away from their ability to foster adaptive management. We saw little in the way of innovative, even risky, experimentation in terms of organizational structure and processes to promote adaptive management; e.g., in terms of new links between research and management. Conflicts between adaptive management/AMAs and other resource functions and administrative units often led to a diminution in effectiveness and efficiency. Other than the AMA coordinators, there was a virtual absence of organizational leadership at any level. Finally, probably the most central component of effective adaptive management—monitoring and evaluation—was administratively segregated and largely absent from on-the-ground efforts in the AMAs.

Collectively, these shortcomings fatally compromised any effort to promote adaptive management as a driving element of the Plan and the role of the AMAs as venues for experimentation, innovation, and vision.

Ethical: Who wins and who loses with adaptive management?—
Thinking and acting adaptively might appear logical and compelling, but it is important to recognize that such behavior leads to costs as well as benefits and that these are not evenly distributed. Lee (1999: 8) noted "there are risks of disclosure which look inappropriate in the eyes of one or more stakeholders." For example, thinning experiments in riparian zones, with the intention of facilitating old-growth structures, carry the possibility that those desired conditions will not eventuate. Or, if they do, adverse impacts on other values, such as salmon, might occur. Or, although such treatments facilitate restoration, the act of human intervention itself constitutes a cost to some interests and will be resisted, irrespective of the scientific merits. Thus, new knowledge—and the management implications it holds—is a benefit to some interests, a cost to others. When costs are revealed, resistance is often not far behind.

Adaptive management implicitly acknowledges that emerging understanding could lead to changes in policies and programs. Such knowledge could reveal that previous practices were poorly founded or ultimately unsustainable. Changing policies requires acknowledging these past errors as well as incurring the costs of finding and implementing new solutions. Implementing new programs might impose specific practices that some find inimical to their interests. In either case, an adaptive management approach implies that agency processes and actions become increasingly transparent and visible, inviting criticism, second-guessing, and critique.

Adaptive management also acknowledges there are multiple ways of knowing the world. In traditional management, expertise was held by scientists and specialists. Knowledge long has been a currency of power, but in an adaptive world, this currency becomes universal and shared, meaning in the final analysis, that power is distributed rather than concentrated.

Among both citizens and many agency staff, the adaptive management concept and the AMA allocation raised significant expectations; again, the mantra of "a new way of business" was repeated by many. There was a legitimate sense of excitement, particularly within many communities adjacent to the AMAs, that this allocation represented places where that new way of business could be fashioned and fostered. But the inertia associated with the old way of business seems to have predominated. The failure to capitalize and build on these expectations as a source of human and political capital was disappointing to many, both in these communities as well as among those agency staff who welcomed the apparent interest in innovation and change. In such an analysis, it is hard to conclude that change and innovation—key qualities of adaptive management—have been a winner. Instead, they appear to have lost to the forces of convention, tradition, and risk aversion.

Pragmatic: Does adaptive management make a difference?—

In response to the rhetorical question, "Does adaptive management work?" Lee (1999: 9) concluded, "We do not know yet." Moreover, given the time scales involved, with both biophysical and socioeconomic systems, it might be a long time before we have a definitive answer. Unfortunately, the nature of the world in which we reside is uncomfortable with, even intolerant of, such a situation. The acrimonious nature of conflict, the demands for immediate resolution and accommodation of individual interests, and the structural nature of budgeting and planning cycles combine to make a "wait and see" stance untenable.

Innovations such as adaptive management can take a decade or more to take hold (Rogers 1995). They face significant challenges; Do the potential gains of the innovation (often unknown) outweigh the risks of departing from tradition (which is known and understood)? How do the benefits of innovation and experimentation, often displaced well into the future and always tentative and provisional, compare to their costs, which are immediate and apparent? How can the threats and fears of change—elusive and often unknown—be weighed against the comforts of conforming with convention and tradition, however spurious and specious that conformity might be? The expectation that the adaptive management directives in the Plan will produce demonstrable evidence of success in only a few years is unrealistic. However, given the social, legal, political, and organizational environments within which the Plan is imbedded, such an inability might foreshadow the conclusion that adaptive management has failed.

Adaptive Management: Too Soon to Know, Too Late to Matter?

At the time of this evaluation, a decade had passed since the ROD was signed. Was this a sufficient period for revealing the outcomes of a major change in how resource management was to be undertaken? Or, was it too early to make any kind of substantive judgment about progress or the lack thereof? Is there evidence that we are on the right path or at least the right trajectory? Do the experiences help identify barriers—internal or external—that require attention? Most importantly, have we been able to capitalize on these experiences, positive and negative, in a manner consistent with the underlying idea of adaptive management: namely, using policies as experiments from which we can learn?

Much has occurred over the past decade. For example, the period from 1993 until the present witnessed a number of events and outcomes associated with adaptive management and the AMAs (box 3). However, although it is important to recognize that time is a critical variable in the successful implementation of any program, it is equally important to acknowledge that there must be appropriate and meaningful markers that help define progress. In the case of adaptive management and the AMAs, are there indications that these efforts are accompanied by the development and implementation of transitional processes that help ensure these programs become institutionalized and an accepted component of the organizational culture? Successful implementation must be measured by more than creation of the AMAs or undertaking an adaptive project in one area.

Our conclusion is that adaptive management and the AMAs have fallen far short of the promise and potential envisioned in the Plan. Whether these shortcomings prove fatal remains to be seen, but in our judgment, turning the program around will require active, positive intervention by a host of players, internal and external. Lacking such proactive intervention, the likelihood of revitalizing adaptive management and the AMAs is low.

What Accounts for Adaptive Management's Disappointing Performance in the Plan?

As discussed in chapter 1, when President Clinton hosted the forest conference in Portland, Oregon, in 1993, there was a palpable sense of despair throughout the forest community in the Pacific Northwest. Local communities faced a dismal economic future, there was concern about the future of old-growth forests and associated species, and the growing acrimonious debate between "preserve" and "develop" advocates increasingly was seen as harmful to the fabric of society.

Box 3

Time Line for Adaptive Management and the Adaptive Management Areas (AMAs)

1992 – Applegate Partnership formed, prior to creation of the Northwest Forest Plan (the Plan).

1993 – Forest Ecosystem Management Assessment Team prepared; option 9 includes specific recommendation for adaptive management and allocation of AMAs.

1994 – Supplemental environmental impact statement, record of decision, creation of AMAs. Appropriation of the Plan funds to support AMA activity. Pacific Northwest Region (R-6) Regional Office establishes coordinating position for AMAs. Federal Advisory Committee Act-based lawsuit initiated against the Plan.

1995 – Appointment of AMA coordinators. Regional ecosystem office (REO) guidelines and review processes published.

1996 – Tuchmann et al. (1996) report on the Plan. Lead scientists for Oregon and Washington AMAs assigned.

1997 – Pacific Northwest (PNW) Research Station meeting on adaptive management, AMAs, and research (Skamania meeting). First AMA guides prepared and reviewed by REO. Variable stand management project on the Five Rivers area of Siuslaw National Forest initiated, testing three treatments.*

1998 – Publication of Pipkin (1998) report. AMA guides continue to be prepared. Plan budget support for R-6 AMAs dropped, PNW financial support withdrawn. Publication of disturbance-based management plan for Augusta Creek, Willamette National Forest (Cissell et al. 1998).

1999 – Preparation of AMA business plan.

2000 – REO white paper on AMAs and standards and guidelines (S&Gs).

2003 – Stankey et al. (2003) evaluation report on adaptive management and AMAs initiated. New legal opinion regarding applicability of S&Gs in AMAs prepared.

2004 – Plan 10-year interpretive report prepared, Plan meeting in Portland, Oregon. The PNW Station Director, Tom Quigley, releases memo on research and AMAs.

2005 – Regional Interagency Executive Committee requests new options to enhancing role of AMAs as learning centers and for inclusion of adaptive management in landscape planning and management.

* The Five Rivers project (Bormann and Kiester 2004) was initiated in the Five Rivers area of the Siuslaw National Forest after efforts to implement an adaptive approach to silvicultural treatments on the North Coast AMA failed owing to the lack of support among area managers and local citizens.

The Plan that emerged from combined efforts of that conference, the FEMAT exercise, and the ROD offered the hope that a significant change of events lay ahead. Within the larger context of the Plan, the strategy of adaptive management was key to progress and change, underlain by improved knowledge, mutual learning, and a commitment to innovation and creative management. Yet, today, much of that hope seems to have given way to cynicism and a sense that little has changed. In particular, the promise and potential of adaptive management largely has been lost, replaced by rhetoric and glib assurances and assertions. As the discussion above regarding the performance of adaptive management and the AMAs relative to the evaluative criteria indicates, we have come up far short of the expectations that prevailed at the time the Plan was created.

What accounts for this? There are a variety of possible explanations, none of which are mutually exclusive.

First, the scientists who initially proposed adaptive management were overly optimistic and naïve. The idea of adaptive management as a strategy involving replication and controls, experimental design, and grounded in modeling simply set the bar too high. Coupled with naivete on the part of those advocating its use in the Plan about the real world context and constraints within which it would have to survive, the concept had little practical likelihood of successful implementation.

Second, because managers and planners were not involved in the FEMAT process, where the adaptive management strategy was proposed initially, there was a lack of ownership in the idea. Moreover, their absence in the discussions about adaptive management meant there was little opportunity for mutual learning between scientists and planners/managers about the definition, role, and rationale for such an approach. Coupled with the ambiguity surrounding the meaning of adaptive management, there never was an opportunity to transform the concept from its scientific and technical origins to one consistent with the demands and constraints of an applied setting.

Third, and deriving from the first two points, the planning and management community did not embrace or accept the concept. In part, this derives from a sense that at its core, adaptive management did not represent a new direction. However, it also led to decisions within the management organizations to accord adaptive management a relatively low priority, with limited staff, funding, and other enabling resources. Leadership was largely absent, leaving field practitioners to find their own way. Rather than a core organizational goal and philosophy, like multiple use, adaptive management remained tangential and incidental.

Fourth, even to the extent that managers and planners saw adaptive management as a potentially valuable strategy, they faced formidable barriers, both internally and externally, in efforts to implement it. A restrictive regulatory and legal environment made it difficult to initiate creative and innovative management programs. In particular, the imposition of the S&Gs created a management environment bounded by rigid, inflexible rules. Expectation of an a priori demonstration of a lack of adverse impacts made risk-taking problematic.

Fifth, even if the preceding aspects could be overcome, there were capacity constraints on the ability of agencies to implement adaptive management. Demands for a management approach that "mimicked" the scientific methods required significant inputs of technical expertise in study design, technical background, statistical analysis, and the like. This also increased the cost of implementation at a time of declining budget support and loss of personnel as a result of downsizing.

Finally, adaptive management, as envisioned in FEMAT and the ROD, was simply not possible in the complex, chaotic and contentious environment within which it was supposed to perform. The biophysical realm consists of such complex relations and interactions that it is extremely difficult to forecast, in any predictive sense, what outcomes will eventuate from different interventions. The economic, social, and political realms are not only complex, but the products of shifting, unpredictable forces that similarly make it difficult to anticipate change. In such a world, perhaps the only tenable management approach is one of incrementalism.

Which of these factors account for the experience in the Pacific Northwest? As suggested above, it is likely a result of components of all of them. Moreover, these factors are not unique to forest management in this region; they can be generalized to other resource sectors and other biophysical, economic, and sociopolitical settings. However, even within this list (box 4), there are areas where flexibilities and options do exist; in other words, some of these barriers and challenges can be addressed, maybe overcome, with leadership, thoughtful planning, and commitment.

Challenges to Making Adaptive Management a Viable Enterprise

Evidence from this evaluation, as well as from the wider literature, suggests that successful implementation of adaptive management faces major challenges. However, it is equally clear that such an approach is essential to dealing with a world of complexity and uncertainty. How can these seemingly disparate conclusions be resolved?

Box 4

Alternative Explanation for What We Observe

- The concept of adaptive management advanced in the Northwest Forest Plan (the Plan) was too academic and set the bar unrealistically high.

    - Forest Ecosystem Management Team (FEMAT) scientists were naive about real world conditions and constraints facing on-the-ground managers.

- Managers and planners were not involved or adequately engaged in the creation of the adaptive management vision, concepts, or processes.

    - Transformation never occurs between FEMAT scientists and those charged with implementing the plan (line officers, staff specialists).
    - Little or no mutual learning between those who designed FEMAT and those who would implement the Plan.
    - Limited understanding by planners and managers as to what adaptive management was intended to achieve.
    - Multiple meanings existed as to what adaptive management implied.

- Managers did not embrace or accept the concept of adaptive management as outlined in FEMAT.

    - Those placed in charge of implementing adaptive management lacked the leadership skills to make the needed transformations.
    - There was a "business-as-usual" mentality, grounded in traditional management culture.
    - Actions did not match words.

- Managers were not allowed to implement adaptive management as it was intended in the Plan.

    -There were both internal and external political constraints that acted to suppress innovation and experimentation.
    - Regulatory agencies imposed constraints that thwarted changes in management practices and there was a limited ability to gain relief from the standards and guidelines.

- Managers were unable to implement.

    - There was a lack of capacity within the management and research organizations to implement fully the adaptive management vision.
    - Conflicting and/or limiting laws and regulations limited experimentation.
    - Adaptive management, particularly as an experimental-based strategy, proved too costly and complex to maintain.

- Adaptive management as envisioned in FEMAT and the Plan is not possible in a chaotic biophysical, social, and political system.

- All of the above.

- None of the above.

In the following sections we suggest several major areas that must be carefully examined and addressed.

Requisite Attributes for Adaptive Management to Succeed

There is a set of requisite attributes that are necessary for any innovative and creative policy initiative to succeed, be it adaptive management, collaborative management, or ecosystem management.

The following attributes are not uniquely tied to adaptive management, but they are essential precursors to any innovative management strategy. In their absence, breaking from the past and engaging in creative, perhaps even controversial, policies and programs, will prove unlikely.

Leadership—

Successful implementation of innovation requires leadership that sets direction, gets the right people in key jobs, creates a sense of vision and legitimacy, creates and maintains an environment for innovation as well as accountability, and mobilizes internal and external support. Of particular importance, leaders must have courage to challenge the status quo. Effective organizational leaders must help cultivate political understanding and support internally and externally among both elected political leaders and the wider body politic. Without such political support, innovative policies will always be at risk. Leadership must also create a "safe" environment for practitioners in a world dominated by risk aversion. Leadership must be displayed not only at the top of both the management and research organizations, but throughout the organizations as well. And leadership must also come from external parties committed to making adaptive management a reality.

Alignment with organizational goals—

A major liability of many initiatives, such as ecosystem management or adaptive management, is that they are often perceived as something "extra" or simply the latest fashion or rhetoric. From this, it is easy to conclude they are also ephemeral or unimportant. Despite widespread discussion of the role of ecosystem management for more than a decade, for example, it remains unclear what it means or implies for day-to-day management, and for the Forest Service, it remains a compartmentalized function at the Washington Office level, belying its integrative objective. For programs such as adaptive management to be successfully implemented, they must become an integrated aspect of day-to-day business. Leadership plays an

Leadership must be displayed not only at the top of both the management and research organizations, but throughout the organizations as well.

especially important role here, helping to promote collaborative and cooperative attitudes and actions across organizational roles and functions. Achieving this might require innovative use of such things as incentives and rewards.

Commitment and will to act—

This attribute overlaps with others such as leadership. This includes acknowledging that past organizational behavior was not adaptive, in the contemporary sense of the term, and that, contrary to recent assertions, adaptive management requires significant changes in organizational structures, processes, and resources. There must be a willingness to acknowledge publicly that insufficient knowledge is available to guide management actions and that in attempting to remedy this deficiency, errors and mistakes will occur. The heart of this attribute, however, is an explicit, visible acknowledgment that adaptive management constitutes something more than "what we've always done." It should be declared as a formal, public statement of policy and it needs to acknowledge that new structures and processes are required. It recognizes that there must be collaboration among various external parties who scrutinize the agency's behavior, such as regulatory agencies, the courts, political actors, and key interest groups. It also calls for organizations to work toward a long-term commitment of adequate personnel and financial resources to sustain adaptive efforts; this is especially challenging in a world of rapid political change and short-term budget cycles.

Capacity to act—

A commitment to act must be supplemented by a capacity to act. That is, organizations must possess the internal resources to act, including time, money, and technical and social expertise and skills (e.g., knowledge, research design, and communication). It also requires the necessary legal and political license to act (e.g., statutory and administrative mechanisms that permit experimentation). In the case of the Plan, this could involve relief from constraining legislation such as the ESA, the NEPA, and the Federal Advisory Committee Act. This might be done through some sort of "pilot" authority. A level of public understanding and acceptance of such an approach also must exist.

Linking words to deeds—

A recurrent criticism from this evaluation is that the idea of adaptive management was not matched by on-the-ground results. The rhetoric of change must be matched by demonstrated actions and outcomes. In the absence of such results, public and political support will prove untenable. This is an especially challenging issue, given that "final" results of many adaptive efforts might be a long time in coming. However, this only highlights the importance of implementing adaptive approaches that include an ongoing involvement by a diverse array of interests to ensure their understanding of the approaches and the creation of realistic expectations.

Clear, shared language and terminology—

Programs such as ecosystem management and adaptive management are particularly vulnerable to confusion resulting from a lack of clarity in meaning. As noted earlier in this evaluation, the concept of adaptive management is subject to multiple interpretations, ranging from any type of incremental behavior to the more formal, experimental-based practice described in the contemporary literature. Clarity of meaning is essential to establishing a clear sense of vision and responsibility; it also is essential to helping frame appropriate public expectations and for useful post-facto evaluations of performance. When concepts mean everything to everybody, they mean nothing.

Agreement on expectations—

Expectations held by various parties, both internal and external, are always key in the successful implementation of any new policy. In the case of adaptive management and the Plan, as discussed in chapter 6, local community expectations were positive and high; the lack of demonstrated results have dashed many of those expectations, further contributing to the tension and distrust between the management agencies and local citizens. Expectations need to be the product of negotiations among interested parties, including managers, scientists, regulators, and citizens; they help define what will occur, what needs to be done to achieve desired ends, and what are realistic outcomes. Failed expectations, whether appropriate or not, can handicap the most important policy; conversely, managing appropriate expectations is one of the major challenges facing policymakers, managers, and scientists.

Explicit roles and responsibilities—

Successful implementation of any innovation requires explicit clarification of who is going to do what, when, where, and why. It thus involves the relations among key actors, both within and external to the management agencies. It helps define needed changes and facilitates coordination. In the specific case of adaptive management, for example, it would define the respective roles of the management organizations charged with Plan implementation and the regulatory agencies, with responsibilities for endangered species. This could help rationalize the relations between the need for species protection and the importance of experimentation and learning. This is easy to say and hard to do.

Continuity—

Innovative initiatives often are characterized by the need for a long-term perspective, and this is especially the case for adaptive management. Many biophysical and socioeconomic issues will require a significant ongoing commitment of time and resources to be satisfactorily examined. Similarly, the adaptive management processes themselves will require a long-term organizational commitment; the relationships among various players, the development of adaptive techniques and strategies, and the integration of results into management programs and policies likely will be emergent properties. Fostering such developments necessitates a stable and ongoing commitment; it also is dependent on a wider political and public understanding of the need for adequate time. Continuity is critical given the asymmetry between actions (short term) and outcomes (long term).

Clear performance benchmarks—

A key role of adaptive management in the Plan was that it was a strategy that would enable new information to be taken into account in testing and validating S&Gs and, indeed, in the long-term implementation of the Plan. This is critical because without such learning, the initial, precautionary, and often restrictive S&Gs become locked in place. What were not clear were the standards of evidence that would be required, either before changes in current policies and practices would occur or when such current policies and practices would be confirmed as appropriate. The key here is not so much the specific outcomes or results of experimentation, but rather, the processes in place through which such judgments occur. Given the complex and contentious nature of the management environment, such processes are necessarily multi-interest; as noted earlier, for example, changing S&Gs involves not only technical issues but social and political as well. In the absence of such processes and a clear declaration as to when "we know enough," any proposed policy change will always be subject to contentious debate.

In the absence of such processes and a clear declaration as to when "we know enough," any proposed policy change will always be subject to contentious debate.

Formal and explicit documentation—

Because innovative programs such as adaptive management typically involve significant departures from past practices, it is critical there be an ability to document the nature of changes, effects, and consequences. Doing so requires a formal, explicit record that is transparent to interested parties. It should be archived, accessible, and open to clear interpretation; it should support replication efforts. It needs to include both process-related information (e.g., how were decisions made, by whom) as well as outputs. Because of the importance of negative feedback in the learning process, documentation must also provide a record of "failures" as well as what were taken to be successes.

Implementing Adaptive Management: Need for a Strategy

Given the requisite attributes described above, there is a need for a purposeful strategy designed to implement an adaptive approach. Such an effort would involve both a general strategy and specific actions that must be taken to act adaptively and to use the results of such an approach in subsequent management. In this section we discuss some of the strategies and steps that might be considered to improve the likelihood that adaptive management can be more implementable.

Despite the promise and potential of adaptive management, efforts to implement it—in the Plan and elsewhere—have foundered. Is adaptive management a case of an idea that while conceptually elegant is practically flawed? Are implementation efforts confronted with such significant barriers—institutional, legal, and cultural—that there is little realistic hope it can be a relevant strategy on which the Plan relies?

This evaluation points to significant problems and challenges. To realize the potential of adaptive management requires substantive and systemic changes—not cosmetic or operational—on the part of land management, research, and regulatory organizations. For example, affecting the kinds of needed changes will require more than simply enhancing the level of coordination among activities such as monitoring and research (Bormann et al. 2006). It will demand interaction and collaboration with external interests and partners; as with any planning approach, adaptive management is ultimately a political activity and successful implementation requires public support.

What are some specific strategies and steps called for to realize adaptive management's potential? The following describes the types of activities to which increased attention by managers, scientists, policymakers, and citizens is required.

Revitalize the Vision of Adaptive Management

Any effort to reinvigorate adaptive management, as an element of the Plan, must be founded on a visible, forceful expression of an organizational commitment to the concept. This commitment must be grounded in recognition that it represents a significant departure from previous planning approaches and will require innovative structures and processes, coupled with specific skills, approaches, and abilities.

Such an effort could take direction from the vision of adaptive management outlined in FEMAT. It should include a diverse variety of actors; resource managers and scientists, policymakers, regulators, nongovernmental organizations (NGOs), and representatives of public and political interests. Although venues in which such discussions could be fostered are not common, the challenge presented here represents an important opportunity for testing various approaches—in many ways, this would be an adaptive experiment in itself. Such deliberations could address a variety of issues; defining adaptive management, the explicit recognition of the risks and uncertainties facing resource management, the limits of existing knowledge in framing informed policies, and so forth.

In short, the purpose of this phase would be to foster a public and organizational consensus that an adaptive approach is appropriate and relevant to manage the region's natural resources for a diverse mix of goods and services. This is an important first step to building the organizational commitment necessary to make adaptive management a distinctive element of the repertoire of planning strategies for operating effectively in today's complex and contentious world.

Acknowledge That Adaptive Management Is a New Way of Doing Business

Although our interviews revealed a recurring belief that adaptive management constituted a "new way of doing business," we found little evidence of any changes in protocols or procedures to support this assertion.

For successful implementation of the Plan, new structures and processes that facilitate adaptive approaches are needed. As outlined above in our discussion of requisite attributes, this begins with specifying of the existing knowledge that underlies some policy or action and the key questions (uncertainties) that must be addressed. This requires formal processes that document the questions being addressed, actions taken (including why, where, and when), the results of implementation and to what extent results are consistent with anticipations (and if they are different, why might this be so?), and how this knowledge might shape subsequent application.

An adaptive approach also has implications for the relations among managers, scientists, and citizens. This begins at the problem formulation stage; what are the key questions for which attention is needed? The personal or experiential knowledge of citizens and managers becomes an important source of input to this process, and procedures are required to tap these sources. This new relationship extends as well to the analysis and evaluation stages because these phases are as much social as they are technical. There are important opportunities to engage stakeholders in the decisionmaking process, and, although the specific authority to make a decision legally will remain with designated officials, an adaptive approach helps foster a situation in which those decisions simply codify the informed consensus of stakeholders.

Adaptive management has been described as mimicking the scientific method (Stankey 2003, Walters 1986). In this sense, it contrasts with traditional management in terms of its explicit question framing, a monitoring program focused on performance evaluation, and the integration of feedback processes into subsequent policy. However, adaptive management also stands in contrast to traditional scientific inquiry. The contextual complexity within which management policies are implemented means that control and replication—standard tools of scientific investigations—will be difficult if not impossible to impose. Also, the sociopolitical ambiguity within which policy implementation occurs adds another layer of complexity. What this implies is that decisionmaking in an adaptive context will always be characterized by professional judgment. Such judgments are inevitable, but adaptive approaches help create an explicit, visible, and traceable environment in which the rationale for those judgments is apparent.

Despite widespread rhetoric about integrated management organizations and decisionmaking processes, conventional resource management remains dominated by reductionism and compartmentalization. Both qualities stand in contrast to what is needed to practice adaptive management. One factor that has confounded efforts to integrate an adaptive approach in the Plan has been the administrative separation of monitoring from adaptive management. Without a coherent and integrated monitoring program, adaptive management simply becomes traditional trial-and-error management, making the ability to discern the effects of management treatments difficult (Todd 2001). For successful implementation, attention must be given to making adaptive approaches and related, supportive functions (such as monitoring and evaluation) a pervasive, holistic endeavor (Stankey 2003).

Focus on Building Effective Processes, Relationships, and Outcomes

In the contentious environment that characterizes natural resources management today, it will take time to build the necessary understanding, credibility, confidence, and trust to act adaptively. This involves the need to consider three distinct, yet related components. First, decisions must derive from sound, transparent **processes**; e.g., public involvement, links between science and management. Second, there must be productive **relationships** among the various actors; citizens, managers, scientists, policymakers. Third, the processes and relationships must lead to **outcomes**; results and decisions that are visible, well-grounded, and relevant.

The relationship among processes, relationships, and outcomes can be applied to our evaluation of adaptive management and the AMAs. For example, in the Applegate AMA, good processes were in place linking citizens, managers, and scientists. There were productive relationships among these three groups, and these relationships and processes helped generate decisions (outcomes) for local resource management. However, the Applegate also illustrates the fragile nature of this process; the loss of key individuals within the management and research community from the AMA planning process and growing conflicts between national environmental interests and local citizens has curbed progress in working adaptively (Rolle 2002). In the Central Cascades, the historically strong relationship between managers and scientists (nurtured in the H.J. Andrews Experimental Forest) helped foster on-the-ground applications of adaptive management that led to important outcomes, especially in implementation of disturbance-based management strategies (Cissell et al. 1998). Yet, limited relations exist between agency and community interests, and processes to promote and facilitate this relationship tend to be traditional approaches, geared to informing people about what is being done. Implementation of processes to facilitate direct citizen engagement in adaptive decisionmaking (framing problems, providing knowledge) has not been evident.

Provide the Skills, Tools, and Protocols Necessary to Be Adaptive

Because experimentation is core to adaptive management, there must be organizational capacity to frame and implement policies so as to ground them in the current best-state-of-knowledge and design them to yield insight and learning to inform subsequent applications. This requires that managers have access to the skills, tools and protocols that enable such an approach, including research design, sampling and survey methodologies, analysis, and interpretation.

This requirement has important implications for research organizations, including development of protocols for activities such as monitoring or design. In some cases, new types of institutional partnerships between researchers and managers might need to be explored; in others, the research role might focus on training and capacity building.

In short, the purpose here is to develop the skills required to implement adaptive experiments and to build organizational capacity to use the resulting information appropriately in decisionmaking.

Join Knowledge to Policy to Enhance Learning

Adaptive management seeks to provide the knowledge needed to manage effectively, particularly when complexity and uncertainty prevail. However, seldom is it the case that we know nothing. It is important that existing knowledge be brought together to assess the current situation and to help frame the key questions that require additional study. The seminal work of Holling (1978) and Walters (1986) noted the importance of the modeling phase where this knowledge could be displayed, shared, and assessed in designing the adaptive experiment most effectively. However, our evaluation found little evidence such efforts had occurred.

Efforts to revitalize the adaptive management element of the Plan must attend to compiling and assessing knowledge relevant to some place or policy. Knowledge is widely dispersed and possessed. It derives from managerial experience, it comes from traditional scientific investigations, and it results from living, working, and playing in places. Such experiential knowledge is often the form of knowing held by local citizens, and although it lacks the traditional characteristics of knowledge as commonly conceived in resource management planning, it nonetheless can offer important insights. Equally importantly, actively seeking and valuing such knowledge can represent a critical step in obtaining legitimacy and credibility among members of the public.

Build Political Understanding and Support to Foster Adaptive Management

Scientific-rational planning has proven effective in a host of contexts. However, its capacity to address the complex, value-laden problems characterizing many natural resource conflicts is limited in dealing with the array of values and interests that affect and, if ignored, stymie planning decisions (Buck et al. 2001, Wondolleck 1988).

Critiques have fostered interest in a variety of alternatives loosely described as "learning-based" (Friedmann 1987). These models do not ignore the technical dimensions that traditional approaches emphasize, but they explicitly add a socio-political element that acknowledges public concerns, values, interests, and knowledge. These models recognize that planning is as much a social and political endeavor as a technical enterprise.

The scientific-rational bias is evident in early formulations of adaptive management (Holling 1978, Walters 1986). Expert opinion was marshaled, hypotheses were formulated, experimentation was initiated through policy implementation, and analyses and evaluations were undertaken to provide insight and to inform subsequent actions. With publication of Compass and Gyroscope (Lee 1993), an important element was added that explicitly acknowledged and incorporated the idea of civic science and drew attention to the inevitable link between planning and the sociopolitical context within which it occurred. Lee argued that planning had to be intimately connected with this larger context if successful implementation were to occur. However, when Lee assessed the role of adaptive management in the Plan, he concluded it was simply a variant of traditional rational planning, coupled with trial and error (Lee 1999). The essential connection with interest politics was neither present nor acknowledged.

Efforts to revitalize adaptive management in the Plan must acknowledge this link. Despite the inclination to blame current difficulties on "politics," it is important to accept that it is within the political environment that public values and interests are revealed. In the absence of public understanding and support, particularly in today's conflict-laden sociopolitical environment, where many parties hold veto power over management agencies and their programs, the ability to implement adaptive management is restricted (Shindler et al. 2002). The social objective of the AMAs—to create opportunities for creative and innovative links with stakeholders—involves more than simply another call for public involvement; it presages fundamental reform in the relationship among citizens (local, regional, national), scientists, and managers in natural resources management.

Three reasons can be cited for better linking adaptive management with the social and political context within which any management program exists. First, it helps acquire the sociopolitical license required to operate aggressively and explicitly in the face of risk and uncertainty. This is critical, given the generally risk-averse social context.

Second, it helps foster learning communities involving multiple stakeholders by creating venues where negotiations among competing interests and values can occur. Stankey and Shindler (1997) have suggested that a potentially valuable role for the AMAs would be to serve as place-based "forums for working through" (Yankelovich 1991) where such negotiations could take place. This is important because the learning that emerges from adaptive approaches sometimes will suggest policies inimical to the interests of certain stakeholders (e.g., harvesting old-growth trees for any reason, thinning in reserves). Because of the value conflicts such outcomes could generate, it is essential the adaptive planning framework be designed so as to facilitate dialogue and openness among conflicting interests to find satisfactory solutions.

Third, it facilitates discussion regarding what it means to learn and how such learning might lead to changes in land management practices. As suggested earlier, such changes involve both technical as well as sociopolitical questions, and efforts to bring about change in the absence of public understanding and political support generally will prove unsuccessful (Shindler et al. 2002).

Rethink Phases and Steps for Implementing Adaptive Management

The earlier discussion of requisite attributes describes a set of necessary conditions that must be addressed prior to implementing an adaptive management strategy. Each of the attributes is essential, although it is recognized that there will be varying levels to which they are met. However, in the absence of any one condition (e.g., leadership, organizational capacity), the likelihood of successful implementation is low.

However when some level of achievement exists for each of these attributes, the stage is set for a serious consideration as to the possibility of implementing an adaptive management strategy. In the following discussion, we describe a set of questions and steps that would need to be addressed as such an implementation process takes place.

To begin, managers need to ask the basic question as to whether an adaptive approach, irrespective of how it is defined, is an appropriate and realistic strategy. Often the answer to this is that an adaptive approach is not required. Some issues and management problems are straightforward; conventional planning approaches are adequate and appropriate to such issues. In other cases, the issues might be of such complexity that traditional scientific inquiry is required, along with the qualities of control and replication that might produce results that eventually filter into more practical terms. Thus, the nature of the underlying management issue might help frame a response to this question. However, it is also necessary to consider the social and political setting as discussed earlier with regard to prerequisite attributes. The legal or political milieu might be such that an adaptive approach, particularly one involving risk to endangered species or other important values, might lack the necessary support to be undertaken.

However, if there is a conviction that an adaptive approach is both appropriate and acceptable, a second question that must be addressed concerns the type of adaptive approach that would be employed. Earlier, we described a variety of ways in which adaptive management has been defined; e.g., passive vs. active. In some cases, it might be possible to rely on existing data or management experience and to infer from these data what the potential applications to a current situation might be. In other circumstances, such data are either lacking or the problem is of such a character that it is necessary to examine it in a fresh light. In these situations, some more active form of adaptive management is called for and it is to these that our attention now turns.

If the decision is made to undertake an active, experimental-based, adaptive management approach (and it is our contention that this was the intent of the adaptive management strategy as outlined in the Plan) a particular set of steps must be undertaken.[5] As suggested earlier, adaptive management involves more than making it up as we go. It is more than simply accommodating new information in an incremental fashion (i.e., "muddling through"). Several of the steps that must be carefully implemented are briefly described below.

Frame the problem—
Adaptive management begins by focusing on the problem, including identifying what, among many, problems will be examined and how that problem is framed. The key here is to obtain a consensus on what question(s) will be the focus of study. This would include a discussion of why the question is important and why it was chosen rather than some other problem. As Clark et al. (1999: 314) suggested,

> Problem framing is one part of, if not the most critical part of integrative processes....Failure to ensure effective problem identification and subsequent action often leads to: stating the problem so it cannot be solved, solving the wrong problem, solving a solution; trying to get agreement on the solution before there is agreement on the problem...

In earlier discussions of adaptive management, Walters (1986) called for the use of modeling to help frame the problem for which an adaptive management approach would be used. The modeling process is a way of coming to agreement on how a particular system operates, what the key variables are, and what the key areas of uncertainty are. Actually building an operational model may or may not occur.

At this stage, there is also a discussion of expectations about outcomes (i.e., What are the likely results of this work?) and how such new knowledge would

---

[5] We acknowledge that it is possible these steps could be addressed in various ways   i.e., there is no single template to guide management actions in fulfilling them   but they must be taken into account, and there must be a clear and visible record of how they are addressed.

inform and influence the decisionmaking process. Finally, because there are many questions and issues inevitably involved, the problem identification and framing phase must involve a diverse range of parties, including managers, scientists, and interested citizens. Such discussions are open and visible.

Document intentions, processes, and outcomes—

A second essential feature of an adaptive-based approach is that it is characterized by extensive documentation. Documentation makes the process transparent and facilitates review by interested and affected parties. In a sense, documentation needs to address the same kinds of questions a journalist would; what was done, by whom, when and where, why. It identifies expectations, assumptions, and the rationale for action. Such information is essential for any possible future replication as well as for eventually assessing the effects of any action (i.e., What were the effects of the action [fire, silvicultural treatment, road closure, etc.] that was taken and how does it compare with what was expected?).

Finally, documentation ensures an accurate record of what happened and why. This includes information regarding the outcomes of any treatment, along with any variations in time and space. It also records discussions about varying, perhaps competing, explanations for the results; e.g., Why didn't we get the results anticipated (the driving question was wrong, we used the wrong methods, our assumptions were flawed, implementation was compromised, etc.)?

Documentation is critical simply because people forget or move and it often can be difficult to later reconstruct exactly the chain of events. It is also important that the documentation process capture those actions and events that later prove to be mistakes and errors; these are often major sources of learning, but in risk-averse settings, there often is a hesitancy to record them.

Documentation also needs to include not only the substantive issues but process-related ones as well. That is, the adaptive management process itself is one characterized by emergent qualities; how relations among various players changed and why, what techniques to involve others were used and how they worked, how decisions were made (consensus, majority, etc.), etc. In this way, documentation provides critical input into not only what is learned (substantive) but also in how learning occurred.

Interpret what was learned—

A third critical element the adaptive management process must engage is the question of how interpretations of results are made and how or whether those interpretations are incorporated into subsequent actions or how they might alter existing

> **It is important that the documentation process capture those actions and events that later prove to be mistakes and errors; these are often major sources of learning, but in risk-averse settings, there often is a hesitancy to record them.**

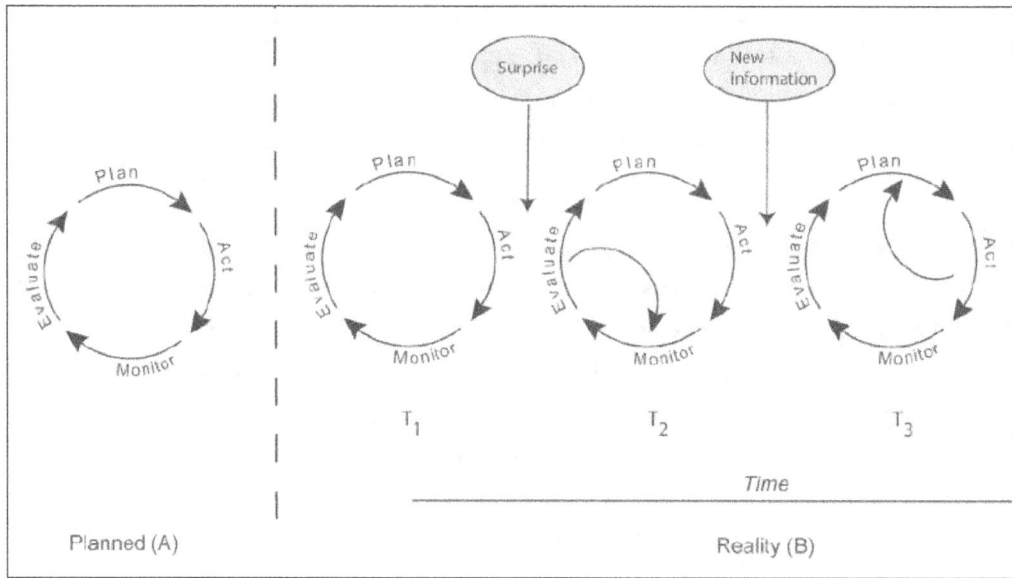

Figure 5   As portrayed in the Northwest Forest Plan, the adaptive management cycle (A) proceeds in an unbroken, linear manner from planning to action, monitoring, and evaluation. In reality (B), the process has a temporal component and is less predictable and more flexible. Unanticipated events including surprises (such as sudden policy changes) and new information emerge, requiring one to stop, reconsider, and perhaps back up. *Figure by Kelly Lawrence.*

policies. This acknowledges that seldom does data speak for itself. Variable interpretations almost always exist, and these are influenced by disciplinary background, experience, interests, and ideology.

Thus, the adaptive process must provide a forum in which debate and discussion about interpretation occurs, what the consequences and implications of alternative perspectives might be, the feasibility of incorporation into actions, and so forth. There must also be discussion about the standards of adequate evidence; that is, when is there sufficient evidence or information to warrant either a change in policy (e.g., when would new information about riparian buffer widths warrant a change in S&Gs?) or confirm that existing standards are valid? There needs to be a consensus regarding the decision criteria that will be used to make policy changes, based on the results of an adaptive management experiment.

As suggested earlier, the present set of allocations and rules embodied in the Plan serve certain interests better than others. Thus, any change will inevitably provoke opposition among some interests and support from others. Such conflicts cannot be avoided, but they can be made an open and explicit part of the process by ensuring debate about the rationale for various interpretations or discussions about long-term impacts, etc.

Evaluate new questions and uncertainty—
Finally, the adaptive process will always reveal new issues, new questions, and new uncertainties. In a general sense, this is acknowledged in the adaptive management cycle (fig. 2); the learning process is cyclic and ongoing. Knowledge is always tentative and provisional. However, contrary to the seemingly straightforward flow of events as depicted in the adaptive management cycle, in reality, it will typically be characterized by numerous false starts, dead ends, unanticipated events, etc (fig. 5). What were seen as key questions suddenly become unimportant, fundamental assumptions about system drivers suddenly are revealed to be false, and so on. The result is that the cycle is filled with points at which progress halts, backs up, and begins again. However, this is the fundamental nature of learning and indeed, many of those false starts and mistakes will be major sources of learning.

Fostering Trust to Support Adaptive Management

A recurring theme from the literature, citizen surveys, and interviews concerns the issue of trust. This is not surprising; hardly any aspect of human relationships is more fundamental than trust. However, it is especially critical to the potential role of an adaptive management approach, given its concern with working on the interface of complexity and uncertainty. Most definitions of trust recognize that there must be a condition of risk for trust to occur; there would be little need for trust if actions could be taken with complete certainty. Trust also requires a state of interdependence; the interests of one party cannot be achieved without reliance on another.

As chapter 2 outlined, the Plan grew out of an environment of distrust. At the time President Clinton came to Portland to host the forest conference, there were sharp divisions across the region between interests representing diverse perspectives: rural-urban, development-preservation, local-national control. The processes through which the Plan evolved were similarly steeped in distrust. The exclusion of managers, planners, and citizens, despite promises of a more collaborative approach, further aggravated the situation (Clark et al. 1998). The exclusion of managers was taken by many as an indication of a lack of trust in their ability to manage the region's forests appropriately. Once completed, the Plan in general, and the adaptive management and AMA programs in particular have fostered unfulfilled expectations, including concerns about promised timber sale volumes, species protection, and a more open, collaborative approach to management.

One implication of this lack of trust is that it compromises the level of social acceptability needed to implement adaptive management. How can this situation be rectified? Two actions seem necessary. First, it must be acknowledged that trust

A recurring message in the literature on collaborative management, with clear implications for adaptive management, is the importance of doing what was promised.

cannot be created in a mechanistic fashion. Trust is an emergent quality of long-term relations, grounded in good faith and followthrough. A recurring message in the literature on collaborative management, with clear implications for adaptive management, is the importance of doing what was promised.

Second, trust is a provisional quality, requiring constant nurturing. It is also asymmetric; whereas the building phase can be lengthy, it can be lost in a moment. Nor is it dichotomous (I trust you or I do not); both trust and distrust can exist simultaneously. Trust can exist between individuals, as we clearly have seen from our interviews and surveys, but if the organization for which the individual works is perceived as untrustworthy, it will be difficult to fashion enduring productive relations.

However, it is also important to recognize that collaboration can occur even in the absence of trust. When trust is absent or limited, rules (e.g., laws such as NEPA or administrative requirements such as the S&Gs) serve to provide a safety net for those interests who engage with agency officials. Even if a trustworthy relationship fails to materialize, these rules provide an assurance that adverse outcomes are unlikely. But this rule-based environment also can help foster interested people sitting down together to debate future forest management issues. Over time, trustworthy relations among different interests can evolve, and these relations can become increasingly important in promoting mutually acceptable policies and programs.

As the discussion in this chapter suggests, the adaptive management process is a highly complex endeavor; it involves much more than simply "plan-act-monitor-evaluate." Beyond the specific phases and steps noted above, it should also be acknowledged that the process, executed properly, involves ongoing, real-time learning and knowledge creation, both in a substantive sense as well as in terms of process. Because all parties need to be engaged from the problem identification stage through to implementation, an adaptive approach largely negates traditional technology transfer. Rather than having a linear, compartmentalized approach in which certain people (scientists) are creating knowledge, and then passing it along to practitioners (managers), with citizens largely relegated to a passive, observer status, an adaptive approach actively engages all parties in all phases, facilitating mutual learning. The result is that not only is the knowledge creation and application process strengthened, but it also results in improved understanding among all parties regarding the rationale for any given policy, meaning that the critical political understanding and support essential for effective implementation is also enhanced.

In Closing

Technically, the vision for adaptive management and AMAs articulated in the NWFP is not working well….So, this appears to external observers to be where adaptive management stands in the Northwest Forest Plan in 2004: at best treading water, at worst sunk (Salwasser 2004: 13).

In the final analysis, efforts to implement an adaptive approach likely will continue because as FEMAT suggests "if we cannot learn to manage adaptively, gridlock and paralysis will continue and both the biological and social dimensions of the federal lands will suffer" (FEMAT 1993: VIII-9). But for any innovative concept to be successful, understanding and support must exist internally and externally. There is little on the horizon that signals the agencies are dealing in any substantial way with the barriers discussed in the literature or in this evaluation to cause one to be hopeful. Rather it seems that more problems and barriers have become evident. And with the failure of adaptive management to gain traction as part of the Plan, new labels and variants have emerged (e.g., Bormann and Kiester 2004). The problem with simply renaming is that the fundamental limitations or barriers remain in place.

Fashioning an adaptive organization is not simply a question of determining exactly what the organizational chart would look like; it is not a question of what boxes and arrows it contains. Adaptive approaches likely are possible under a variety of organizational structures, from the conventional to the exotic. It is important to remind ourselves that in FEMAT, adaptive management as a strategy was seen as consistent with any of the possible options under consideration. Although adaptive approaches likely would benefit from certain enhancements in the administrative, legal, and policy landscape, such approaches could be implemented under any one of a variety of circumstances, including the technical-rational model that dominates current planning and management efforts. The key to successful implementation, under any administrative arrangement, is not found in the boxes and arrows of an organization chart, but in the level of commitment, leadership, and political will that is present. Thus, the central question is not one of the mechanics of the organizational structure, but one of the extent to which different structures and processes are likely to nurture the necessary requisites of an adaptive approach.

Efforts to reinvigorate adaptive management in the Plan must begin with a clear, unequivocal commitment (in both words and deeds) on the part of the management and research organizations to foster such approaches. Much has been said about the importance of leadership; without it, there is little reason to believe that

The key to successful implementation, under any administrative arrangement, is not found in the boxes and arrows of an organization chart, but in the level of commitment, leadership, and political will that is present.

adaptive management (or any innovative policy initiative) can succeed. Leadership provides vision, direction, and support; it helps create a sense of legitimacy and importance; it can foster tolerance for the inevitable errors that occur when confronting uncertainty; and it can help create an organizational appreciation for the concept of learning as an output of management (Bormann et al. 1999). However, it is important to recognize that the presence of leadership not be limited to agency heads (e.g., regional forester, state director). Leadership is not just a hierarchical concept; it must occur at multiple levels both internal and external to the agencies. Despite the difficulties in implementing the AMA program, the coordinators and lead scientists provide useful examples of leadership at field and implementation levels. However, there must also be commitment within the specialist staffs, within the regulatory community, and among key external interests.

As the previous discussion about the link between technical planning and interest politics suggests, there must be an aggressive effort undertaken to work with those stakeholders who possess "veto power" over agency actions. Unfortunately as Salwasser (2004: 4) reported, "mistrust is the dark heart of wicked problems (King 1993) and according to many students of the current situation regarding federal forest stewardship mistrust is high and pervasive among many participants." This is critical in the risk-averse environment that characterizes natural resource management. Some of the parties are easily identified; the regulatory agencies, for example, have important and difficult obligations with ensuring that agency programs do not place endangered species at inordinate risk. However, as the literature suggests, under conditions of uncertainty, what constitutes such "inordinate risk" might not be immediately apparent. Thus, there is a need for thoughtful and careful experimentation to improve the state of knowledge to ensure appropriate and effective protection. Nonetheless, risks will remain an inevitable part of such efforts, and agency specialists, scientists, and decisionmakers must initiate a dialogue with the regulatory community to find ways to negotiate effective solutions and build trust among the agencies and citizens they serve.

Such dialogue also must embrace other key stakeholders, including the political community, special interest groups, and local citizens. Given high levels of public access to legal and political institutions and the pressure to secure political and legal remedies for intransigent problems, agencies must create new processes to build understanding and support for adaptive approaches. This would include improving understanding of the consequences of the failure to expand the knowledge required for managing the species, uses, and values that drive natural resource management today.

There is a need to be more thoughtful in creating new ways to implement adaptive management. We need to work hard at picking the right place, the right time, the right problem, and the right people. In a review of adaptive experiences in river management in North America, Ladson and Argent (2002) identified several conditions associated with effective adaptive management efforts: jurisdictional simplicity, few points of possible intervention, the presence of credible science, a modeling phase that was sufficiently complex to represent the system accurately but simple enough that it could be completed and used, early evidence of successful implementation, and a sense of community among stakeholders. These are useful criteria by which possible pilot projects (perhaps with formal pilot authority) to implement adaptive management under the auspices of the Plan might be evaluated.

It is important that attention be given to picking the right people to involve in such a project. Both line officers and staff should be comfortable with complexity and ambiguity and both should possess sufficient technical competency along with skills in working with others. Not everyone possesses such abilities; lessons from the diffusion literature (Rogers 1995) would be a helpful guide in identifying the skills, dispositions, and experiences that would best ensure the likelihood of success.

In the case of the AMA system, it is difficult not to conclude that the number of areas diminished the opportunities for success. In the future, it would seem fruitful to consider focused attention, efforts, and resources on establishing at least one demonstrable success (which might or might not involve an existing AMA) before attempting to implement a regionwide program. This is particularly important, given the limited financial resources available in support of adaptive management and the AMAs. From this small start, designed to achieve the early success to which Ladson and Argent (2002) referred, the idea and the experiences could diffuse to other contexts.

Adaptive management was envisioned as a bold, innovative response to the need to better integrate new or emerging knowledge into decisionmaking. Achieving its potential, however, has been difficult, and future progress will require equally bold, innovative leadership at both technical and political levels. Technically, it calls for development of protocols and techniques that facilitate learning and its integration with other decisionmaking factors. Politically, it calls for support and endorsement of engaging risk and uncertainty explicitly and of ensuring adequate resources and support. Just where this leadership will come from is not clear.

Creating new ways to implement adaptive management will be neither quick nor cheap. Although some might believe that adaptive approaches will deliver quick results at minimal costs, Walters (1997) has observed this is seldom the case. Again, this suggests the need for enduring political understanding and support.

Adaptive management will necessitate fundamental changes in how resource management is reviewed and undertaken. It has the capacity to change the dialogue among resource managers, citizens, and scientists, making them partners from the problem-formulation stage through to implementation and evaluation. This will diminish the distinction between knowledge-producers and knowledge-users. It will also dramatically alter how we think about technology transfer, replacing the linear, compartmentalized model that characterizes current approaches, replacing it with a pervasive, ongoing exchange of knowledge exchange, testing, and validation (Miner and Stankey 2000).

It is important that we acknowledge that complex challenges (social, ecological, and economic) will continue to confront us. New information might provide useful insight for resolving specific problems, but it will generally reveal as many questions as it does answers. In such a context, adaptive approaches are a necessary component of the survival kit for society.

Finally, it is important that any future adaptive management exercise be given sufficient time to develop. Throughout this report, we have noted that adaptive management represents a significant change in the way natural resource management is done. Time is required for the innovative demands of this approach to be addressed, in part, because the biophysical and socioeconomic systems that an adaptive approach addresses require time for effects and consequences to play out, and because the qualities that facilitate adaptive thinking (inclusion, collaboration, trust, confidence, etc.) are emergent properties. That is, these qualities cannot be imposed or simply and easily acquired; they result from prolonged interactions undertaken in a good-faith context. Arbitrary deadlines cannot be set to force such outcomes.

> It is now 10 years after FEMAT and the Northwest Forest Plan and we have squandered one of the boldest learning opportunities created on federal lands to increase our capacity for adaptive management of dynamic, uncertain forest ecosystems to sustain their ecological integrity, resilience and productivity for the suite of values for which these lands are held in the public interest (Salwasser 2004: 18).

Metric Equivalents

When you know:	Multiply by:	To get:
Inches	2.54	Centimeters
Miles	1.609	Kilometers
Acres	.405	Hectares

References

Agee, J.K. 1999. Science review. In: Johnson, K.N.; Swanson, F.; Herring, M.; Greene, S., eds. Bioregional assessments: science at the crossroads of management and policy. Washington, DC: Island Press: 288-292.

Allan, C.; Curtis, A., comps. 2002. Notes from an adaptive management workshop. Rep. 171. Albury, New South Wales, Australia: Johnstone Centre, Charles Sturt University: 15-16.

Allenby, B.R.; Richards, D.J. 1994. The greening of industrial ecosystems. Washington, DC: National Academy Press. 259 p.

Ashworth, M.J. 1982. Feedback design of systems with significant uncertainty. Chichester, United Kingdom: Research Studies Press. 246 p.

Barber, B.R. 1984. Strong democracy: participatory politics for a new age. Berkeley: University of California Press. 320 p.

Baskerville, G.L. 1995. The forestry problem: adaptive lurches of renewal. In: Gunderson, L.H.; Holling, C.S.; Light, S.S., eds. Barriers and bridges to the renewal of ecosystems and institutions. New York: Columbia University Press: 37-102.

Bernstein, B.B.; Zalinski, J. 1986. A philosophy for effective monitoring. In: Oceans 86 monitoring strategies symposium. Washington, DC: Marine Technology Society: 1024-1029. Vol. 3.

Birman, B.F.; Kennedy, M.M. 1989. The politics of the national assessment of chapter 1. Journal of Policy Analysis and Management. 8(4): 613-633.

Blahna, D.J.; Yonts-Shepard, S. 1989. Public involvement in resource planning: toward bridging the gap between policy and implementation. Society and Natural Resources. 2(3): 209-227.

Blumenthal, B.; Haspeslagh, P. 1994. Toward definition of corporate transformation. Sloan Management Review. 35(3): 101-106.

Bormann, B.T.; Kiester, A.R. 2004. Options forestry: acting on uncertainty. Journal of Forestry. 102: 22-27.

Bormann, B.T.; Lee, D.C.; Kiester, A.R.; Busch, D.E.; Martin, J.R.; Haynes, R.W. 2006 [In press]. Adaptive management and regional monitoring. In: Haynes, R.W.; Bormann, B.T.; Martin, J.R., eds. Northwest Forest Plan—the first 10 years (1994-2003): synthesis of monitoring and research results. Gen. Tech. Rep. PNW-GTR-651. Portland, OR: U.S. Department of Agriculture, Forest Service, Pacific Northwest Research Station. Chapter 10.

Bormann, B.T.; Martin, J.R.; Wagner, F.H.; Wood, G.W.; Alegria, J.; Cunningham, P.G.; Brookes, M.H.; Friesema, P.; Berg, J.; Henshaw, J.R. 1999. Adaptive management. In: Johnson, K.N.; Malk, A.J.; Sexton, W.T.; Szaro, R., eds. Ecological stewardship: a common reference for ecosystem management. Oxford, United Kingdom: Elsevier Science Ltd.: 505-534.

Brewer, G.D. 1973. Politicians, bureaucrats, and the consultant: a critique of urban problem solving. New York: Basic Books. 291 p.

Bridges, W. 1991. Managing transitions: making the most of change. Reading, MA: Addison-Wesley Publishing Co. 130 p.

Brunson, M.W.; Kruger, L.E.; Tyler, C.B.; Schroeder, S.A., tech. eds. 1996. Defining social acceptability in ecosystem management: a workshop proceedings. Gen. Tech. Rep. PNW-GTR-369. Portland, OR: U.S. Department of Agriculture, Forest Service, Pacific Northwest Research Station. 142 p.

Buck, L.E.; Geisler, C.C.; Schelhas, J.; Wollenberg, E., eds. 2001. Biological diversity: balancing interests through adaptive collaborative management. New York: CRC Press. 465 p.

Busing, R. 1994. Detailed review of research needs and issues defined through analysis of the FEMAT report. Research plan to support implementation of ecosystem management. Portland, OR: Research Work Group, Interagency Implementation Team. 14 p. Appendix 4.

Caldwell, L.K. 1998. The National Environmental Policy Act: an agenda for the future. Bloomington, IN: Indiana University Press. 209 p.

Cissel, J.H.; Swanson, F.J.; Grant, G.E.; Olson, D.H.; Gregory, S.V.; Garman, S.L.; Ashkenas, L.R.; Hunter, M.G.; Kertis, J.A.; Mayo, J.H.; McSwain, M.D.; Swetland, S.G.; Swindle, K.A.; Wallin, D.O. 1998. A landscape plan based on historical fire regimes for a managed forest ecosystem: the Augusta Creek study. Gen. Tech. Rep. PNW-GTR-422. Portland, OR: U.S. Department of Agriculture, Forest Service, Pacific Northwest Research Station. 82 p.

Clark, R.N.; Meidinger, E.E.; Miller, G.; Rayner, J.; Layseca, M.; Monreal, S.; Fernandez, J.; Shannon, M. 1998. Integrating science and policy in natural resource management: lessons and opportunities from North America. Gen. Tech. Rep. PNW-GTR-441. Portland, OR: U.S. Department of Agriculture, Forest Service, Pacific Northwest Research Station. 22 p.

Clark, R.N.; Philpot, C.; Stankey, G.H. [N.d.]. Framework for NWFP Research. 9 p. Unpublished discussion paper. On file with: U.S. Department of Agriculture, Forest Service, Pacific Northwest Research Station, 400 N 34th, Suite 201, Seattle, WA 98103.

Clark, R.N.; Stankey, G.H.; Brown, P.J.; Burchfield, J.A.; Haynes, R.W.; McCool, S.F. 1999. Toward an ecological approach: integrating social, economic, cultural, biological and physical considerations. In: Johnson, N.C.; Malk, A.J.; Sexton, W.T.; Szaro, R., eds. Ecological stewardship: a common reference for ecosystem management. Oxford: Elsevier Science Ltd. III: 297-318.

Clarke, J.N.; McCool, D. 1996. Staking out the terrain: power and performance among natural resource agencies. 2nd ed. Buffalo, New York: State University of New York Press. 279 p.

Colfer, C.J. Pierce; Prabhu, R.; Wollenberg, E.; McDougall, C.; Edmunds, D.; Kowero, G. 2001. Toward social criteria and indicators for protected areas: one cut on adaptive comanagement. In: Buck, L.E.; Geisler, C.C.; Schelhas, J.; Wollenberg, E., eds. Biological diversity: balancing interests through adaptive collaborative management. New York: CRC Press: 293-312.

Cortner, H.J.; Moote, M.A. 1999. The politics of ecosystem management. Washington, DC: Island Press. 179 p.

Cortner, H.J.; Shannon, M.A.; Wallace, M.G.; Burke, S.; Moote, M.A. 1996. Institutional barriers and incentives for ecosystem management: a problem analysis. Gen. Tech. Rep. PNW-GTR-354. Portland, OR: U.S. Department of Agriculture, Forest Service, Pacific Northwest Research Station. 35 p.

Creswell, J.W. 1998. Qualitative inquiry and research design. Thousand Oaks, CA: Sage Publications. 326 p.

Curtis, A.; Birckhead, J.; DeLacy, T. 1995. Community participation in landcare policy in Australia: the Victorian experience with regional landcare plans. Society and Natural Resources. 8(5): 415-430.

Delli Priscoli, J.; Homenuck, P. 1990. Consulting the publics. In: Lang, R., ed., Integrated approaches to resource planning and management. Calgary, AB: The Banff Centre for Continuing Education: 67-79.

Dietz, T.; Dolak, N.; Ostrom, E.; Stern, P.C. 2003. The drama of the commons. In: Ostrom, E.; Dietz, T.; Dolak, N.; Stern, P.C.; Stonich, S.; Weber, E.U., eds. The drama of the commons. Washington, DC: National Academy Press: 3-35.

Dryzek, J.S. 1987. Rational ecology: environment and political economy. Oxford, United Kingdom: Basil Blackwell Ltd. 270 p.

Fairfax, S.K. 2005. When an agency outlasts its time: a reflection. Journal of Forestry. 103(5): 264-267.

Falanruw, M.V.C. 1984. People pressure and management of limited resources on Yap. In: McNeely, J.A.; Miller, K.R., eds. National parks, conservation, and development: the role of protected areas in sustaining society. Washington, DC: The Smithsonian Institution Press: 348-354.

Forest Ecosystem Management Assessment Team [FEMAT]. 1993. Forest ecosystem management: an ecological, economic, and social assessment. Portland, OR: U.S. Department of Agriculture; U.S. Department of the Interior [and others]. [Irregular pagination].

Franklin, J.F. 1994. Adaptive management areas. Journal of Forestry. 92(4): 50.

Friedmann, J. 1987. Planning in the public domain: from knowledge to action. Princeton, NJ: Princeton University Press. 501 p.

Graham, A.C.; Kruger, L.E. 2002. Research in adaptive management: working relations and the research process. Res. Pap. PNW-RP-538. Portland, OR: U.S. Department of Agriculture, Forest Service, Pacific Northwest Research Station. 55 p.

Gray, A.N. 2000. Adaptive ecosystem management in the Pacific Northwest: a case study from coastal Oregon. Conservation Ecology. 4(2): 6. http:///www.consecol.org/vol4/iss2/art6. (April 22, 2001).

Grumbine, R.E. 1994. What is ecosystem management? Conservation Biology. 8(1): 27-38.

Guerrero, M.C.S.; Pinto, E.F. 2001. Reclaiming ancestral domains in Pala'wan, Phillipines: community-based strategies and perspectives on adaptive collaborative management. In: Buck, L.E.; Geisler, C.C.; Schelhas, J.; Wollenberg, E., eds. Biological diversity: balancing interests through adaptive collaborative management. New York: CRC Press: 423-447.

Gunderson, L. 1999. Stepping back: assessing for understanding in complex regional systems. In: Johnson, K.N.; Swanson, F.; Herring, M.; Greene, S., eds. Bioregional assessments: science at the crossroads of management and policy. Washington, DC: Island Press: 27-40.

Gunderson, L.H.; Holling, C.S.; Light, S.S., eds. 1995. Barriers and bridges to the renewal of ecosystems and institutions. New York: Columbia University Press. 593 p.

Haber, S. 1964. Efficiency and uplift: scientific management in the progressive era, 1890-1920. Chicago, IL: University of Chicago Press. 181 p.

Halbert, C.L. 1993. How adaptive is adaptive management? Implementing adaptive management in Washington State and British Columbia. Reviews in Fisheries Science. 1: 261-283.

Hirt, P.W. 1994. Conspiracy of optimism: management of the national forests since World War II. Lincoln, NE: University of Nebraska. 416 p.

Holling, C.S. 1978. Adaptive environmental assessment and management. London: John Wiley. 377 p.

Holling, C.S. 1995. What barriers? What bridges? In: Gunderson, L.H.; Holling, C.S.; Light, S.S., eds. Barriers and bridges to the renewal of ecosystems and institutions. New York: Columbia University Press: 3-34.

Jansson, B.-O.; Velner, H. 1995. The Baltic: the sea of surprises. In: Gunderson, L.H.; Holling, C.S.; Light, S.S., eds. Barriers and bridges to the renewal of ecosystems and institutions. New York: Columbia University Press: 292-374.

Johnson, B.L. 1999. Introduction to the special issue: adaptive management—scientifically sound, socially challenged? Conservation Ecology. 3(1): 10. URL:http://www.consecol.org/vol3/iss1/art10. (January 4, 2000).

Johnson, F.; Williams, K. 1999. Protocol and practice in the adaptive management of waterfowl harvests. Conservation Ecology. 3(1): 8. http://www.consecol.org/vol3/iss1/art8. (January 7, 2000).

Johnson, K.N.; Herring, M. 1999. Understanding bioregional assessments. In: Johnson, K.N.; Swanson, F.; Herring, M.; Greene, S., eds. Bioregional assessments: science at the crossroads of management and policy. Washington, DC: Island Press: 341-376.

Johnson, K.N.; Swanson, F.; Herring, M.; Greene, S., eds. 1999. Bioregional assessments: science at the crossroads of management and policy. Washington, DC: Island Press. 398 p.

Johnson, K.N.; Franklin, J.F.; Thomas, J.W.; Gordon, J. 1991. Alternatives for management of late-successional forests of the Pacific Northwest. A report to the Agriculture Committee and the Merchant Marine and Fisheries Committee of the U.S. House of Representatives. Washington, DC. 59 p. Unpublished report. On file at: College of Forestry, Oregon State University, Corvallis, OR 97331.

Junker, S. 1999. The perfect storm. New York: HarperCollins. 256 p.

King, J. 1993. Learning to solve the right problems: the case of nuclear power in America. Journal of Business Ethics. 13: 105-116.

Korten, D.C.; Klauss, R., eds. 1984. People-centered development: contributions toward theory and planning frameworks. Hartford, CT: Kumarian Press. 333 p.

Kotter, J.P. 1995. Leading change: why transformational efforts fail. Harvard Business Review. March-April: 59-67.

Kuhn, T. 1970. The structure of scientific revolutions. Chicago: University of Chicago Press. 210 p.

Kvale, S. 1996. Qualitative inquiry and research design. Thousand Oaks, CA: Sage Publications. 402 p.

Ladson, A.R.; Argent, R.M. 2002. Adaptive management of environmental flows: lessons for Murray-Darling Basin from three large North America rivers. Australian Journal of Water Resources. 5(1): 89-101.

Lawrence, R.L.; Daniels, S.E. 1996. Public involvement in natural resource decisionmaking: goals, methodology, and evaluation. Corvallis, OR: Forest Research Laboratory, Oregon State University. 49 p.

Lawrence, R.L.; Daniels, S.E.; Stankey, G.H. 1997. Procedural justice and public involvement in natural resources decision making. Society and Natural Resources. 10(6): 577-589.

Lee, K.N. 1993. Compass and gyroscope: integrating science and politics for the environment. Washington, DC: Island Press. 243 p.

Lee, K.N. 1995. Deliberately seeking sustainability in the Columbia River Basin. In: Gunderson, L.H.; Holling, C.S.; Light, S.S., eds. Barriers and bridges to the renewal of ecosystems and institutions. New York: Columbia University Press: 214-238.

Lee, K.N. 1999. Appraising adaptive management. Conservation Ecology. 3(2): 3. http://www.consecol.org/vol3/iss2/art3. (January 4, 2000).

Lindblom, C. 1959. Scientific objectivity and values. In: Webb, L.J.; Kikkawa, J., eds. Australian tropical forests: science-values-meaning. Melbourne, Victoria, Australia: Commonwealth Scientific and Industrial Research Organisation: 133-141.

Lunch, W.M. 1987. The nationalization of American politics. Berkeley: University of California Press. 408 p.

McLain, R.J.; Lee, R.G. 1996. Adaptive management: promises and pitfalls. Environmental Management. 20(4): 437-448.

Messick, D.M.; Bazerman, M.H. 1996. Ethical leadership and the psychology of decision making. Sloan Management Review. Winter: 9-22.

Michael, D.N. 1973. On learning to plan—and planning to learn. San Francisco: Jossey-Bass Publishers. 341 p.

Michael, D.N. 1995. Barriers and bridges to learning in a turbulent human ecology. In: Gunderson, L.H.; Holling, C.S.; Light, S.S., eds. Barriers and bridges to the renewal of ecosystems and institutions. New York: Columbia University Press: 461-488.

Miller, A. 1999. Environmental problem solving: psychosocial barriers to adaptive change. New York: Springer-Verlag. 239 p.

Mills, T.J.; Quigley, T.M.; Everest, F.J. 2001. Science-based natural resource management decisions: What are they? Renewable Resources Journal. 19(2): 10-15.

Miner, C.L.; Stankey, G.H. 2000. Influencing the adoption of forestry innovations: a case example from the United States [Abstract]. In: Forests and Society: the role of research. Abstracts of Group Discussions, Vol.11.

Moore, S.A. 1995. The role of trust in social networks; formation, function, and fragility. In: Saunders, D.A.; Craig, J.L.; Mattiske, E.M., eds. Nature conservation 4: the role of networks. Surrey, United Kingdom: Beatty and Sons: 148-154.

National Research Council. 1999. Downstream: adaptive management of Glen Canyon Dam and the Colorado River ecosystem. Washington, DC: National Academy Press. 230 p.

Nyberg, J.B.; Taylor, B. 1995. Applying adaptive management in British Columbia's forests. In: Proceedings of the Food and Agriculture Organization/Economic Commission for Europe/International Labour Organization international forestry seminar. Prince George, BC: Canadian Forest Service: 239-245.

Overbay, J.D. 1993. Memorandum to recipients of the Scientific Analysis Team report, dated March 1993. Washington, DC: U.S. Department of Agriculture, Forest Service.

Parson, E.A.; Clark, W.C. 1995. Sustainable development as social learning: theoretical perspectives and practical challenges for the design of a research program. In: Gunderson, L.H.; Holling, C.S.; Light, S.S., eds. Barriers and bridges to the renewal of ecosystems and institutions. New York: Columbia University Press: 428-460.

Pinkerton, E. 1999. Factors in overcoming barriers to implementing co-management in British Columbia salmon fisheries. Conservation Ecology. 3(2): 2. http://www.consecol.org/vol3/iss2/art2. (February 23, 2001).

Pipkin, J. 1998. The Northwest Forest Plan revisited. Washington, DC: U.S. Department of the Interior, Office of Policy Analysis. 117 p.

Rayner, J. 1996. Implementing sustainability in west coast forests: CORE and FEMAT as experiments in process. Journal of Canadian Studies. 31(1): 82-101.

Regional Ecosystem Office [REO]. 2000. Standards and guidelines and the adaptive management area system. Adaptive Management Area Work Group, Paper Number 1. Portland, OR. 14 p.

Robertson, F.D. 1991. Memorandum to the Regional Foresters. Silvicultural practices, clearcutting. On file with: USDA Forest Service, Washington Office, Auditors Building, 201 14th Street, SW, at Independence Avenue, SW, Washington, DC 20250.

Robertson, F.D. 1992 (4 June). Letter to Regional Foresters and Station Directors. Ecosystem management of the national forests and grasslands. On file with: USDA Forest Service, Pacific Northwest Research Station, Pacific Wildland Fire Sciences Laboratory, 400 N 34th, Suite 201, Seattle, WA 98103.

Roe, E. 1996. Why ecosystem management can't work without social science: an example from the California northern spotted owl controversy. Environmental Management. 5: 667-674.

Rogers, E.M. 1995. Diffusion of innovations. 4th ed. New York: Free Press. 519 p.

Röling, N.G.; Wagemakers, M.A.E. 1998. Facilitating sustainable agriculture: participatory learning and adaptive management in times of environmental uncertainty. Cambridge, United Kingdom: Cambridge University Press. 318 p.

Rolle, S. 2002. Measures of progress for collaboration: case study of the Applegate Partnership. Gen. Tech. Rep. PNW-GTR-565. Portland, OR: U.S. Department of Agriculture, Forest Service, Pacific Northwest Research Station. 13 p.

Rossi, P.H.; Freeman, H.E. 1993. Evaluation: a systematic approach. Newbury Park, CA: Sage Publications, Inc. 488 p.

Rubin, H.J.; Rubin, I.S. 1995. Qualitative interviewing: the art of hearing data. Thousand Oaks, CA: Sage Publications. Pgs.

Salafsky, N.; Margoluis, R.; Redford, K. 2001. Adaptive management: a tool for conservation practitioners. Washington, DC: Biodiversity Support Program, World Wildlife Fund, Inc. 136 p. http://fosonline.org/resources/Publications/AdapManHTML/adman 1.html. (September 17, 2003).

Salwasser, H. 2004. Adaptive management and the federal Northwest Forest Plan. A paper presented to the Ecological Society of America annual meeting. Portland, OR. 20 p. Unpublished report. On file at: College of Forestry, Oregon State University, Corvallis, OR 97331.

Schelhas, J.; Buck, L.E.; Geisler, C.C. 2001. Introduction: the challenge of adaptive collaborative management. In: Buck, L.E.; Geisler, C.C.; Schelhas, J.; Wollenberg, E., eds. Biological diversity: balancing interests through adaptive collaborative management. New York: CRC Press: xix-xxxv.

Schumucker, Elizabeth F. 1996. Adaptive management from FEMAT to ROD to practice. 6 p. Unpublished paper. On file with: USDA Forest Service, Pacific Northwest Research Station, Pacific Wildland Fire Sciences Laboratory, 400 N 34th, Suite 201, Seattle, WA 98103.

Scientific Analysis Team [SAT]. 1993. Viability assessments and management considerations for species associated with late-successional and old-growth forests of the Pacific Northwest. The report of the Scientific Analysis Team. Portland, OR: U.S. Department of Agriculture, Forest Service. 530 p.

Seidman, I. 1998. Interviewing as qualitative research: a guide for researchers in education and the social sciences. 2nd ed. New York: Teachers College Press. 143 p.

Senge, P.M. 1990. The fifth discipline: the art and practice of the learning organization. New York: Currency Doubleday. 423 p.

Shands, W.E. 1992. Public involvement, forest planning, and leadership in a community of interests. In: Proceedings, Society of American Foresters convention: an evolving tradition. Richmond, VA: Society of American Foresters: 364-369.

Shannon, M.A.; Antypas, A.R. 1997. Open institutions: uncertainty and ambiguity in 21st-century forestry. In: Kohm, K.A.; Franklin, J.F., eds. Creating a forestry for the 21st century: the science of ecosystem management. Washington, DC: Island Press: 437-445.

Shannon, M.; Graham, A.; Antypas, A. 1997. Learning to innovate: innovating to learn: a social and organizational assessment of the adaptive management areas. 11 p. Unpublished report. On file with: USDA Forest Service, Pacific Northwest Research Station, Pacific Wildland Fire Sciences Laboratory, 400 N 34th, Suite 201, Seattle, WA 98103.

Shannon, M.; Sturtevant, V.; Trask, D. 1995. Organizing for innovation: a look at the agencies and organizations responsible for adaptive management areas: the case of the Applegate AMA. Report submitted to the Interagency Liaison, Forest Service and Bureau of Land Management, Applegate Adaptive Management Area. Medford, OR. 28 p.

Shindler, B. 2003. Implementing adaptive management: an evaluation of AMAs in the Pacific Northwest. In: Shindler, B.; Beckley, T.; Finley, C., eds. Two paths to sustainable forests: public values in Canada and the United States. Corvallis, OR: Oregon State University Press: 210-225.

Shindler, B.; Aldred-Cheek, K. 1999. Integrating citizens in adaptive management: a propositional analysis. Conservation Ecology. 3(1): 9. http://www.. consecol.org/vol3/iss1/art9. (May 22, 2001).

Shindler, B.; Aldred-Cheek, K.; Stankey, G.H. 1999. Monitoring and evaluating citizen-agency interactions: a framework developed for adaptive management. Gen. Tech. Rep. PNW-GTR-452. Portland, OR: U.S. Department of Agriculture, Forest Service, Pacific Northwest Research Station. 38 p.

Shindler, B.; Neburka, J. 1997. Public participation in forest planning: eight attributes of success. Journal of Forestry. 91(7): 17-19.

Shindler, B.; Steel, B.; List, P. 1996. Public judgments of adaptive management: an initial response from forest communities. Journal of Forestry. 94(6): 4-12.

Shindler, B.; Toman, E. 2002. A longitudinal analysis of fuel reduction in the Blue Mountains: public perspectives on the use of prescribed fire and mechanized thinning. Corvallis, OR: Department of Forest Resources, Oregon State University. 76 p.

Shindler, B.; Wright, A. 2000. Watershed management in the central Cascades: a study of citizen knowledge and the value of information sources in the lower South Santiam Basin. Corvallis, OR: Department of Forest Resources, Oregon State University. 90 p.

Shindler, B.A.; Brunson, M.; Stankey, G.H. 2002. Social acceptability of forest conditions and management practices: a problem analysis. Gen. Tech. Rep. PNW-GTR-537. Portland, OR: U.S. Department of Agriculture, Forest Service, Pacific Northwest Research Station. 68 p.

Slocumbe, D.S. 1993. Implementing ecosystem-based management. BioScience. 43(9): 612-621.

Socolow, R.H. 1976. Failures of discourse: obstacles to the integration of environmental values into natural resource policy. In: Tribe, L.H.; Schelling, C.S.; Voss, J., eds. When values conflict: essays on environmental analysis, discourse, and decision. Cambridge: Ballinger Company: 1-33.

Smith, G.R. 1997. Making decisions in a complex and dynamic world. In: Kohm, K.A.; Franklin, J.F., eds. Creating a forestry for the 21st century: the science of ecosystem management. Washington, DC: Island Press: 419-435.

Stankey, G.H. 2003. Adaptive management at the regional scale: breakthrough innovation or mission impossible? A report on an American experience. In: Wilson, B.P.; Curtis, A., eds. Agriculture for the Australian environment. Albury, New South Wales, Australia: Charles Sturt University: 159-177.

Stankey, G.H.; Bormann, B.T.; Ryan, C.; Shindler, B.; Sturtevant, V.; Clark, R.N.; Philpot, C. 2003. Adaptive management and the Northwest Forest Plan: rhetoric and reality. Journal of Forestry. 101(1): 40-46.

Stankey, G.H.; Clark, R.N.; Bormann, B.T. 2005. Adaptive management of natural resources: theory, concepts, and management institutions. Gen. Tech. Rep. PNW-GTR-654. Portland, OR: U.S. Department of Agriculture, Forest Service, Pacific Northwest Research Station. 72 p.

Stankey, G.H.; Shindler, B. 1997. Adaptive management areas: achieving the promise, avoiding the peril. Gen. Tech. Rep. PNW-GTR-394. Portland, OR: U.S. Department of Agriculture, Forest Service, Pacific Northwest Research Station. 21 p.

Stokstad, E. 2005. Learning to adapt. Science. 309: 688-690.

Taylor, B.; Kremsater, L.; Ellis, R. 1997. Adaptive management of forests in British Columbia. Victoria, BC: Forest Practices Branch, Ministry of Forests. 93 p.

Thomas, J.W.; Forsman, E.D.; Lint, J.B. [and others]. Viability assessments and management considerations for species associated with late-successional and old-growth forest of the Pacific Northwest. Portland, OR: U.S. Department of Agriculture, Forest Service. 530 p.

Thomas, J.W.; Verner, J. 1992. Accommodation with socio-economic factors under the Endangered Species Act—more than meets the eye. Transactions of the 57th North American wildlife and natural resources conference. Washington, DC: Wildlife Management Institute: 627-641.

Todd, C. 2001. Identifying the weakest link: adaptive management of the reintroduction of a threatened fish. Watershed (November): 6-7. Canberra, ACT, Australia: Centre for Freshwater Ecology, University of Canberra.

Tuchmann, E.T.; Connaughton, K.P.; Freedman, L.E.; Moriwaki, C.B. 1996. The Northwest Forest Plan: a report to the President and Congress. Portland, OR: U.S. Department of Agriculture, Forest Service, Pacific Northwest Research Station. 253 p.

Tugwell, R.G. 1940. The superpolitical. Journal of Social Philosophy. 5(2): 97-114.

U.S. Department of Agriculture, Forest Service. 1996. Adaptive management areas: 1996 success stories. Portland, OR: Pacific Northwest Region. 24 p.

U.S. Department of Agriculture, Forest Service; U.S. Department of the Interior, Bureau of Land Management [USDA and USDI]. 1994. Record of decision for amendments to Forest Service and Bureau of Land Management planning documents within the range of the northern spotted owl. [Place of publication unknown.] 74 p. [plus attachment A: standards and guidelines].

U.S. Senate. S. Doc. 115. 1963. A university view of the Forest Service. [Bolle Report]. 91st Cong. 2d sess., Washington, DC: Government Printing Office. 33 p.

Van Cleve, F.B.; Simenstad, C.; Goetz, F.; Mumford, T. 2003. Application of "best available science" in ecosystem restoration: lessons learned from large-scale restoration efforts in the U.S. Product of the Puget Sound Nearshore Ecosystem Restoration Project, Nearshore Science Team. 38 p. http://www.pugetsoundnearshore.org. (March 16, 2004).

Volkman, J.M.; McConnaha, W.E. 1993. Through a glass, darkly: Columbia River salmon, the Endangered Species Act, and adaptive management. Environmental Law. 23(4): 1249-1272.

Wallace, M.G.; Cortner, H.J.; Burke, S. 1995. Review of policy evaluation in natural resources. Society and Natural Resources. 8(1): 35-47.

Walters, C.J. 1986. Adaptive management of renewable resources. New York: Macmillan. 374 p.

Walters, C.J. 1997. Challenges in adaptive management of riparian and coastal ecosystems. Conservation Ecology. 1(2): 1. http://www.consecol.org/vol1/iss2/art1. (January 22, 2001).

Walters, C.J.; Gunderson, L.; Holling, C.S. 1992. Experimental policies for water management in the Everglades. Ecological Applications. 2: 189-202.

Westley, F. 1995. Governing design: the management of social systems and ecosystems. In: Gunderson, L.H.; Holling, C.S.; Light, S.S., eds. Barriers and bridges to the renewal of ecosystems and institutions. New York: Columbia University Press: 391-427.

Wildavsky, A. 1998. Searching for safety. Bowling Green, OH: Social Philosophy and Policy Center and Transaction Publishers. 253 p.

Wilkinson, C.F. 1992. Crossing the next meridian: land, water, and the future of the West. Washington, DC: Island Press. 376 p.

Wilkinson, C.F.; Anderson, H.M. 1987. Land and resource planning in the national forests. Washington, DC: Island Press. 396 p.

Williams, R.L. 2001. Public knowledge, preferences and involvement in adaptive ecosystem management. Corvallis, OR: Department of Forest Resources, Oregon State University. 137 p. M.S. thesis.

Wondolleck, J.M. 1988. Public lands conflict and resolution: managing national forest disputes. New York: Plenum Press. 263 p.

Wondolleck, J.M.; Yaffee, S.L. 1994. Building bridges across agency boundaries: in search of excellence in the U.S. Forest Service. Research report submitted to the USDA Forest Service, Pacific Northwest Research Station. Seattle, WA. 90 p.

Wondolleck, J.M.; Yaffee, S.L. 2000. Making collaboration work: lessons from innovation in natural resource management. Washington, DC: Island Press. 277 p.

Yaffee, S.L. 1994. Wisdom of the spotted owl: policy lessons for a new century. Washington, DC: Island Press. 430 p.

Yankelovich, D. 1991. Coming to public judgment: making democracy work in a complex world. Syracuse, NY: Syracuse University Press. 290 p.